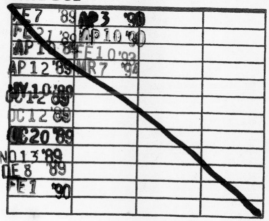

# POLICY AND
# BUREAUCRACY

*by*
## CHARLES E. JACOB
*Vassar College*

### NEW PERSPECTIVES
### IN
### POLITICAL SCIENCE

## D. VAN NOSTRAND COMPANY, INC.
### PRINCETON, NEW JERSEY
**TORONTO**  **NEW YORK**  **LONDON**

## To Gale

---

D. VAN NOSTRAND COMPANY, INC.
120 Alexander St., Princeton, New Jersey
(*Principal Office*)
24 West 40 Street, New York 18, New York

D. VAN NOSTRAND COMPANY, LTD.
358, Kensington High Street, London, W.14, England

D. VAN NOSTRAND COMPANY (Canada), LTD.
25 Hollinger Road, Toronto 16, Canada

---

---

Published simultaneously in Canada by
D. VAN NOSTRAND COMPANY (Canada), LTD.

---

---

# Preface

THIS BOOK SEEKS TO OPEN A FEW DOORS TO THE HOUSE OF POLITI-
cal knowledge. While in short space only a few rooms can be in-
spected, the hope is that some light will penetrate the dark corners
of those rooms labeled "policy" and "bureaucracy." Total illumi-
nation can come only—if ever—with the help of many other
specialized guides.

Obviously, these doors have not been breached at random, hap-
hazardly. Any author setting out on such a tour carries with him
certain preconceived notions, evaluations of what is most significant, and orders of priority that are his own property. (This is,
after all, the only real property the author of a book of this sort
can call his own.) Thus I have not even discussed certain traditional administrative notions, such as "line" and "staff," but have
spent some considerable time looking at the sociological aspects
of bureaucracy. In the area of business policy I have limited my-
self rigorously in the discussion of antitrust to allow more room
for a consideration of the politics of the modern corporation. In
the discussion of national security I have sacrificed a detailed
description of major institutions in order to consider the role of
private research groups and the scientific community in this vital
area of policy. And so on.

I have done all this in the hope that students—either in intro-
ductory political science courses or in more specialized policy-
administration courses—will find a book like this a useful supplement to traditional, detailed analyses available elsewhere. I would
not have written this book had I thought of it as just one more
repetition of existing "short studies."

Like all composers of syntheses, I owe more intellectual debts
than I can count. The vast body of literature in this field, which
I have called upon and borrowed from freely, receives only partial
credit throughout. I have been led to this literature in two ways.

Most recently, I have been prompted repeatedly to look farther and deeper by challenging students in my public policy course at Vassar College. At a more formative stage my interest was aroused by a corps of academic mentors who combined scholarly precision with political wisdom and imagination. Mario Einaudi, Andrew Hacker, and—most of all—Clinton Rossiter are hereby cited for their various contributions to this writer's development. Any shortcomings in the present text are signs of lessons the student failed to learn, not that the teacher failed to teach.

Finally, special thanks are due to my friend and editorial guide, William G. Andrews of Tufts University: first, for suggesting that I might take up this study, and second, for his helpful suggestions after reading the manuscript. Franklin L. Burdette, likewise, labored over the manuscript and contributed to its improvement. Mildred Tubby served as a skilled and efficient typist; and the Vassar College Committee on Research acted as a generous benefactor in making a summer grant available for the preparation of the manuscript. I alone am responsible for any errors committed in spite of these several aids and comforts.

CHARLES E. JACOB

*Poughkeepsie, New York*

# Contents

## PART II. AREAS OF POLICY                                 107

**PART I**

# The Formulation of Policy

# CHAPTER 1

# The Evolution of
# the Governmental Process

POLICY AND ADMINISTRATION, THOUGH ONCE THOUGHT TO BE separate entities, must be viewed as two interrelated parts of the same governmental process. When we speak of policy we usually mean a principle, plan, or course of action. When we speak of administration we are talking about the management of governmental affairs. Since policy making implies formulation and administration implies execution or implementation, it would appear that two different kinds of acts must be distinguished. Yet the two acts are not as separable as they might appear at first sight. Obviously, without policy there can be no administration. And without administration policy is empty and meaningless. These two processes are further interrelated by the effect of each on the scope and operations of the other. That is, *what* is to be done determines, in part, *how* it is to be done. Likewise—though less often acknowledged—the *what* is partially determined by the *how*.

To explore this paradox further we must consider the components of policy and administration. Policy is motivated by needs, derived through calculation by people, and conditioned by choices of values. The needs motivating policy may be real or merely apparent. The calculation may be rational or nonrational. The people may be intelligent, experienced, and dedicated, or they may be extremely limited, time-serving novices. The values may be humanistic, egoistic, blindly ideological, or confused. Though all these components play a part in policy making, and their relative weight varies with the situation, values are usually the ultimate determinants of policy. Values condition the perception of need for a given policy, but, if the process of policy making is characterized by nonrational, unintelligent calculation, the values to be served by the policy are unlikely to be sustained. In any case, once a policy is formulated, to be meaningful, it must be executed. In order to be executed effectively, certain necessary components of administration must come into play.

Administration implies the existence of policies to be carried out and requires people, organized in offices, calculating means of implementation that are, again, conditioned by values. The people (administrators) may be intelligent and competent or ineffective. The organization may be structurally efficient and satisfying or conflict-producing and dysfunctional. The calculation of means may be rational or nonrational. The values may be the same as those of the policy maker or *different*.

This, then, is the crucial nexus of the policy-administration relationship. Policy making may be weak or in error, in which case administration is severely limited. On the other hand, administration, either because of structural or personal ineffectiveness, or lack of sympathy and commitment to the policy, can undermine it or change its content. The degree of discretion exercised by administration has come to be recognized in its true significance: policy making is not limited to those whose title endows them with the function.

Policy making (or as it is sometimes more loosely characterized, decision making) and administration together constitute the chief business of government. It is not, of course, the only business of government. Modern democratic man has come to expect his government to fulfill a representative function and a justice dispensing function as well. That is, government should, in one way or another, represent the interests of society and guarantee the rights and liberties of citizens under a Rule of Law, as interpreted by the courts.

It is the chief business of government, however, that concerns us here. The exercise of the policy making and administrative functions implies the exercise of power. Power may be defined as the influence of one group or person over another. In most societies, this influence is granted (through deference to legal norms or ideological considerations) to the wielders of power by those over whom it is exercised. This transforms power into legitimate authority. In the United States all political power has its legal source in the Constitution. It is, thus, to this source that we must look to gain an understanding of the traditional norms and forms of American government.

## THE ESTABLISHMENT OF CONSTITUTIONAL NORMS

The constitution that emerged in 1787 was a document born of very mixed feelings on the part of the drafters. A general conviction that a new basic law was needed was prompted by the realization that the Union, under the Articles of Confederation, was at the brink of disintegration. Reasons for this malaise were easy to find. Congress, under the Articles, was little more than a convention of ambassadors from sovereign states. In order for anything of importance to be accomplished by this Congress, a vote of two-thirds was required. Even so, when this extraordinary majority did act, no means of compelling compliance from the individual states existed. There was no executive organ as such. The fact that the "laws" of the confederation were viewed as being no more than recommendations is no better typified than by the common refusal of the states to accede to the tax levies of the Congress.[2]

It was a long step, however, from the recognition of the need for a new constitution to the acceptance of one. The Framers were above all realistic men, well acquainted with the dynamics of political power as they operated in their day. Realizing that a constitution amounts to a grant of powers, and fearing abuses of power, they tempered the grant with a stern catalogue of limitations. Being eighteenth-century men, the surest way they knew of limiting power was by dividing it. They had read their Montesquieu and drawn the appropriate moral: Political power is of three kinds—executive, legislative and judicial. The most salutary means of preventing abuses of power is to prohibit the same officials (whether the one, the few, or the many) from exercising all three kinds of power. They proceeded, then, to construct a governmental apparatus based upon the separation of these three types of power and strengthened it with an elaborate system of countervailing checks to balance them.

A few comments are in order at this point about the handiwork of the Framers. In the first place, no clear distinctions can be based upon the *nature* of the powers exercised by the three branches.[3]

The Founders created and labeled three sectors of government and listed some examples of functions they expected each sector to perform. In establishing identifiable institutions—President, Congress, and the Supreme Court—they prescribed certain powers to be exercised by each. What made these powers precisely executive, legislative, or judicial in nature, however, and more important, what would be the nature of then unspecified powers that were to develop was left unanswered. That there would ensue an overlapping of powers was inevitable, and that this would lead to jealousies and conflict was foreordained. The shrewder of the Founding Fathers anticipated the overlapping at the outset. Thus, Madison took pains to justify the inevitable by quoting Montesquieu as saying that separation of powers does not mean:

> that these departments ought to have no *partial agency* in, or no *control* over, the acts of each other. His meaning . . . can amount to no more than this, that where the *whole* power of one department is exercised by the same hands which possess the *whole* power of another department, the fundamental principles of a free constitution are subverted.[4]

Yet it is precisely the fact that there would be many instances of "partial agency" and that new functions—requiring the exercise of new powers—would develop, that has raised so many obstacles to the making and execution of policy. The storm center of conflict in policy making has, of course, been over the relations between President and Congress. Nevertheless, the fact that administration—the execution of the business of government—was rather left in institutional limbo has led to problems of another order in American government.[5] The responsibility and accountability of the administrative officialdom have been more difficult to assure because of imprecise institutional placement.

If the fear of tyranny through abuse of governing powers was primarily responsible for the triadic form of government that was established in the Constitution, this fear likewise accounts in no small measure for that other outstanding and unique feature of the new American Constitution: federalism. It was not enough to divide power functionally; it had further to be bisected regionally. The Framers realized that securing the adoption of the new Constitution would be difficult enough since, to many, the barriers to tyranny envisioned in the charter were perilously weak fortifications. They knew that without the reservation of a notable quantum of the governing power to the states the document would never achieve the necessary ratification at the hands of the several states. In this sense, even if the wisdom of federalism *per se* had not recommended itself to the Framers—and it did to a vast majority of them—some type of sharing arrangement would have had to be invented for reasons of political expediency. As it was, proponents of the Constitution had to present strong briefs to the various state legislatures, arguing that in reality the states would retain their integrity and hold the balance of power under the new Constitution.

The most eloquent pleas in favor of the integrity afforded to the states by the new Constitution were made by the Federalists in their fight for ratification in New York. James Madison maintained that the powers delegated to the national government were actually few and well defined; that those reserved to the state governments were many and broad; and, indeed, that the states would possess powers that "will extend to all the objects which, in the ordinary course of affairs, concern the lives, liberties and properties of the people, and the internal order, improvement, and prosperity of the State." [6] Beyond this, Madison titillated the nerve of provincial pride in allowing that the spirit of localism—the attachment of the people to local institutions and local officials—would be a natural and automatic obstacle to distant, federal attempts at aggrandizement. In one fleeting concession to the possibility of federal pre-eminence, Madison wrote a few lines that are worth considering today if only for their prophetic wisdom:

If, therefore, as has been elsewhere remarked, the people should in future become more partial to the federal than to the State governments, the change can only result from such manifest and irresistible proofs of a better administration as will overcome all their antecedent propensities. And in that case, the people ought not surely to be precluded from giving most of their confidence where they may discover it to be most due. . . . [7]

Fortunately for the Federalists, the contingency of future federal pre-eminence suggested by Madison was not sufficient in the minds of his constituents to destroy the elaborate structure of arguments in favor of probable state superiority. The claims made about effective state powers together with the limitations afforded by the separation of powers laid to rest most of the fears about potential tyrants, and the Constitution was safely adopted.

One way of summarizing the conventional wisdom of the times that appealed to nearly all those who were concerned with constitution making is to reiterate simply that the best of all possible governments envisioned was a limited government. The tasks of government were to be kept to a minimum, and ambitious attempts by the governors were to be checked at every turn by constitutional limitations. The prevailing attitude was not one that asked what government could do for the people, but rather one that feared what government might do *to* the people. This attitude was reflected not only in the formulations already considered but was further "constitutionalized" in the Bill of Rights. That series of Amendments, beginning: "Congress shall make no law . . . ," and continuing with a catalogue of specific restrictions on the right of government to interfere with the liberties of the people, provides eloquent testimony to the fear of government. The concluding Tenth Amendment attempts definitively to bottle the evil genii of political power: "The powers not delegated to the United States by the Constitution, nor prohibited by it to the States, are reserved to the States respectively, or to the people."

Before turning from the norms of political thought of those who created American governmental institutions to a consideration of their evolutionary development, we are bound to ask why political mechanisms devoted to insuring limited government were built into the Constitution. The answer is to be found in an intermingling of thought, experience, and economic interest.

*Political Thought.*   At the base of all political systems lie certain assumptions, whether expressed or implied, about the nature of society and man's place in it. The dominant source of ideas that influenced the constitution makers was the tradition of English Whig philosophy. The name Locke is most often cited to represent the philosophic tradition that shaped the ideas of the Founders. It is true that Locke lent philosophical respectability to the concept of a separation of powers (later refurbished by Baron Montesquieu), the idea of contract, and the preferred position of property ownership, on the one hand; it is also true that he spoke the rhetoric of inalienable rights and the right to revolution, on the other. While the latter were of great utility in the revolutionary period of American history and contributed notably to the spirit of the Declaration of Independence, they held little effective sway over the constitution makers as political architects. In 1787 the more conservative elements of Lockian philosophy were cited. The permissive and optimistic elements in Locke, carried to their logical conclusion by French Romanticists, might appeal to a Sam Adams or a Tom Paine; they held little allure for a John Adams, an Alexander Hamilton, or a Gouverneur Morris. These gentlemen had been raised on the spartan diet proffered by the Puritan, colonial, theocratic tradition. Man was not seen as a repository of all the virtues. Borrowing from Rousseau, one might say man was thought to be rather more savage than noble. In short —and to shift philosophers again—man, as the Founders viewed him, fitted the image created by Hobbes more than any other. He was a mixture of good and evil, but, for the purpose of framing institutions of government, it was safer to consider him potentially ignorant, selfish, and aggressive. These qualities could be expected to inhere in both the governed and the governors. This attitude explains two overriding features of the Constitution: the limitations placed upon democracy (to limit the governed) and the internal institutional counterweights (to limit the governors).

Fear of the excesses of the people could be documented in endless variations in the remarks of the delegates to the Convention. Let one example suffice. In the debate over the form of election for the Presidency, Mr. Gerry can be cited as remarking: "A popular election in this case is radically vicious. The ignorance of the people would put it in the power of some one set of men dispersed through the Union & acting in Concert to delude them into any appointment." [8]

From this general attitude flowed the constitutional provisions for election of the President by a special body of electors, provisions for fixed terms of office, provisions for an indirectly elected, and presumably more aristocratic Senate, and a host of others designed to place the institutions of government at a safe remove from the immediate reach of the people.

That the same frailties of human nature had to be counteracted in the governors themselves is no better rationalized than in a famous passage from *Federalist* Number 51:

Ambition must be made to counteract ambition. The interest of the man must be connected with the constitutional rights of the place. It may be a reflection on human nature that such devices should be necessary to control the abuses of government. But what is government itself but the greatest of all reflections on human nature? If men were angels, no government would be necessary. If angels were to govern men, neither external nor internal controls on government would be necessary. In framing a government which is to be administered by men over men, the great difficulty lies in this: you must first enable the government to control the governed; and in the next place oblige it to control itself. A dependence on the people is, no doubt, the primary control on the government; but experience has taught mankind the necessity of auxiliary precautions.

Thus men could attempt wisely to frame institutions with built-in limitations in order to preserve their liberties. Yet such objects of human ingenuity would not suffice in the absence of the loyalty of the people to the system itself. The best means, it seemed, to assure popular loyalty was through appeals to a traditional, higher standard—the standard of Law. Law had always held a high position in the minds of the colonial Americans. The various formulations of law might be contradictory or inconsistent; yet the "law that there is a Law" was unexceptionable. The overseers of the Puritan theocracies had preached God's Eternal Law. Domestic intellectuals had called upon the Higher Law, or natural law, in that rationalist form that Locke had identified as the law of self-preservation. The great English jurists, Coke and Blackstone, played important roles in transporting common law traditions through their treatises into the colonies. And in 1787, the Constitution itself *embodied* the Higher Law, taking novel validity, as Professor Corwin has pointed out, as a statute emanating from a sovereign people.[9] The sanctity ascribed to law as the great impersonal regulator of the relationships among men is important not merely for the historical role it played in the establishment of American institutions, but the more important because its vitality is renewed as each new generation of Americans pursues its political quests.

*Political Experience.* The idea of constitutionalism was not one of theoretical origins alone. Before 1787 the colonists had created, tested, and modified different forms of political charters. Some had been rejected, others adapted and used as real governing instruments. Incipient forms of constitution making can be seen in the Mayflower Compact (1620) and the Fundamental Orders of Connecticut (1639). Still later, more advanced charters were developed, such as the Fundamental Constitutions of Carolina and William Penn's Frames of Government. At the Union level the Articles of Confederation bespeak the colonial penchant for developing fundamental charters of government out of the crucible of needs and experience. Each of these examples attests to belief in the wisdom of "a government of laws rather than men."

Colonial religious sectarianism provided another source of experience in dealing with human problems by institutional means. In fact, Clinton Rossiter has seen a direct intellectual link between church and state: "The Puritan theory of the origin of the church in the consent of the believers led directly to the popular theory of the origin of government in the consent of the governed." [10] In many ways, some obvious, others more subtle, answers to church questions were applied to political questions. The Protestant ethic of individualism itself was one that applied more generally to social, economic, and political affairs. The corollary contempt of these religious individualists for centralization and bureaucratic hierarchy carried over into the political-institutional realm. On the one hand, articles of association and compacts made within the separatist churches taught a rudimentary lesson in internal self-government. On the other, a growth in the recognition of the rights of differing and dissenting sects in a free society led naturally to an acceptance of a plurality of interests and an adoption of mechanisms designed to balance and check antagonistic interests.

The outstanding analogy to self-regulation in church affairs is found in the spirit of localism that developed in the preconstitutional period. Citizen participation in local affairs (even though the eligible participants were strictly limited by suffrage and property qualifications) and a jealous guardianship of local integrity against colonial intrusions were reflected in a fear of strong central government in 1787. This attitude was most vociferously expressed against executive prerogative, and the prime target of disdain was the body of colonial bureaucrats, English and Loyalist American alike. Jefferson echoed the feelings of many a local burger and town selectman when he complained in the Declaration of Independence that the mother country had ". . . erected a multitude of New Offices and sent hither swarms of officers to harass our people, and eat out their substance."

The legacy of colonial political experience was a mixed one. A government of laws was seen as a requisite of the good society. Yet there was an abiding suspicion of government, a suspicion that grew as governmental institutions became geographically more remote than immediate; more centralized than dispersed; more executive or administrative than popular; and finally, more complex than simple and understandable to the meanest citizen.

*Economic Interests.* The relationships we have thus far considered contributed to the quest for divided, limited government. Indeed, had these been the only influences at work in Philadelphia, the governmental apparatus that emerged would have been more self-restrained than it was. Yet powerful forces, in the form of economic interests, contended for a federal government that was also capable of energetic initiatives. Representatives of the landed and manufacturing interests, together with those who were not but who sought to safeguard from populist challenges what they considered an element of stability, progress, and prosperity, opted for a constitution that would afford maximum protection of property rights. Madison, considering the sources of faction and instability in government, pleads in *Federalist* Number 10 for the protection of inequality:

> The diversity in the faculties of men, from which the rights of property originate, is not less an insuperable obstacle to a uniformity of interests. The protection of these faculties is the first object of government. From the protection of different and unequal faculties of acquiring property, the possession of different degrees and kinds of property immediately results. . . .

Later in the same paper Madison itemizes the prevailing fears of agrarian, populist sentiment when he denounces: "A rage for paper money, for the abolition of debts, for an equal division of property, or for any other improper or wicked project. . . ."

And what was it, more specifically, that the propertied classes sought in the new government? They were concerned to see property rights receive protection through the sanctity of contract; to see revenue and tariff policies administered by a responsible central government; and to see a part of the public treasury allocated for the encouragement and promotion of commerce and industry. To these ends there were both positive and negative routes. Of the former, a central government empowered to act in each area and blessed with financial independence and integrity was at the top of the list of general priorities. It was effected through the extensive listing of congressional powers in Article I, Section 8; through the potentially great powers of the chief executive and through the clear constitutional statement concerning the supremacy of federal law. Of the latter—the negative route—limitations on the powers of the states and of the people were essential. This desire characterizes such provisions as the indirect election of the President, the presidential veto power, the appointment rather than election of senators, and the very existence of the Supreme Court. Each of these institutional devices satisfied, in part, the needs of the men of property to protect themselves from radical state legislatures, insurgent congressmen, and political movements representing frontier populism.

It would be misleading to imply that the Constitution which emerged was the handiwork of a cabal of business entrepreneurs. The constituent debates reveal that the men of property did not satisfy all their wants. Various proposals for general disfranchisement of nonproperty-holders and similar aristocratic provisions were defeated in convention by the forces of popular democracy. Finally, it must be noted that, while the establishment of institutions of a certain character was important in giving direction to future national political life, the real test was to come in the operation of these institutions. Institutional structure itself is static; it becomes dynamic through function. Thus the character of the functionaries—those who make the institutions work—is of paramount importance. A clue to the future, in this connection, is the fact that at the end of the eighteenth century the concept of the stake in society, indeed of general aristocratic superiority, was widely, if not universally, held.[11] This factor is of vital importance in studying the evolution of the fundamental norms of government in the nineteenth century.

## INSTITUTIONAL RELATIONSHIPS: THE FIRST HUNDRED YEARS

Considering the brief period of time the Federalists held political power in the nation, the governing mode they established is significant out of proportion to their short tenure as a political party. Doubtlessly this is so because their men were the *first* to practice the art of government within the framework of the new institutions and because they were some of the keenest minds and most skillful practitioners of politics in our history. What they did was bound to be important. Their chief operating assumption was that a rational and salutary conduct of the affairs of government could only be achieved by experts. They had in mind not experts in any narrow, specialized sense but rather men of uncommon education, broad experience, and professional training. In 1789 this meant clearly men of the upper class. Though they unabashedly maintained an aristocratic preference, they were not spokesmen for an irresponsible aristocracy. They admitted the wisdom of a check on the rulers by a popular assembly while resolutely denying the capacity of that assembly to formulate sound public policy. The predisposition of the Federalists for government for the people, by an elite of the people, had corollaries in the acceptance of a considerable measure of centralization in government and in a preference for the prerogatives of a vigorous executive. Federalist practice followed closely the counsel of that leading Federalist, Hamilton, expressed forcefully in the Seventieth Number of the *Papers:*

> Energy in the executive is a leading character in the definition of good government. It is essential to the protection of the community against foreign attacks; it is not less essential to the steady administration of the laws; to the protection of property . . . to the security of liberty against the enterprises and assaults of ambition, of faction, and of anarchy.

Since the chief aims of the Federalists were to re-establish public credit, encourage business and manufacturing activity, and protect the peace and stability of the nation, they were compelled by their quests to utilize as much central authority as they could constitutionally justify. Hence they became loose constructionists where provisions concerning federal power were concerned. Beyond this, the closest student of administrative developments in this period, Leonard White, has noted that, in shaping the governmental structure, the Federalists saw to it that leadership was lodged in "national rather than state agencies at the crucial points."[12] In the actual operation of the new government, the Federalists under Washington's leadership organized themselves efficiently, were conscientious, competent, and maintained a system of responsibility that narrowed down to individual officials held directly accountable.

In respect to the governing function, the advent of Jefferson to the Presidency justified once more the French epigram, *Plus ça change, plus c'est la même chose.* Jefferson the democrat, the agrarian, the man of the people, inherited and continued the Federalist establishment. While the sage of Monticello appeared to place a more restrictive construction on the Constitution, he soon became convinced of the practical wisdom of a vigorous exercise of executive powers. While he could not accept an aristocracy of wealth and birth which recommended itself to John Adams, he believed in a form of aristocracy nevertheless. Writing to his old political foe, Adams, in 1813 he conceded:

> For I agree with you that there is a natural aristocracy among men. The grounds of this are virtue and talents. . . . The natural aristocracy I consider as the most precious gift of nature, for the instruction, the trusts, and government of society. . . . May we not even say, that the form of government is the best, which provides the most effectually for a pure selection of these natural *aristoi* into the offices of government? [13]

Jefferson was too much of a gentleman not to accept a gentlemanly principle of rulership. This high regard for an ethic of quality, integrity, responsibility, disinterested service, and leadership, carried on by Jefferson, has been reasserted throughout American history; one would hope it continues to have appeal in the age of mass man. Yet there was a real difference between the patrician aristocracy of Adams which reflected a distrust of the people and the republican aristocracy of Jefferson which reflected a faith in people and the ultimate rectitude of popular majorities.

The distinction can be seen still more clearly with the coming of Jacksonian democracy. With that upsurge of the frontier, strident seaboard appeals for aristocratic privilege fell on deaf ears. A new breed of political functionary came into being. Richard Hofstadter has noted that between 1812 and 1821 six western states were admitted to the union along with constitutions that provided for universal white manhood suffrage. A new source of power in the ballot spawned brokers of that power. These politicos practiced a fine political art in representing social and economic constituencies that had theretofore been largely ignored.[14] By 1820 the Federalist Party was dead. When Jackson came to the Presidency in 1828, he brought with him the accumulated grievances of a class that felt itself historically underprivileged. A war was conducted against privilege as symbolized by the manufacturers in general and the National Bank in particular. The political bastions of privilege were assailed in the name of popular democracy, as the Jacksonians swept away the gentlemanly establishment and substituted a spoils system. The logic of the spoils system was simple and arresting as Jackson stated it in his first Annual Message to Congress:

> The duties of all public offices are, or at least admit of being made, so plain and simple that men of intelligence may readily qualify themselves for their performance, and I can not but believe that more is lost by the long continuance of men in office than is generally to be gained by their experience. . . . In a country where offices are created solely for the benefit of the people no man has any more intrinsic right to official station than another.[15]

The Jacksonians held that both the making and administration of public policy were matters that required good common sense, experience, and no more. Theory and expertise alike were eschewed. The consequence of this doctrine when put into practice was twofold. On the one hand a real democratic leavening occurred in the political process whereby the interests of the middle and lower classes were paid heed. On the other hand, there was a diminution in administrative expertise, impartiality, and intellectuality. This was a phenomenon of great portent for the development of the administrative system: The politicians were now officially pre-eminent over the bureaucrats. At the same time, it is interesting to note that the volume of governmental business was increasing at a rate that required an extension of the administrative family. By the middle of the nineteenth century a bureau system, characterized by a high degree of autonomy and independence, had developed within the various executive departments.[16] Thus, while the Jacksonians curtailed upper class dominance of the administrative complex they did not inhibit the growth of the complex itself. This is but one element of the paradox of executive energy expended within a popular democratic movement. For while Jackson himself opposed the Hamiltonian ends to which the central, executive-dominated state was directed, he was thoroughly Hamiltonian in his exercise of executive power, particularly in his use of the veto and his attempts to lead Congress.

This paradox contained the seeds of a future division in thought about the abiding problem of presidential-congressional relations created by the separation of powers. Twenty years after the breakup of the Federalist Party, the Whigs elected their first President and remain historically important more for their restrictive theory of presidential power than anything else. In many ways the Whigs resembled the early Republicans (Jefferson in theory, though not in practice) in their suspicions of federal power and executive authority. In turn, Jackson and the new Democrats, notably James K. Polk, found themselves challenging the strict constitutional constructions that were to become the first principle of Whiggery. In fact, as Leonard White notes, the Democrats even went the Federalists one better when, in their attempts to dominate Congress, they declared that the President was as representative of the people as Congress was.[17] The contest between President and Congress would be carried on throughout American history to the present, sometimes conducted under partisan banners, at other times simply resulting from a clash of institutional loyalties. That the contest actually turns more upon personalities and issues than upon party loyalties is demonstrated historically by the taste of Republicans (Lincoln and Theodore Roosevelt) for executive energy as well as Democrats (Jackson, Wilson, and Franklin Roosevelt).

The period from the end of the Civil War to the turn of the century was, with few exceptions, an unproductive one in terms of the development of the art of government. The overseers of what has been called the Republican Era could boast of nothing that compared with either the patterns of leadership established by the Federalists and carried on by the Jeffersonians or the democratic political revolution that was presided over by the Jacksonians and their successors. During the greater part of this period, the Whig theory of government accurately describes what occurred in practice. Presidents who followed Andrew Johnson to office were hard put to repair the damage done to the Presidency in the immediate postbellum period. Congress, having sampled the fruits of supreme political power, fought to retain that supremacy by tightly exercising the leading strings it imposed on presidential policy. It was in this period that the congressional oligarchy of committee chairmen and House Speakers came into its own.[18] Only toward the end of the period, when the rumblings of reform were beginning to be heard, were any solid accomplishments registered. The establishment of the Civil Service Commission in 1883 and of the Interstate Commerce Commission in 1887 was but a hint of sweeping institutional changes that were to come in the next half century.

In the post-Civil War period the doctrine of *laissez faire* reigned supreme over the land. The industrial revolution that was taking place was presided over by a coterie of irresponsible tycoons who brought to perfection the practice of monopoly finance capitalism. The state had immobilized itself by its meek adherence to the prescription of let-alone. Public morality sank to new depths; corrupt office seeking was rife; and congressional government was often the collective tool of selfish financial interests.

Of the two substantial reforms that were effected, the establishment of the Interstate Commerce Commission came about almost by accident. Indeed, there was real public pressure for the regulation of railroad rates. That Congress was unable to withstand this pressure sufficiently was due more to the vicissitudes of its own operating rules than to strong majority conviction in favor of reform. The House of Representatives, which never had really approved the scheme, found itself pressured into accepting at the final stages a compromise conference committee report.[19] Of such mean circumstances are eventful accomplishments sometimes born.

Civil Service reform had been on the public agenda since Grant's time. In fact, Grant had established a commission in 1871 (again, by the devious route of a rider attached to an appropriations bill), but congressional antagonism frustrated this attempt at a merit system. When the Pendelton Civil Service Act passed in 1883, after a tortuous amble through the legislative labyrinth, major credit was due to a high-minded pressure group—the National Civil Service Reform League—and the public-spirited leadership of such men as Carl Schurz and Charles Bonaparte. And it was a momentous piece of legislation. It gave the President authority over the rules and regulations governing federal appointment, established an open, competitive examination system, and guaranteed the protection of the classified service against political pressures. Finally, as White has pointed out, the establishment of the system implied a recognition of presidential responsibility over the whole range of disparate administrative agencies.[20] Though not appreciated at the time, this constituted a significant victory for presidential claims to administrative leadership. Nevertheless, the impulse to sweeping change and reform was satisfied only after the Progressives had brought a full realization of the existing political malaise to public attention.

## THE PROGRESSIVE ERA OF REFORM

To speak of the Progressive Movement, as is often done, is to speak in a vague, generic sense. Actually there was not *a* Progressive Movement, but several movements involving quests from different regions of the country, simultaneously and at different times, for a whole catalogue of social, economic, and political reforms. There were the "hayseed radicals" of the Midwest who felt the oppressive resuls of scarce money and blamed business, the city, and plutocratic government.[21] With all the injured indignation they could summon up, a people hard put upon wallowed in the sentiment of the agrarian myth.[22] In meetings in Cincinnati, St. Louis, and Omaha, they were harangued and aroused to a delirious pitch by spirited leaders, such as the improbable Ignatius ("Atlantis Ignatius") Donnelly, and out of it all came: "Bryan! Bryan! Bryan!—the peerless leader, the shining knight of the West." [23] The storm clouds out of the Midwest produced thunderous revolts that catapulted into legislative power insurgents like Robert M. LaFollette of Wisconsin, Albert B. Cummins of Iowa, and Albert J. Beveridge of Indiana.

Contemporaneously, the social justice aspect of the progressive endeavors was forging ahead in the Midwest and East. Child labor, a perennial source of shocked consciences, came under the guns of the Consumers' Leagues and such organizations as Chicago's Hull House. The action of these dedicated bands bore swift results as revealed by the fact that in 1900 twenty-four states and the District of Columbia had no minimum wage requirements, while, by 1914, only one state remained without a minimum wage law on its statute books. Similarly, with reference to the conditions of women workers in 1896, New York initiated a trend toward limiting women's hours of work, a precedent quickly followed by Massachusetts, Nebraska, Michigan, Colorado, Washington, and Tennessee. By 1917, thirty-nine states had enacted hours legislation.[24] Further social reforms, such as industrial accident insurance programs, were initiated during the opening decade of the century, giving pioneer initiative to even greater demands.

The cities of America, marked by widespread corruption, provided another battle site to absorb the reforming zeal of progressives on the move. "Bath House" John Coughlin and "Hinky Dink" Kenna, along with their less magnificently identified counterparts in the cities across the land, regularly promised and delivered the votes on election day in return for jobs and influence. Contaminated water, bad sewage disposal, and unpaved streets were the fruits of the machinations of the bosses and their clients. A distinguished visitor from abroad, James Bryce, was forced to conclude that what Lincoln Steffens, the muckraking journalist, had called the "shame of the cities" was indeed the most conspicuous failure of the United States.[25] Popular pressure at the local and state levels of government was sufficient in many cases to bring about valuable practical reforms, if only in piecemeal fashion. Major reform at the national level required nothing less than a full-scale assault on the reigning dogma of *laissez faire*. In the end, it was the successful refutation of the philosophy of negative government which constituted the lasting achievement of the intellectual leaders of the Progressive Era. For once old inhibitions against vigorous and pervasive government action had been removed, the American polity had taken a long step forward on the road to a general walfare state supported institutionally by a rapid increase in the size, responsibilities, and powers of the administrative arm. To the conservative of 1900 as to the conservative today, such a course was fraught with peril. To the progressive of 1900 as to the liberal today, such a course constituted an inescapable recognition that society had changed and comparable changes in the governing institutions were sources of opportunity and justice.

The implications of the changes wrought in the classical norms and forms of American government in the twentieth century will be a major focus of attention in the remaining pages of this book.

At this point, it may prove useful to preview in brief some "scenes from the coming attractions."

(1) SEPARATION OF POWERS. Even though the Federalists did not view the three branches as watertight compartments and accepted, as Madison noted, the view that one branch would have a "partial agency" over the acts of the others, they could not have imagined the extent to which a sharing of powers and an *extensive* agency of one over the others would develop. The two striking features of twentieth-century American national government are the expansion of the Presidency and the growth of administration which, while sometimes considered "executive" in function, often operates independently of the three branches. Although the constitutional checks on each branch imposed by the others still exist, they have long since lost their potency as strict balancing mechanisms. Thus, Congress can override presidential vetoes, but the vast majority of vetoes are sustained; Congress can reconstitute the Supreme Court or the Senate can refuse to accept presidential appointments, but neither falls within the limits of the probable; indeed, even Congress' constitutional function of lawmaking is shared through delegated legislation to administrative agencies and a partial acceptance of executive leadership; finally, to cite a more extreme example, only Congress has the constitutional right to declare war, but this had become meaningless by the middle of the twentieth century. On the other hand, the constitutional skeleton of presidential powers has over the last few decades been clothed with powerful muscle. Indeed, some would argue that the executive has become literally muscle-bound, its presidential nervous system unable to control the bureaucratic appendages. A plethora of new agencies, independent regulatory commissions, public corporations, and "advisory" groups operates an administrative complex sometimes beyond the limits of specific presidential control. The Supreme Court, once a conservative bulwark against ambitious exercises of executive prerogative, has apparently come to accept the imperatives of positive government and regularly provides judicial rationales for a liberal construction of policy making powers.

(2) FEDERALISM. It is a truism to say that the balance of powers between the states and the national Government has

shifted radically in the direction of national pre-eminence. The sheer weight and scope of services that American citizens have come to expect of government has been too much for the states to handle. Urbanization and industrialization together with a high degree of mobility have combined to produce problems that can only be met adequately with the resources of the national government. Conservation, highways, educational systems, urban renewal, and much more are all projects that require massive expenditures and a degree of planning and co-ordination unavailable to the states. Where the states *have* been able to provide for the needs of a new society, they have often refused to assume the burden, with the result that citizens have transferred a large measure of their loyalties from the states to the national government. An ambitious and resourceful exercise of state powers might, in some cases, have filled the vacuum of needs from day to day, but it is difficult to imagine how the states could meet the challenges posed by such emergencies as war, depression, recession, and natural disaster. Beyond this, an increased regard for social justice in our times has produced increased federal intervention in traditional areas of state competence where basic rights are being denied citizens.

(3) LIMITED GOVERNMENT. The sum total of changes in institutional relationships is manifested in a steep reduction of the limits on governmental action. A necessity for the regulation of private group activity—particularly that of business, labor, and agriculture—in a complex industrial society has brought about a merger of the spheres of public and private life. The use of the comerce power, the taxing power, and the enforcement of the Bill of Rights have all taken a toll of property rights while augmenting other human and social rights. In short, a subtle change in philosophy about the relations of man to man, and man to the state, has occurred. The individualistic ethic of our forebears has given way to a social or co-operative ethic that seems to accord more realistically with the times.

(4) DEMOCRACY. The balance of democracy in our times is a difficult one to assess. In the sense that democracy means greater opportunity for the people to achieve their desires and aspirations politically, *quantitatively* we are more democratic than ever. Public officials must appeal to a wider and wider variety of groups for

public favor. Senators have been elected popularly since 1916. The suffrage has been widened. In our grandparents' generation, women were admitted to the polls; in our own time, Negroes are gradually winning basic political rights. In the sense that democracy means widespread, educated participation in politics and an exacting exercise of control over the decision makers, *qualitatively,* we may not have progressed far. The very complexity of policy making in the modern state necessitates battalions of experts to carry on the work of policy formulation and execution in each specialized area of government. The layman citizen is thus placed in a position of having to choose among vague alternatives insofar as he can affect policy at all. Final frustration ensues when, even after the citizen has made his vague choice, his elected representatives are unable to translate aspirations into policy or to make policy effective through administration.

Many of the problems attending the rise of Big Government have long been recognized. As far back as 1887 Woodrow Wilson initiated a discussion which continues to the present day concerning the place of administration in modern government.[26] Wilson conceived of administration as being separate from politics, and he believed that the only rational and responsible system of government was one in which policy is set forth in broad outline by the lawmakers, leaving the detailed execution to administrators endowed with wide discretion. The professor of politics at Princeton who was later to become President of the United States realized that the unhampered discretion he sought for administrators could be safely granted only if the officials could be held accountable. He saw the solution to his problem in a hierarchical system in which an official at the apex of the organization would be held publicly accountable. It is a tribute to Wilson's prescience that this general theory is nearly universally accepted today. The difficulty, of course, lies in the translation of theory into practice. In the chapters which follow, we shall examine some of the obstacles which arise along the road to this goal, beginning with an investigation into the nature of bureaucratic organization.

## REFERENCES

1. Of definitions of power there are many. Although a proper elaboration of any definition could easily fill the pages of this book, the simple

relationship stated above will serve our purposes. For essays on the theme of power, see Bertrand Russell, *Power: A New Social Analysis* (London: Unwin Books, 1962); H. D. Lasswell and A. Kaplan, *Power and Society* (New Haven: Yale University Press, 1950); and Robert Dahl, "The Concept of Power," *Behavioral Science,* II (July, 1957), pp. 201-215.

2. Max Farrand, *The Framing of the Constitution of the United States* (New Haven: Yale University Press, 1913), pp. 3-4.

3. See William Bondy, "The Separation of Governmental Powers," *Studies in History, Economics, and Public Law,* ed. by the Faculty of Political Science of Columbia University (New York: Columbia University, 1896), pp. 133-318.

4. Alexander Hamilton, James Madison, and John Jay, *The Federalist Papers,* Clinton Rossiter (ed.), No. 47 (New York: Mentor Books, 1961). Italics in the original.

5. This is not to say that the Founders had no concept of the importance of administrative power. It is to say that they could not achieve a consensus on the knotty problem of the locus of this power. Those who favored a strong, central government had no doubts about its proper location in the executive branch. Hamilton states it flatly in *Federalist* No. 72: "The administration of government, in its largest sense, comprehends all the operations of the body politic, whether legislative, executive or judiciary; but in its most usual and perhaps in its most precise signification, it is limited to executive details, and falls peculiarly within the province of the executive department."

6. *Federalist,* No. 45.

7. *Federalist,* No. 46. Madison goes on to note for the record that this is a highly unlikely contingency.

8. Gaillard Hunt and James Brown Scott (eds.), *The Debates in the Federal Convention of 1787 Which Framed the Constitution of the United States of America, Reported by James Madison* (New York: Oxford University Press, 1920), p. 323.

9. Edward S. Corwin, *The "Higher Law" Background of American Constitutional Law* (Ithaca: Cornell University Press [Great Seal Books], 1955).

10. Clinton Rossiter, *Seedtime of the Republic* (New York: Harcourt Brace & Company, 1953), p. 53.

11. See especially Vernon L. Parrington, *Main Currents in American Thought,* 3 vols., Volume I, *The Colonial Mind* (New York: Harcourt Brace & Company [Harvest Books], 1954), Book 3; and Charles A. Beard, *The Economic Basis of Politics and Related Writings,* compiled and annotated by William Beard (New York: Vintage Books, 1958), Part IV.

12. Leonard D. White, *The Federalists* (New York: The Macmillan Company, 1948), p. 509.

13. Quoted in Leonard D. White, *The Jeffersonians* (New York: The Macmillan Company, 1951), p. 549.

14. Richard Hofstadter, *The American Political Tradition* (New York: Vintage Books, 1955), p. 50.

15. Quoted in *ibid.*, p. 51.

16. Leonard D. White, *The Jacksonians* (New York: The Macmillan Company, 1954), p. 538.

17. *Ibid.*, p. 564.

18. For a classic description and critique of the system, see Woodrow Wilson, *Congressional Government* (originally published in 1885) (New York: Meridian Books, 1956).

19. Peter Woll, *American Bureaucracy* (New York: W. W. Norton & Co., Inc., 1963), p. 37.

20. Leonard D. White, *The Republcian Era, 1869-1901* (New York: The Macmillan Company, 1958), p. 364.

21. Russel Nye, *Midwestern Progressive Politics* (East Lansing: Michigan State College Press, 1951), pp. 71-75.

22. Richard Hofstadter, *The Age of Reform from Bryan to F.D.R.* (New York: Alfred A. Knopf, 1956). Hofstadter performs some careful exploratory surgery on rural society, living off the myth of the precious yeoman, but growing aware of the techniques of the acquisitive, commercial society. See Chapter I, "The Agrarian Myth and Commercial Realities."

23. Nye, *op. cit.*, p. 70.

24. Arthur S. Link, *American Epoch* (New York: Alfred A. Knopf, 1955), pp. 70-71.

25. James Bryce, *The American Commonwealth,* 2 vols., 2nd ed., rev. (New York: The Macmillan Company, 1891), Vol. I, p. 637.

26. Woodrow Wilson, "The Study of Administration," *Political Science Quarterly,* II (1887), pp. 197-222.

# CHAPTER 2

# Bureaucracy in Society and State

THE ORGANIZATIONAL REVOLUTION

The roots of governmental change are extensive, taking their source from a changing American society. Only a misreading of American history would suggest that novel institutional developments were a product of the programmatic notions of theorists and ideologists. Our politics have always followed a pattern drawn from practical needs and popular aspirations rather than ideal prescriptions. Perhaps at once the most comprehensive and meaningful way of viewing institutional modifications is to look upon them as a reflection of changes in the *organizational* structure of society. One immediately identifiable change has been in size. A more interesting and informative quest, however, looks to the mode of accommodating ever greater numbers to environment. Beyond this, one might be moved to consider the ethical implications of increased size and modified structure.[1] A preliminary task, however, is the identification of some of the more striking quantitative aspects of the organizational revolution.

In contrast to the kind of society we shall be describing as contemporary, life in the preindustrial past was characterized by smallness and self-sufficiency. Very often the family and small community comprised the sphere of social intercourse. Mobility was extremely limited, and frequently horizons did not extend beyond immediate geographical regions. The individual, whether farmer, artisan, or tradesman, could realistically consider himself an autonomous producer, largely responsible for his own destiny. Of course, organizations existed, but they were, for the most part, small and social in nature. Organization meant the community church, the fraternal order, the sewing circle, or perhaps the grange. The one-room schoolhouse and the small, denominational college (drawing its enrollment from a minute and well-to-do segment of the whole population) characterized the educational system. Relationships were more man to man than man to the organization. Relative isolation and a lack of technology produced an environment that demanded a maximum degree of self-sufficiency and individual responsibility. It is a small wonder that when nineteenth-century Social Darwinists applied the doctrine of the survival of the fittest to humankind, social prescription seemed to accord with experience.[2] As the pace of industrialization quickened in the latter half of the nineteenth century, economic theory reiterated the rural values of individualism and competition. Economic practice, as we shall see, was devoted to quite different techniques. By the end of the nineteenth century a number of social eruptions on the once prosaic landscape had signaled the revolutionary transformation that was to take place in the twentieth.

In outlining the contours of the organizational revolution, it is fitting to begin with the economic transformation that took place in the decades following the Civil War. Kenneth Boulding has noted: "In the Western world the organizational revolution has gone hand in hand with a rapid rise in the over-all productivity of the society—a rise which was going on before the great growth of organizations, but which does not seem to have been abated by them."[3]

A major source of this economic growth is to be found in expanding technology and mechanization. The tremendous growth in transportation facilities from the 1870s onward provided the stimulus for rapid industrialization. The completion of the railroad network crossing the country by the 1890s, followed by automotive and air transportation in the twentieth century, created the mobility necessary to sustain a giant industrial complex. The revolution in communications brought by the telegraph, telephone, radio, and television has contributed to the solution of problems posed by mere geography. In our own time the efficient division of labor through assembly line techniques, the development of new machinery, and indeed the whole trend toward automation have meant that fewer men can produce, distribute, and exchange more goods and services in a shorter period of time. Statistically, this increase in productivity can be gauged by the ever mounting

gross national product (total national output of goods and services). In 1875 the GNP stood just over $7 billion, by 1900 it had
more than doubled to $15.7 billion, and by 1920 it had quadru-
pled itself. In 1940 the GNP exceeded $100 billion, and in the
next twenty years it had multiplied fivefold, exceeding in 1960,
$500 billion.[4]

Yet another vital prerequisite to expansion was the change that
overcame the *organization* of production. In a competitive atmosphere, economies of size were sought through efficient division of
labor and the corollary development of specialization in the productive process. Concomitantly new relationships were created
among men in the process of making a living. The hallowed
dynamic of competition was soon recognized to have destructive
as well as constructive effects, and entrepreneurs resorted to combination in order to mitigate these effects.[5] In the 1870s and
1880s the great trust empires grew. The lore of the "robber
barons" is effulgent with tales of John D. Rockefeller and his
Standard Oil combine, Andrew Carnegie's gigantic steel empire,
Henry Clay Frick in coal, Morgan and Harriman in railroads, and
many lesser luminaries. The technique of the financial trust combined with the modern corporation abetted the trend toward
concentration, and in 1933 Berle and Means reported that nearly
half the corporate wealth of the United States was controlled by the
200 largest corporations.[6] A still more revealing consequence of
the modern corporation as a form of economic organization is the
contrast it presents to the image of the autonomous property owner
of bygone days. The most significant conclusion that Berle and
Means reached was not the fact of concentration—which had
been public knowledge since the turn of the century—but the
separation that had developed between ownership and control.
Through a variety of legal devices, such as the pyramiding of
stock, the issuance of nonvoting stock, the use of proxies, and the
assurance of management control, the thousands of shareholders
in a corporation (very often the largest single interest being a
fraction of one per cent) exercise no control over the decision
making process.[7]

Rising productivity and the fruition of the modern corporation
begat sweeping changes in the occupational structure of the nation. Increasingly over recent decades, Americans have become

employees of the big organization. This trend is partially indicated by dramatic numerical increases in those occupational groups typically serving the large organization. Whereas in 1910 in a total work force of 38 million, professional, nonfarm technical and managerial workers numbered approximately 4 million; clerical workers, approximately 3.8 million; and semiskilled workers, approximately 5.5 million. In 1960 with a total work-force of 66.7 million, these groups had increased disproportionately as follows: professional-technical-managerial, 14.5 million; clerical, 9.8 million; and semiskilled, 12.7 million. During the same time period, unskilled workers remained approximately the same.[8] Another way of viewing the occupational trend is to note the sharp decreases in the farming and self-employed sectors. In 1860, of total employment, 58 per cent was agricultural; by 1900 that percentage had dropped to 37.5; in 1960 only 8.5 per cent of the labor force was involved in farming. Similarly, at the turn of the century, nearly one-quarter of the work force was self-employed, whereas by 1960 that proportion had declined to 13.7 per cent.

Of the nearly 87 per cent of the labor force that works for someone else, it may be estimated that half of these employees serve the big organizations in an environment characterized by "size, standardization, impersonality, exquisite specialization, hierarchy and dependence."[9] The kinds of organizations employing vast work forces are characterized by, but by no means limited to, the large corporations. A survey by *Fortune Magazine* done in 1965 indicates that the 500 largest industrial corporations employed 10.4 million. General Motors led in size, providing employment for over 600,000; the Ford Motor Company employed over 300,000; and ten others employed over 100,000 each. The average work force of the 500 corporations was over 20,000 workers each.[10] The largest banks (Bank of America, Chase Manhattan, and Morgan Guaranty Trust), the largest life insurance companies (Metropolitan, Prudential, and Equitable Life), the largest merchandising companies (Great Atlantic & Pacific, Sears Roebuck, and Montgomery Ward), and the largest transportation facilities (New York Central Railroad, Pennsylvania Railroad, and Pan American World Airways) all employ massive numbers in their organizations. As Presthus has noted, the great utilities like American Telephone and Telegraph, the armed forces, and the mammoth universities similarly provide employment for additional millions.[11]

It is further interesting to note that, while agriculture as a vocation has diminished greatly, a trend toward increased size and concentration in individual units similar to industry has appeared. The move is in the direction of the large commercial farm, utilizing the fruits of the latest farm technology and machinery and operating along industrial lines. From 1900 to 1959 the total number of farms declined from 5,737,000 to 3,703,000; during the same period, large, commercial farms of the 1000 acre-and-up class increased from 47,000 to 136,000. Correspondingly, 44 per cent of the farms representing the larger commercial enterprises accounted for 90.8 per cent of market sales while the other 56 per cent accounted for only 9.2 per cent of the market.[12] The family plot of Jeffersonian lore appears to be giving way to an organizational structure patterned after the modern corporation.

Since the great industrial corporations, private commercial agencies, and mammoth universities are usually located in or around cities, it is not surprising that a trend toward urbanization has been another of the indices of the revolution in social organization. The reversal in the circumstances of habitation over the past century has been startling. In 1860, 80 per cent of our people lived in rural areas and 20 per cent in urban; by 1900 the urban proportion had doubled, but we were still 60 per cent rural. In 1960 this was more than reversed, with a population that was 70 per cent urban and 30 per cent rural. There is evidence that we are perhaps even more "urbanized" than we are urban according to census figures. That is, through the mass media of communications which knit the nation together we seem to be developing a rather homogeneous and essentially urban consciousness. The newspapers we read have declined precipitously in number while increasing vastly in circulation bringing about heavy concentration. A few great chains account for well over half of newspaper circulation in the country. Similarly, the programs we listen to on radio and watch on television are largely produced by the great networks. Whether the viewer resides in Kenosha, Wisconsin; Laramie, Wyoming; or Texas City, Texas, he absorbs images of social reality created in New York or Los Angeles.

The trend toward size, concentration, and standardization is also revealed by the growth of fraternal, professional, and educational organizations in which the modern American participates. The archetype of these organizations seems to be federationist and bureaucratic. Eighteen million American workers are organized into unions, and the giant AFL-CIO federation, overwhelming all others, accounts for nearly 85 per cent of all unionists. Social and fraternal organizations have massed. There are nearly 3 million American Legionaires, 1.2 million Elks, 1.3 million Odd Fellows, over a million Knights of Columbus, a half million Rotarians, and 2.2 million (predominantly rural) members of 4-H Clubs.[13] We also take our higher education in a big way as the small, rural college gives way more and more to the imposing state university, or even federation of universities. With nearly 4 million students now enrolled in colleges and universities, the top 20 in enrollment account for well over half a million. The multi-campus University of California system enrolls over 50,000, and the College of the City of New York over 100,000. Anticipated doubling and trebling of college enrollments in coming decades assure the continuance of the trend toward the "multi-versity."

As a people we have become accustomed to the big organization. Indeed, there is probably a consensus among us that many rewards have accrued as a result of our organizational genius. Others have identified a number of socially questionable by-products of the great transformation.[14] In any case, given the circumstances of growth in every direction on the North American continent, the revolution was inevitable. Nor should it be at all surprising that bigness in all walks of life has been reflected in Big Government. The crude features of the organizational revolution in government can be documented quantitatively as they have been for society as a whole. The growth in the number of the government employees, increased budgetary expenditures, and a broadening in the range of governmental activities provide convenient criteria by which to judge the extent of change.

In 1860 civilian employees of the federal government numbered about 50,000. By the turn of the century that number had grown to over 200,000. Even at this point cabinet department heads conducted a great deal of the business of their departments personally, aided by clerks who were just making the transition from laboriously hand-copied records to the use of the typewriter. In our own century government employment has grown approximately twelve times its 1900 size, reaching 2,445,598 in 1962. These figures in themselves, however, tell only a part of the story. The greatest measure of growth has taken place in the executive branch—specifically in the administrative arm. Only slightly more than one per cent of federal employees work outside the executive branch. Another way to look at the variability of change might be to consider that since the first decade of this century the membership of Congress has remained stable; the size of the House was fixed at 435 in 1912, and, with the exception of the admission of two new states' Senate delegations, the Upper House has now grown. Of course, Congress has permitted itself a few thousand additional aides, but the significance of its growth has been minimal. For a longer time the Supreme Court has remained a body of nine. From time to time additional courts and judges are added to the federal system, signifying the growth of judicial business, but this growth is again inconsiderable. Likewise, there is still only one President, but the growth of the establishment of his administrative helpers in this century from slightly over 200,000 to 2.4 million is the hallmark of our bureaucratic age.

One humorous explanation for this growth, which also contains a measure of serious wisdom, has been codified as "Parkinson's Law." The "Law" is actually a general principle based upon two laws: the law of "multiplication of subordinates" and the law of "multiplication of work." In the first instance, overburdened civil servants hire assistants in pairs. This provides, in turn, two important benefits since fear of each other's promotion sets up a healthy competition between the assistants and at the same time keeps them too busy to contemplate taking the boss's job. In the second instance, work must be multiplied rather geometrically in order to fill the time of the assistants and, eventually, that of the two additional sub-assistants whom they, in the nature of things, will each employ.[15] While internal momentum does play a part in the expansion of administrative officialdom, the needs created by wars, depressions, and other emergencies are surely the major spurs to governmental growth.

Another index of the size of the governmental function is the magnitude of government expenditures. An idea of the general upward trend is revealed by noting that in 1875 total federal expenditures amounted to $274.6 million; by 1900 this figure had nearly doubled, reaching $520.9 million; and in 1965 it reached a peacetime high of 97.5 *billion*. The gradual, steady increase in expenditures has exploded sharply during the years of our great wars. Thus, while in 1875 the government spent little more than a quarter billion, ten years earlier in the final year of the Civil War federal expenditures had exceeded one billion dollars for the first time in our history. Similarly, in 1919 at the close of World War I expenditures had reached $18 billion from which point they dropped sharply until the 1940s. A slightly different and particularly revealing dimension of the increase in government spending is revealed when we compare the amounts cited to the increasing total productive output (GNP). In 1900 federal expenditures constituted 3.3 per cent of the GNP whereas in 1963 they were 15.8 per cent of GNP. Thus government spending has risen far out of proportion to total productivity and has continued at a rather high rate in the post-World War II years. The immediate cause of continued high expenditures is the fact that such a large proportion of the federal budget (running close to two-thirds during most of the postwar period) is devoted to military and defense spending. If one were to assume that the cold war would be liquidated in the coming years we might anticipate a leveling off of expenditures somewhat, though certainly not to prewar levels. The reason for this is simply that government does more and is expected to do more in our times than ever before.

Ultimately, it is this widened range of governmental activities that explains a larger administrative establishment, greater expenditures, and, one might add, a greater federal debt rate. The myriad activities government now performs have long histories and complex sources and will be considred more fully at a later stage. For the present, let a few general factors underlying the advent of Big Government be set forth. The rapid growth and reorganization of the economic structure, coupled with the expiration of the dogma of *laissez faire,* have endowed government with a largely expanded role as regulator or policeman over our "economic republic." Each new commission, bureau, or agency charged with the oversight of some economic activity—transportation, communications, trade, the system of exchange, or labor-management relations, to mention but a few—means more civil servants, more office space, and more expenditures. Likewise, the acceptance of the philosophy that government should act to help citizens in economic distress, and even more, that government should *plan* to avoid, or at least to cope with unavoidable distresses, has further added to the role of modern government. Perhaps the outstanding recent example of government's acceptance of this latter obligation was given when congress passed the Employment Act of 1946 (by large bipartisan majorities in both houses) which commits government to encourage and promote a maximum level of employment and production. A third major cause of big government is the new world-wide role that has developed on the United States in this century. Unexcelled productivity and industrial capability have made of America a great world power. Paradoxically, this national power cannot be exercised independently or in isolation. Power breeds responsibility for its use. In a world of contending powers and power blocs the State must, of necessity, expend a greater share of its product and its energies in tending to its international affairs. One aspect of the acceptance of these responsibilities by the American government may be cited. From the time of its inception in 1948 to 1962 the Mutual Security Program for allocating foreign aid made available some $64 billion to nations around the world.

These, then, are the broad outlines of the organizational revolution that has occurred in the course of a lifetime. Yet the revolution has been far from a mere statistical one. Without order and authority a revolution soon develops into anarchy. However, the challenge has been met, and modern man has perfected bureaucracy as the system for ordering events and achieving goals rationally. For the remainder of this chapter, we shall identify and evaluate a number of the peculiar characteristics of this widely misunderstood phenomenon.

## THE ANATOMY OF BUREAUCRACY

Bureaucracy may be thought of as a complex system of men, offices, methods, and authority which large organizations employ in order to achieve their goals.[16] Since bureaucracy is characteristic of large organizations, much of what follows will be as true of private bureaucracies like the modern corporation and the university as it is of public bureaucracy found in government. And while our primary concern is to understand the nature of governmental administration, examples drawn from private bureaucracy are relevant in elucidating the operation of public bureaucracy. Bureaucratic patterns of organization did not suddenly spring forth, full-blown, in the last century. There are records of ancient bureaucracy that have long fascinated the historian and sociologist. It is the elaboration and predominance of bureaucracy in modern society and government that make its consideration so vital to the contemporary political scientist. The first major attempt to theorize extensively about the nature and significance of bureaucracy was made by the eminent German sociologist, Max Weber (1864-1920). Our debt to Weber's pioneering efforts is immense, and it must be with his careful formulation of an ideal type that we make our point of departure on the way to understanding modern bureaucracy. For convenience, Weber's construct may be set down in terms of the four systematic elements of our definition: (1) men, (2) offices, (3) methods, and (4) authority.

(1) The bureaucrats, or men who hold office in a bureaucracy, are vocationally oriented. They have reached office by route of a particular course of training in a specialized field. The division of labor required by the large organization demands specialized technical qualifications from its officials. In general, the job of the bureaucrat is one of management—either of persons or things— a service which he contributes to the organization in return for his livelihood. In addition, according to Weber, appointment to office rather than election is characteristic of the professional bureaucrat. The official as a rule enjoys high status in society. His status, or social esteem, results from educational and technical or professional accomplishments which are usually symbolized in certificates, university degrees, or other records of achievement. Additional status is lent by the institution or office in which the bureaucrat works. Officeholding is actually more than a vocation; it is a career. The official is promoted in a series of ascending steps throughout his career. He normally holds claim to tenure in his office and is removable only for cause. Likewise, he is paid a fixed salary which is dependent not upon how much work he performs but rather on the position of his office in the total organization. Salary increases follow promotion to the next, higher level, and it is characteristic of the compensation system to include a pension

after retirement. In sum, the career of the official is characterized by his relationship primarily to the organization office (bureau) rather than to another *person.* Duties, obligations, and loyalties are directed toward the institution itself.[17]

(2) The bureaucratic office is characterized by a special area of competence. It is one, perhaps small but indispensable, part of the total organizational matrix. Its relationship to the other offices of the organization is determined by the principle of hierarchy. It is subordinate and accountable to offices above it and receives subordination and accountability from those offices resting beneath it. Matters of direction, control, and discipline flow from the top down in step fashion. As Weber has noted, although control is exercised formally through the hierarchy, ideally the essence of this control is control by knowledge. Knowledge in an administrative system is of two kinds. Specialized, technical knowledge is one source of power; in practice, experience and an acquaintance with office methods, practices, and conventions are other sources of superior knowledge and power. In the typical bureaucratic unit there is a total separation between the use and ownership of the means of production or administration. As *employees,* officials use the furniture, machinery, libraries, laboratories, or other resources of the organization during their regular working hours. Thus all the appurtenances of the position are borrowed by the official, and he is accountable for their use to the organization. This contributes to a final characteristic of the bureaucratic system—its formalistic impersonality. Neutral norms and procedures, applying to all, excepting none, and creating an atmosphere of impersonal equity are hallmarks of ideal bureaucracy.[18]

(3) The methods by which bureaucracy operates are basically an outgrowth of the system of offices which characterizes it. Within the hierarchy each office operates according to established rules and norms. The object of such an atmosphere is to enhance the efficiency of the office and the psychic well-being of the official. The bureaucrat can calculate an appropriate course of action within the rules and be assured that his acts are justified or "safe." This mode of behavior explains in part the heavy reliance upon records and files which is typical of bureaucracy. All communications must be prepared in multiple copies and records of all conversations, orders, and transactions must be systematically

filed away for future reference. The system of recorded precedents promotes efficiency and uniformity within the office and supports individual official acts with predictability.[19]

(4) The system of authority which Weber found most appropriate to the modern bureaucratic organization was one based upon rational-legal grounds. The reason Weber regarded this basis of authority as superior to alternative sources was not merely because it was becoming more common in his own times, but because he felt it was by far the most efficient. As Peter Blau has noted, Weber's analysis of bureaucracy is a *functional* one.[20] His foremost concern was to find what system of authority would produce the highest degree of goal achievement for the organization. A system of authority deriving from impersonal, abstract legal norms based upon rational calculations by legislators, constitution makers, or entrepreneurs and applying equally to all members of the organization constituted, for Weber, the maximum of efficiency. Law was deemed corporate in nature, and obedience to the law was given by the official in his capacity as a member of a corporate group. In practice, the official obeys a superior person, but obedience is not really given to the person but to the office which is a legitimate personification of the rational-legal order.[21]

Weber admitted two other types of legitimate authority to his analysis—traditional and charismatic. Authority finding its source in traditional grounds has been widely exercised throughout history. What makes such authority legitimate is its appeal to the sanctity of long-established practices and conventions. In turn, the sanctity of the traditions vests with status those who interpret and apply them. A tradition-based authority system can be bureaucratic, employ a large administrative staff, and yet violate the ideal bureaucratic canon of formalistic impersonality since officials in such a system give loyalty to persons directly and primarily rather than to legal norms. The third type of legitimate authority Weber analyzed is charismatic. Whereas under traditional systems, authority becomes personalized (and, thereby, less efficient), under charismatic rule all authority is totally personal, drawing legitimacy from no other source than the command of a superhuman, otherworldly leader. Such leadership is inspirational in nature, and, as long as charisma persists, the godlike determinations of the charismatic leader are accepted as legitimate and absolute by his followers. Pure charisma is decidedly nonbureaucratic in that such authority, depending on the whim of the leader, totally rejects routine. However, Weber concluded that over a period of time, with the establishment of a system of succession, charisma could become routinized. In this instance, charisma could function authoritatively within a bureaucratic framework.[22] Weber realized that the three types of authority he described seldom exist in pure form and that any given administrative system can be based upon elements of two, or even all three, forms of legitimacy. Yet the ideal Weberian type—and the one with which we are most closely familiar—is the rational-legal bureaucratic system.

## BEYOND WEBER

Many of the characteristics of bureaucracy that Weber has outlined for us would be familiar to the contemporary citizen on the basis of his experience. Such concepts as hierarchy, routine, formality, standardization, "paper work," rules, and regulations all seem to accord accurately with our image of modern administration in the big organization. Yet when we look more closely at bureaucracy in operation we are bound to conclude that practice diverges rather widely at many points from the Weberian ideal type. This is true for two reasons. First, Weber's construct is partially limited in its applicability to the social and political context in which he lived. Second, the construct is, within its own terms, a one-sided statement of reality. That is, Weber was so concerned to point out the functional utility of a rational-legal bureaucratic system that he failed to pay sufficient attention to internal characteristics that *inhibit* the rational goal achievement he seeks.

The social and political environment of Western Europe, and particularly of Germany, in Weber's time provided a more commodious setting for the smooth operation of a rigid bureaucratic system than does contemporary America. In our times a plurality of competing groups contend for social recognition and political power and find justification in an egalitarian ethic. Essentially, because of democratic expectations which thrive and strive in this society, administrative bureaucracy is not immune to pressures from a variety of diverse sources. Bureaucracy must live within a fluid class system rather than the highly stratified one to which

Weber was attuned. Politically, the separation of powers considered in Chapter 1 has made bureaucracy subject to undulating institutional pressures that it cannot anticipate or gauge with precision. An example or two may give substance to these generalizations. One branch of the American bureaucracy is charged with the regulation of various aspects of economic life. The Federal Communications Commission, for example, in granting franchises for new television channels finds itself subject to the importunities of the television industry; the Federal Power Commission in regulating rates rarely acts totally oblivious to the claims of private power industries; nor can the Secretary of Agriculture (or the President) make farm policy disregarding the opinions of clientele farm organizations. Furthermore, in any of these cases, should a fearless bureaucrat attempt to follow what he considers the most rational course of action independently, he would find himself blocked not only by private clientele groups but also by their allies and spokesmen in Congress.

Bureaucracy is also challenged in the American institutional context by sporadic interference from the legislative branch. An extreme example of the havoc that one man can create over a whole department is the wide range of techniques used by the late Senator Joseph McCarthy in his battles with the Department of State. Officials were publicly denounced, policy objectives distorted, and personal agents employed within the department by the Senator in order to bring into disrepute the entire establishment. On such occasions the remarks of Max Weber about the security of officials in a bureaucratic system seem chimerical. Less extreme examples of congressional interference—for laudable motives and base—are limitless. Many a congressman denounces bureaucrats for short-sighted, irresponsible behavior; many another congressman denounces the bureaucrats out of jealousy of their expertise or their prerogatives.

Since in modern America public officials are drawn from a rather wide range of regional, class, and ethnic backgrounds, administration is not the preserve of any one group or stratum of society. While this is considered laudable in an ideological sense, it has resulted in a bureaucracy that has no particular claim to high status. The third assistant secretary is not nearly the object of esteem in the United States that he is in Great Britain or Germany. This is merely a function of a less stratified society, possibly augmented by occasional waves of anti-intellectualism. Finally, the existence of great occupational mobility coupled with the availability of higher financial rewards outside government service have made the public bureaucracy less stable and more subject to circulation among the officials than Weber anticipated. It is not uncommon for the young law graduate to gain a few years' experience in the Securities Exchange Commission and then move on to a more lucrative career in a corporation law firm.

Additional qualifications of Weber's ideal type are not related to any particular social or political context but are produced out of the bureaucratic syndrome itself. Fundamentally, a bureaucratic system is a social system, a system in which interpersonal relations cannot be ignored or overcome by an impersonal reign of office routine as Weber suggested. Indeed, it has been shown on numerous occasions that attempts to impose what appear to be highly rational organizational schemes on a given set of bureaucratic employees meet with frustration and produce consequences in opposition to the goals sought (dysfunction). A reason for such administrative failure is that unfortunately (or otherwise) human beings do not always function rationally. Understanding this, social scientists have recently come to the conclusion that a rewarding source of insight into the bureaucratic process is to be found in the study of personality. Thus Robert Presthus in his study of *The Organizational Society* has fruitfully applied some of the theories of the psychiatrist, Harry Stack Sullivan. Sullivan, having addressed himself to the question of the degree to which personality is a result of social interaction, suggests that one way to interpret irrational and sometimes dysfunctional official behavior within bureaucracy is to determine whether *situations* are anxiety producing or anxiety relieving. The manner in which employees attune themselves to situations arising in a bureaucratic context may be more dependent upon individual personality traits or drives and reactions to other personalities than upon the impersonal factors of an office environment. In a provocative attempt to theorize about different patterns of accommodation to bureaucracy, Presthus has suggested three types. "Upward-mobiles" react to the bureaucratic situation with zest, loyally accepting authority, operating efficiently—keenly aware of status differentials, and taking pleasure in their service to the organization. "Indifferents," on the other hand, fail to identify with the aims and conventions of their employer organizations. Though functional, their bureaucratic position is seen as a means of making a living. Beyond that, they are alienated from their work, taking refuge in outside, psychically "meaningful" preoccupations. The third type of accommodation that Presthus percieves is that of the "ambivalent," the least fortunate of the three types, both from his own and the organization's point of view. He is caught between a craving for the rewards offered by the big organization and his contempt for the bureaucratic methods that are the price of these rewards. Personally, he is unhappy and frustrated; organizationally, he is dysfunctional.[23]

A further critique of Weber's ideal type must deal not only with acts of omission, such as his inability to apply personality theory, but also with the frequent inapplicability of some of his choice canons of bureaucracy. A useful, but by no means exhaustive, consideration of three principles of bureaucracy—formality, predictability, authority—will indicate that they are far less rigid in application than Weber imagined. Bureaucratic formality, for example, can be a highly functional trait of organizations. It may provide an atmosphere wherein personally antagonistic employees can cooperate effectively in furthering organizational goals because communication and the official integrity of each is maintained under the protective cover of bureaucratic protocol. On the other hand, it is a deficient view of bureaucracy that fails to take into account the importance of *informal* organizations. Informal organizations are so much a part of bureaucracy (formal organization) that one writer has concluded the latter could not operate without the existence of the former.[24] One purpose of informal organization is to act as an escape valve for the expression of personal desires, motives, and needs for which there is no place in the formal organization. For example, companionship has no place in bureaucracy, but an informal creation of friendships among highly compatible persons may enhance morale and increase productivity. Alternatively, it is possible that if friendship groups harden into prepossessing cliques, intergroup or interpersonal antagonisms may result in bad morale and dysfunction. In either case, informal organization is vitally important to the efficiency of bureaucracy. Peter Blau discusses an instructive case study of cohesiveness and efficiency which resulted from informal organization in a federal law enforcement agency. Officials of the agency made frequent investigations, the interpretations and results of which required skill and care in the use of principles of auditing, accounting, and legal reasoning. Occasionally, some officials would be uncertain of their methods but avoided questioning their superior since they felt this would reflect unfavorably on their own capabilities. Instead, they regularly violated an agency rule prohibiting contacts among agents working on different cases. The contacts were usually among close friends and were often carried on under a disguise accepted by both parties which gave the consultations a character of casual conversations not directly related to a specific case. The advice-giver received satisfaction in the status he felt as a consultant to a colleague, or simply because he was able to help a friend. The advice-receiver was enabled to do his job satisfactorily and to avoid the official onus of incapacity. Morale was high because of the cohesive atmosphere of the office, and total efficiency was improved.[25]

Predictability has long been considered a desirable attribute, within and without the bureaucratic context. Elementary common sense teaches that an individual will be more at ease and more effective in his work if the consequences of his actions are carefully laid out in specific rules and regulations. Yet this commonplace, like so many others, depends for its validity on the situation and the position of the individuals concerned. A study of industrial bureaucracy convinced Alvin Gouldner that precise predictability in employee relations was by no means always desirable or productive of efficiency from the point of view of organization leaders. Particularly at the lower levels of the organization, matters concerning promotion, wage increases, or conditions of dismissal were purposely made as unpredictable as possible. The rationale behind this approach dictated that insecurity and anxiety would produce greater motivation, perhaps interpersonal competition, and higher productivity.[26] This situation, of course, has been a key motivation to unionization and the establishment by means of labor contracts of norms governing conditions intimately affecting workers. Nonetheless, from the point of view of a superior, there is good reason to avoid a careful structuring of the work environment of his subordinates. An overprecise delineation of workers' rights and duties may make it extremely difficult to exact performance beyond the strict norm when the organization is confronted with pressing needs. In such a situation, a manager must resort to authoritative sanctions or draw for persuasion upon a fund of good will. Every organization needs a "Catch-22." [27]

This brings us to the heart of a final qualification of bureaucratic rules: the complexity of authority. "Legality" may well be the fundamental basis of bureaucratic authority; the securing of constant compliance with all the laws of the organization, however, discloses a source of challenges to the modern bureaucratic official. Weber thought largely in terms of sanctions where rules were violated. Yet a strict and frequent application of sanctions may have the unintended consequence of reducing morale and efficiency in any organization. We are all familiar with rules that are honored in the breach. It is often the better part of wisdom for an official to be permissive about his subordinate's adherence to certain book rules. Even so authoritarian an organization as an army finds it useful at times to wink at its own rules. This is particularly true in crises and combat situations when the normal stiff formality of military address and salute between officers and enlisted men gives way to a preference for informality and camaraderie which are productive of much greater efficiency. In any organization an official endowed with manipulative skills may well be able to dispense almost entirely with coercive sanctions and secure compliance with organizational objectives by creating social obligations. The very act of disregarding specific rules that matter little can create a bond of friendship between superior and subordinate that will permit the former to exact higher efficiency from the latter as a matter of social reciprocity. To identify just one more source of authority not related to coercive sanctions, consider the position of a Nobel Prize winner in a large scientific institute or government agency. Such a person's advice, opinions, or directives are likely to be accepted unquestioningly by his subordinates out of motives of respect or even adulation. The prerogatives of professionalism and expertise and the intraorganization status they create are of greater significance in modern bureaucracy than Weber imagined.

## THE POLICY ROLE OF THE PUBLIC BUREAUCRACY

In modern government, bureaucracy has come to be equated with administration, and, for practical purposes, this is not an erroneous equation. For as we have seen, the vast majority of government bureaucrats is employed in the administrative arm of government. To be sure, an organizational pattern that is bureaucratic in nature exists in the legislative branch with its elaborate system of committees, hierarchies, and sharply articulated formal and informal rules. At a later stage, we shall consider the implications of bureaucracy in the area of legislative policy making. For the present, however, public bureaucracy may be taken to mean administration. Traditionally, the function of administration has been assumed to be the implementation of public policy; the making of policy was the prerogative of the sovereign representatives of the people. The very term applied to administrators—civil *servants*—indicates their traditional status of subordination in government. Hence, to speak of the "policy role" of the public bureaucracy is to fly in the face of constitutional norms and ideological prescriptions. But fly we must if we are to gain a realistic understanding of the multifaceted nature of policy making in American government today.

The initial point of access by bureaucrats to the regions of policy making is discovered in the exercise of the legitimate function of implementation. In theory, Congress (or Congress *and* the President, if a friendly atmosphere prevails) decides policy needs and sets forth its determinations in public law. Administrative handmaidens then translate statute book provisions into governmental activity. An example is in order. In 1934 Congress passed a Securities and Exchange Act by which it established a Securities and Exchange Commission. The job of the Commission is to protect the interests of the public and of investors against malpractices in the financial and securities market. It does this largely through its licensing authority under which it may approve or deny, revoke or suspend operating licenses to stock exchanges and brokers. It may permit or withhold the registration of securities for trading on the market. Its membership of five commissioners and staff of 800 have nearly unlimited discretion in regulating securities according to their view of the public interest. Its example is repeated many times in other agencies that have been delegated broad powers to regulate, according to the common rubric, in the "public interest, convenience, and necessity." No meaningful definition of policy making could be conjured to exclude the activities of such administrative agencies.

A more direct instance of bureaucratic participation in the policy making process is the exercise of the rule making authority granted to many agencies by Congress or simply assumed in practice through custom and usage. A railroad wishing to increase its fares, or discontinue service on one of its lines, must consult rules established by the Interstate Commerce Commission and not congressional lawmakers directly. Directives, orders, and commands issue daily from the offices of federal agencies, departments, bureaus, and commissions. Each of these makes or states policy affecting the rights of individuals, the character of economic life, and the destiny of the nation. An example of one such order that aroused a certain amount of congressional criticism was a 1963 directive from the Pentagon authorizing military commanders to declare "off limits" areas close to their bases where "relentless segregation" was being practiced.[28]

Less tangible means of administrative policy making than rule making or discretionary implementation are to be found in the use and even dependence upon administrative advice by Congress and the executive in their policy making labors. The same causes that fostered the growth of bureaucracy necessitate the use of bureaucratic expertise in reaching policy decisions. Rational courses of action can only be taken on the basis of consultations with expert, specialized intelligence. A presidential decision to invade Cuba, raise the tariff on bicycle imports, or outlaw discrimination in public housing can only be reached after careful consultations with experts in foreign policy, economics, and law. Congress is equally dependent on the information and advice offered by the downtown bureaucrats. To be sure, congressional committees are organized functionally to deal with a limited segment of the legislative terrain, such as taxes, commerce, agriculture, or labor. Problems in each of these major areas, however, are bound to be so complex that the most experienced legislator would find it impossible to depend upon his own resources in formulating policy. In some cases legislators become lost in the maze of information offered by bureaucratic specialists. The following colloquy from a committee hearing, in which a legislator attempts to reach a rational conclusion about the selection of various naval craft by the Defense Department, is suggestive:

> SECRETARY MCNAMARA: It is a question of antisubmarine emphasis versus antiaircraft plus antisubmarines. The three DE's are almost exclusively for antisubmarine warfare. The two DEG's had some desirable capability beyond antisubmarine warfare.
>
> Our chief problem is antisubmarine warfare, and it seemed to me wise to consider putting in three antisubmarine warfare ships instead of two that had some antiaircraft capability.
>
> MR. HARDY: I can't disagree with any of these things—they are completely over my head—but I am trying to explore how we arrive at the specific things we have.[29]

Beyond all these means of participation in the policy process, bureaucracy has an additional persuasive technique which it sometimes employs in the shaping of policy. As spokesmen for particular problem areas of economic and social life, bureaucrats represent natural constituencies or clientele groups in society. For example, farmers are keenly interested in the work of the Department of Agriculture; the military is immediately affected by Defense Department policy; organized labor concerns itself with the Department of Labor and the National Labor Relations Board. Consequently, in the process of attempting to influence policy, it is not uncommon for any of these or other agencies to enlist the support of their clientele organizations. (On the other hand, it is just as common for clientele agencies to pressure the bureaucrats for policies favoring their clients.) In any case, effective working alliances are developed between private interest groups and public bureaucrats in favor of common policy goals. Hence, in a situation where the Department of Defense and the military services are united in support of particular policies, it is exceedingly difficult for either the President or Congress to oppose them effectively. Occasionally, differences on policy matters develop between administrator and clientele. In such a situation the elements of conflict, bargaining, and shifting coalitions—which are the substance of politics—come into play. The bureaucrat does not always win out in the policy struggle; the point worth emphasizing is that he nearly always does participate in it.

## BUREAUCRACY UNDER FIRE

Even a brief discussion of the role of the public bureaucracy would be deficient if it failed to take account of the wide range of criticisms of the system. Ironically, one category of complaints often heard denounces the alleged inefficiency of bureaucracy. Although the basic motive of a bureaucratic system is the rational and efficient achievement of goals, it is undeniable that bureaucracy carries within it the seeds of its own inefficiency. The heavy reliance on rules, regulations, and canons of procedure can, and sometimes does, have the consequence that the bureaucrat is so preoccupied with procedural niceties as to lose sight of substantive goals. As the sociologists phrase it, a "displacement of goals" —in which means become ends—is an occupational hazard of bureaucracy. Occasionally, a state of trained incapacity develops where a bureaucratic technician is so adept at a very specialized skill applicable in a specific context that a change of context renders him incapable.[30] A similar criticism of bureaucratic procedure is the inordinate amount of routine paper work that characterizes any sizable office. What the French call *La paperasserie,* the Germans, *vielschreiberei,* and Americans, "red tape," is a universal bureaucratic component of inefficiency. An amusing story making the conversational circuit in Washington was reported in *The New York Times* in 1963. It tells of a government clerk who received dozens of papers daily which he read, initialed, and deposited in his "out" basket. One day a report meant for another office found its way to his desk, and he followed the usual reading, initialing, and dispatching routine. Two days later the report was returned with this memorandum attached: "This document was not designed for you to handle. Please erase your initials and initial the erasure." [31]

Such elements exist in all bureaucracy, but it is wise to place them in perspective. Bureaucracy as a system should not be considered hopelessly inefficient as a whole merely because we can point to specific examples of inefficiency. Curiously, our attitudes about bureaucratic inefficiency and red tape vary, depending upon *which* bureaucracy we are talking about. One sees much handwringing about governmental bureaucratic waste. I have yet to hear horror stories about an inefficient General Motors Corporation or an inefficient American Telephone and Telegraph Company. Presumably, however, these large organizations are not miraculously immune to bureaucratic deficiencies.

A more serious criticism of public bureaucracy addresses itself to the obviously great power exercised by administrators and questions whether administrative discretion can possibly be made clearly responsive and accountable to elective officials and, in turn, to the public. It is difficult to deal with this question satisfactorily. For, on the one hand, one may say with confidence that extreme fears of a despotism conducted by power-crazed bureaucrats are not rationally based upon anything we know about administrators as individuals or bureaucracy as a dynamic force. On the other hand, only the most sanguine observer would ignore the implications of a vast and complex establishment of appointed officials exercising wide discretionary use of delegated legal powers. It would seem that the most the citizen can ask is that the administrator be a man of integrity and good judgment and that he conduct his office with a regard to the professional criteria of excellence which apply to his specialized area of operations. Moreover, the other branches of government are not helpless before the specter of bureaucratic power. Frequently Presidents issue executive orders governing various aspects of the administrative process, shifting personnel, changing functions, reorganizing agencies, and so on. An outstanding example is President F. D. Roosevelt's issuance of Executive Order 8248 in 1939 which created, with a single stroke, the Executive Office of the President. His successors have liberally altered the composition of the executive office to meet their own needs and the requirements of changing governmental relationships. Likewise, Congress plays a part in the governing of administration through committee checks, reorganization plans, and the setting of procedural standards. Thus in 1946 Congress passed the Administrative Procedure Act which applied specified judicial standards to administrative conduct.[32]

A corollary of the concern about the discretionary authority of administrators is the twofold charge that they either exercise too much policy initiative in pressing for schemes of economic or social change, or that they act as a collective drag on progress in government because of bureaucratic inertia. Again, both charges can be documented with appropriate case studies. Certainly it cannot be gainsaid that administrators are capable of bringing about profound shifts in economic and social relationships. In the first Kennedy administration the persistent application of administrative pressures by such agencies as the Civil Rights Division of the Justice Department, the Interstate Commerce Commission, and other agencies and departments quietly brought about an increased enjoyment of basic civil rights by Negroes. On the other hand, Philip Selznick shows in a careful study how the administrators who manage the Tennessee Valley Authority have altered the goals of the original plan. Initially they played an important part in lifting the standard of life in the Valley area; in the long-term course of development, however, the bureaucratic face hardened, and conservative pressures inhibited the fruition of some advocates' goals for the program.[33] It is in the nature of bureaucracy to be capable of both spirited action and stubborn delay. Thus the bureaucrat must harden himself to the ambivalent criticism of getting nothing done and doing it in an irresponsible way.

CONCLUSION

The development of new economic and technological forces during the last seventy-five years has produced a revolution in the organizational life of American society. Thus transformation has been characterized by size, concentration, and standardization in public and private life. Bureaucracy has been perfected as the system for organizing the new forces at work. The co-ordination of highly specialized talents and activities on the principle of hierarchical divisions whose relationships are governed by rules and regulations—both formal and informal—constitutes the genius of bureaucracy. The system is not perfect largely because the human beings who operate it and operate within it are not perfect.

The reason bureaucracy is so important in a public sense is that it has come to share an important position of leadership in policy making. This new role is so prominently exercised as to be responsible for the assignment of the descriptive title, "Administrative State" to contemporary American government. But there are other—more traditional—centers of leadership in American politics. In the chapter which follows, we shall divert our attention to these major sources of policy leadership and their relationships to bureaucracy.

### REFERENCES

1. For a thoughtful analysis of this problem, see Kenneth E. Boulding, *The Organizational Revolution* (New York: Harper and Row, 1953), especially Part I. A more recent inquiry is to be found in Harlan Cleveland and Harold D. Lasswell (eds.), *Ethics and Bigness* (New York: Harper and Row, 1962).

2. The best investigation of this social current is found in Richard Hofstadter, *Social Darwinism in American Thought,* rev. ed. (New York: George Braziller, Inc., 1959). See also Sidney Fine, *Laissez Faire and the General Welfare State* (Ann Arbor: University of Michigan Press, 1956), especially Chapters 2-5.

3. Boulding, *op. cit.,* p. 35.

4. Simon Kuznets, *National Product Since 1869* (New York: National Bureau of Economic Research, 1946), pp. 52, 119; and US Bureau of the Census, *Statistical Abstract of the United States: 1962,* 84rd ed. (Washington, D.C., 1962), p. 314.

5. *United States Industrial Commission,* 19 vols., *Preliminary Report on Trusts and Industrial Combinations* (Washington, D.C., 1900), Vol. I, p. 9.

6. Adolf A. Berle, Jr., and Gardiner C. Means, *The Modern Corporation and Private Property* (New York: The Macmillan Company, 1933), p. 19.

7. *Ibid.,* Chapter 5.

8. US Bureau of the Census, *Historical Abstracts of the United States, 1789-1945* (Washington, D.C., 1949), p. 65, and *Statistical Abstracts: 1962,* p. 226. All statistics hereafter cited in this chapter are taken from these two sources unless otherwise indicated.

9. Robert Presthus, *The Organizational Society* (New York: Alfred A. Knopf, 1962), p. 79.

10. "The Fortune Directory," *Fortune Magazine,* LXXII (July, 1965), pp. 149-168.

11. Presthus, *op. cit.,* pp. 79-80.

12. Committee for Economic Development, *An Adaptive Program for Agriculture* (New York, 1962), Appendix A; and Committee for Economic Development, *Toward a Realistic Farm Program* (New York, 1957), p. 13.

13. *Encyclopedia of American Associations,* 2nd ed. (Detroit: Gale Research Co., 1959), *passim.*

14. See, for example, William H. Whyte, Jr., *The Organization Man* (Garden City: Doubleday Anchor Books, 1957); David Riesmann, *et al., The Lonely Crowd* (Garden City: Doubleday Anchor Books,

1953); and Paul Goodman, *Growing Up Absurd* (New York: Random House, 1960).

15. *Economist* (November 19, 1955), pp. 635-637; see also C. Northcote Parkinson, *Parkinson's Law* (Boston: Houghton Mifflin Co., 1957).

16. This is designed to be a simple working definition similar to that set forth in John M. Pfiffner and Robert V. Presthus, *Public Administration*, 4th ed. (New York: The Ronald Press Co., 1960), p. 40. Of course, any definition of a phenomenon such as bureaucracy is subject to a variety of formulations depending on choices of emphasis.

17. *From Max Weber: Essays in Sociology*, trans. by H. H. Gerth and C. Wright Mills (New York: Oxford University Press, 1958), pp. 198-204.

18. Max Weber, *The Theory of Social and Economic Organization*, trans. by A. M. Henderson and Talcott Parsons (Glencoe, Ill.: The Free Press, 1947), pp. 330-333, 340.

19. *Ibid.*, pp. 331, 332.

20. Peter M. Blau, *Bureaucracy in Modern Society* (New York: Random House, 1956), p. 32.

21. Weber, *Theory of Social and Economic Organization*, pp. 329-330.

22. *Ibid.*, pp. 341-386.

23. For the full description of these three patterns of accommodation, see Presthus, *Organizational Society*, Chapters 6, 7, and 8. See also Robert K. Merton, "Bureaucratic Structure and Personality," *Social Forces*, XVII (1940), pp. 560-568.

24. Chester I. Barnard, *The Functions of the Executive* (Cambridge: Harvard University Press, 1948). Chapter 9 of this pioneering work deals with the relations between formal and informal organizations.

25. Blau, *op. cit.*, pp. 50-52.

26. Alvin W. Gouldner, "Discussion of Industrial Sociology," *American Sociological Review*, XIII (1948), pp. 396-400. See also Gouldner, *Patterns of Industrial Bureaucracy* (Glencoe, Ill.: The Free Press, 1954).

27. In a grimly humorous satirical novel about military life and military bureaucracy, Joseph Heller has bombardier Yossarian desperately anxious to take leave of his plight as an air force bombardier after forty-four missions. Yossarian hits upon the idea of pleading insanity. He is assured by the air force doctor that, while insanity is a legitimate cause for grounding airmen, his quest is in vain:

"You mean there's a catch?" [Yossarian asked.]

"Sure there's a catch," Doc Daneeka replied. "Catch-22. Anyone who wants to get out of combat duty isn't really crazy." (Joseph Heller, *Catch-22* [New York: Simon and Schuster, 1961], p. 45).

28. *The New York Times*, August 1, 1963, p. 1. It is interesting to note that opponents of the directive questioned its propriety and not its legality.

29. House Committee on Armed Services, 88th Cong., 1st Sess., *Hearings,* "Military Posture and H. R. 2440, to Authorize Appropriations during Fiscal Year 1964, for Procurement, Research, Development, Test and Evaluation of Aircraft Missiles, and Naval Vessels for the Armed Forces, and for Other Purposes" (Washington, 1963), p. 555.
30. This state of affairs and similar phenomena are discussed in Merton, "Bureaucratic Structure and Personality," pp. 560-568.
31. *The New York Times,* July 29, 1963, p. 8.
32. 60 Stat. 237 (1946), 5 USC Nos. 1001-1011. For a discussion of the major details of the Act, see Woll, *American Bureaucracy,* pp. 101-104.
33. Philip Selznick, *TVA and the Grass Roots* (Berkeley and Los Angeles: University of California Press, 1949). See also John Ed Pearce, "The Creeping Conservatism of TVA," *The Reporter,* January 4, 1962, pp. 31ff.

## CHAPTER 3

# The Dispersal of Leadership—I

### THE POLITICS OF PLURALISM

AN INVESTIGATION OF THE PROCESS OF POLICY MAKING WOULD be simplified if we could consult the Constitution, statutes passed by Congress, and the rules of procedure governing legislative bodies, confident that these sources hold the answers to our quest. Such simplicity, however, is misleading, and such confidence would be misplaced. In some cases, a closer scrutiny would reveal that several governmental institutions *shared* leadership in the making of policy; in others, we would discover that the institutions themselves merely reflected and ratified policies which were derived from *other* sources of leadership entirely. To understand more fully the complexity of policy formulation we must recognize the *group* basis of politics.

People behave both as individuals and as members of groups. A group is usually considered to be a collection of people who share certain characteristics and who frequently interact on the basis of those shared characteristics.[1] The marks of commonality knitting people together in groups are numerous, some of the more important being regional, occupational or professional interests, ethnic background, social standing, religious preferences, and so on. It is characteristic of groups to develop interests which the members pursue in common in order to uphold or advance shared group values. When this happens a political interest group is born. For pressure exerted upon society through government is a typical and natural activity of group interests. This phenomenon was described over a half-century ago in an uncompromising manner by Arthur Bentley:

53

All phenomena of government are phenomena of groups pressing one another, forming one another, and pushing out new groups and group representatives (the organs or agencies of government) to mediate the adjustments. It is only as we isolate these group activities, determine their representative values, and get the whole process stated in terms of them, that we approach to a satisfactory knowledge of government.[2]

While we might disagree with the proposition that *all* phenomena of government are group phenomena, we would readily agree that groups play a vital part in the political process. In order to be effective instruments for the achievement of their goals, groups must be organized adequately for the efficient application of whatever resources they may command. Common bases of group strength are large numbers, plentiful financial resources, or social prestige. Any given group may be endowed in one or more of these categories. For example, the primary strength of organized laborers consists in the numbers for which a body like the AFL-CIO can speak and secondarily in the monetary resources at its disposal. An interest group like the National Association of Manufacturers finds its greatest strength in its treasury whereas a professional body like the American Medical Association probably finds its greatest resource in the general prestige of doctors. The means by which well-organized interest groups seek a political accommodation of their values through enactment of appropriate policies are described by David Truman as the dynamics of access.[3] That is, to be effectively influential, interest groups must gain access to the ultimate makers of decisions concerning their interests. The techniques by which access is gained vary widely and a few representative types will be considered in this chapter and the next.

Given the existence of a large number of interest groups seeking different and often conflicting policies, an accurate description of the normal state of policy making is one of conflict and bargaining. For several reasons bargaining normally follows conflict in a politically stable situation such as exists in the United States. At the outset, we may assume that no single group is so powerfully situated that it can work its will all the time. Hence it must make concessions to other groups in order to assure allies in future bargaining situations. Furthermore, group life is characterized by overlapping memberships. Individuals are typically members of more than one group and, when cross-pressured by conflicting interests, may shift their allegiances from one to another group. Since group membership is thus apt to be unstable, interest organization leaders can ill afford to adopt uncompromising stands on any given issue. Take, for example, the position of the American Medical Association which in principle is opposed to all public health insurance programs. Its constituency of doctors, and their larger constituency of patients, include people who feel the need and desire for some sort of federal medical aid program. Thus AMA compromises and shifts its opposition from the question of the principle involved to the extent of coverage and methods of financing such programs.

At the highest level of bargaining over policy, politicians assume the role of brokers among conflicting interests. Thus at the ultimate and most important point, bargaining takes place among the leading decision makers.[4] These leaders may be identified typically to include, in addition to private interest group representatives, high political party functionaries, such important bureaucrats as department heads and bureau chiefs, and congressional committee chairmen. Thus the framework of policy making is in reality much broader than the legal-institutional mechanisms we are accustomed to consider.

The "group basis" analysis of policy making inevitably gives rise to normative questions and often provokes value-based opposition. In the first place, the idea of private groups "pressuring" (an adverse value-laden word) governmental officials appears to some an unseemly and even sinister concept of politics. And, of course, where great sums of money are invested in questionable techniques, the *means* of exercising influence may have an unhealthy character. On the other hand, the pursuance of interests on a group basis can be considered no more than a modern exercise of the basic right to petition one's government. Others close their eyes to group theory because they feel it leaves no place for individual, meaningful activity. We can all think of examples where individual agency has been responsible for momentous policy decisions. The pluralist concept of politics simply asserts that group agency is the *predominant,* not exclusive, characteristic of policy formulation. In some cases students of group activity have damaged the cause of understanding by a resort to moralizing.

That is, in order to make a virtue of the existence of group activity, they have concocted a theory of equilibrium according to which all groups eventually balance one another off in the bargaining process. The result is a policy that represents the golden mean and perhaps even the embodiment of the democratic aspirations of "the people." This is a dangerously close approach to the proposition that whatever is, is right.[5]

Some scholars adopt a more extreme view, rejecting both the legal-institutional approach and the group theory (with or without equilibrium variations) as valid interpretations of policy making. For these people, the true answers to our questions are to be found in the machinations of *elite* bodies. Elitists argue that only certain groups, usually of highest social and economic standing, count in the policy process. This notion casts out the idea of bargaining in favor of one of co-operation, or even conspiracy among the various elements making up a political elite. The exact composition of the elite is a matter of disagreement which creates additional problems for elite theorists in presenting their cases. The idea of a closed corps of manipulators carrying on behind our backs (or under our noses) is an old one. In the 1930s James Burnham was convinced that the day was not far off when the technicians and managers in our society would take over permanently.[6] More recently C. Wright Mills published his influential exploration of a new ruling class, *The Power Elite*. The form Mills' power elite takes is that of an interlocking directorate composed of top business leaders, the upper levels of the military hierarchy, and an influential coterie of appointive political officials. Operating in concert, the members of the elite:

> . . . severally and collectively, now make such key decisions as are made; and that given the enlargement and centralization of the means of power now available, the decisions that they make and fail to make carry more consequences for more people than has ever been the case in the world history of mankind.[7]

To the extent that groups in society do vary considerably in the degree of influence they can exert, such elitists as Mills perform a service in shocking us out of the romantic notion that major policies are made in a kind of town meeting of interested and relatively equal groups. Nonetheless, elite theories tend to prove too much, in that a monopoly of whatever groups are taken to be most powerful is often *assumed* to be responsible for all major policy. Furthermore, an elite must have some measure of stability; yet a closer look at obviously important groups in society reveals that their importance and influence is subject to considerable change. The major groups upon which Mills stakes his theory are obviously powerful; yet the military influence, for example, is a relatively recent occurrence produced by an unstable world situation. Likewise, could it reasonably be argued that the scientific community (which plays no part in Mills' interlocking directorate) is an uninfluential participant in the policy making process, given the current emphasis on science and technology?

One is led to the conclusion that the closest approach to understanding the dynamics of the policy process is to accept the concept of bargaining among leaders who speak for a plurality of changing groups, having unequal sources of power and differing degrees of success at various stages of the struggle. There are several consequences of this state of affairs: Policy is nearly always a compromise which may be irrational because so many conflicting interests have been taken into account. The most highly organized bargainers may well not be the most numerous, and thus minority interests are often overrepresented. Finally, any potentially central source of leadership is dispersed as a result of the institutional context of the policy process in America. The fundamental constitutional norms discussed in Chapter I continue to assure that *"no unified, cohesive, acknowledged, and legitimate representative-leaders of the 'national Majority' exist in the United States."* [8] The fractionalization of leadership is the theme of the succeeding pages.

## PRESIDENTIAL LEADERSHIP

There are few constitutional provisions which directly endow the President with policy making powers, but most modern presidents seek to achieve maximum mileage out of the ancient vehicle described in Article II. The great proportion of presidential leadership consists in his attempts to persuade others to do his bidding. In this *indirect* way he most vitally participates in the policy process. Having said this, let us consider the limited constitutional powers at the disposal of the President. His prerogative of delivering messages to Congress has come to be a means for introducing legislation he wishes that body to act upon. Even the effective use of this power, however, depends almost entirely upon his ability to persuade the legislators that the projects he has introduced should perforce be enacted. Specific persuasive techniques are the personal property of each President—a function of his style—but all presidents make use of certain basic tactics. Among these, his role as leader of his party permits the President to bring political pressures to bear. This tactic, however, is of limited value since our decentralized two-party system places no particular premium on party regularity or party loyalty among congressmen. On occasion the President can resort to another of his constitutional prerogatives—the power of making appointments—to influence legislators. To individual congressmen, the prospect of a share of the available patronage is sometimes beguiling enough to assure a favorable vote on a presidential bill. The aura of majesty that surrounds the institution of the Presidency is a resource which all chief executives draw upon to lead Congress. Few legislators can resist the opportunity to accompany the President on social outings, have dinner at the White House, or appear in presidential company before television and news cameras. The borrowing of such presidential status usually comes with a price tag, and the form of currency is most often legislative support. Finally, if all other techniques are exhausted, the President may attempt to bring popular pressure to bear on Congress by direct appeals to the nation in favor of his proposals. Franklin Roosevelt's invention and use of the "fireside chat" illustrated how useful a tool this can be.

A second power which permits the President to participate directly in the policy making process is the executive veto. At first sight this seems to be a mere negative device and one that is also limited, since a two-thirds majority of both houses can override a presidential veto. Yet by means of the *threat* of a veto, delivered for purposes of bargaining, the President may bring about favorable alterations in measures in the course of the legislative process. Likewise, in practice Congress's ability to override vetoes by an extraordinary majority is not as significant as it may seem. Historically, the great proportion of presidential vetoes have been sustained. Thus, as closely as one can calculate, between

1789 and 1962 Presidents vetoed some 1840 bills of which only 73 (or 4 per cent) were subsequently overridden.

For the greater fund of policy shaping tools the President possesses, he has Congress to thank rather than the Constitution directly. In all major areas of government the legislators have made important delegations of authority to the executive. The Employment Act of 1946, mentioned earlier, places direct responsibility on the President for long-term economic planning and provides him with a Council of Economic Advisers to help formulate policy. The Atomic Energy Act of 1946 transfers to the executive branch the authority to decide on the use of fissionable materials, the direction of experiment and research, the production of weapons, and the equipment of the national arsenal. The National Security Act of 1947 permits the President, with the help of a National Security Council, to co-ordinate foreign, domestic, and military policy. In 1934 Congress passed the Reciprocal Trade Agreements Act which permitted the President to shape trade and tariff policy through the device of negotiating tariff levels by executive agreement. The original act was renewed several times until 1962 when a new Trade Expansion Act extended executive authority considerably by permitting the President to cut tariffs by 50 per cent over a five-year period and to eliminate altogether tariffs on certain categories of goods largely supplied by Common Market countries.[9]

The sum of all the President's powers—constitutional, statutory, and that inherent power of prestige attaching to the office—make of the man an unequaled force in the bargaining process. Though they are the most notable, the President's struggles with Congress are not the *only* instances of the use of the power of persuasion. He must apply his hortatory talents to his own subordinates, to the leaders of important private organizations, and to the nation as a whole. He is often required to play the role of the great mediator, attempting to bring solutions to conflicts between resolute interests. Labor versus management; one branch of the armed forces versus another; state agencies versus federal agencies—each provides the setting for contests we are all accustomed to witness, and in which the President cannot long avoid playing a part. As Professor Neustadt has demonstrated, in order to be a successful mediator, the President must protect his professional reputation and uphold the prestige of his office before his many constituencies.[10] A suggestive account of President John F. Kennedy's fulfillment of the roles of mediator, and subsequently persuader, may be drawn from the steel crisis of 1962.

The background of the crisis properly begins in January of 1962. An abiding problem of the post-World War II economic climate had been a steadily rising inflationary spiral caused by successive increases in wages and prices. In the *Economic Report* of 1962, the Council of Economic Advisers had set forth policy "guideposts" which established maximum rates of price and wage increases deemed noninflationary. In the weeks that followed the January *Report,* the President and his lieutenants were intimately involved in negotiations between the steel industry and steel unions over a wage contract. The attempt at informal mediation was designed to bring about a noninflationary contract for the pace-setting steel industry and thus encourage adherence to Economic Advisers' guideposts. It appeared that executive mediation had been crowned with success when on April 6, 1962, an appropriately noninflationary contract was signed by the United Steelworkers of America and the eleven largest steel companies.

Five days later, headlines of newspapers across the nation announced that the US Steel Corporation had raised its steel prices by $6 a ton; within hours, several other major steel concerns announced identical increases. At this point, mediation gave way to what could only by considered presidential persuasion in its most vigorous form. To serialize the elements of presidential influence applied gives some insight into the extent of executive resources: (1) At a press conference on the afternoon of the day of the announcement, President Kennedy denounced the act as an "unjustifiable and irresponsible defiance of the public interest," which showed "utter contempt for the interest of 185,000,000 Americans." (2) In an apparent attempt to persuade companies that had not yet increased their prices to hold the line, the Undersecretary of Commerce telephoned the board chairman of Inland Steel and the President himself had a long-distance conversation with the Chairman of the Kaiser Steel Corporation in California. (3) The Federal Trade Commission announced a planned inquiry into the possibility of illegal collusion among the companies making identical increases. (4) The Anti-Trust Division of the Justice Department, making liberal use of the FBI, looked into the question of violations of either the Sherman or Clayton Anti-Trust Act. (5) The Treasury Department decided to have another look at its plan to ask for higher depreciation rates giving tax benefits to companies for plant improvement. (6) Secretary McNamara announced that the Defense Department had ordered steel contractors to transfer orders to steel companies that had *not* raised prices. (7) Finally, in both houses of Congress relevant committees began to plan their own investigations.

Just seventy-two hours after the initial announcement of a price increase by the US Steel Corporation, Roger Blough, chairman of the board, reported that his company had rescinded its action, ending the three-day crisis. Seldom have the potentialities of presidential persuasion been so vividly demonstrated.[11]

As potent a device as the power of presidential persuasion is not without its limits. Congress, for example, freely exercises its right to say "No" to the most willful and skillful of chief executives. Just how often Congress has done precisely that can be judged by the proportion of presidentially sponsored bills the legislators have passed in recent years. The four Congresses with which President Eisenhower dealt in the years 1953-1960 enacted, on an eight-year average, 48 per cent of his legislative requests. President Kennedy in his first two years succeeded in persuading the 87th Congress to pass only 46.3 per cent of his proposals.[12] Even low figures do not take into account the fact that often the executive proposals that Congress *does* enact are in a form quite different from the original requests.

In some cases the Supreme Court poses a judicial negative before policy determinations of the President. Thus when in 1952 President Harry Truman, determined to end a strike in the steel industry, ordered the steel mills to be seized and operated by the federal government, the Supreme Court swiftly found his action unconstitutional. The pleas of the President that his act was justified by the emergency of the Korean War and validated by the inherent powers of his office found little sympathy among the justices.[13] In the early years of the New Deal, the Court invalidated many of the Roosevelt administration's major acts. No president can safely make policy disregarding the possible judicially determined constitutional consequences.

While it is clear that the President encounters difficulties in having his policies enacted or sustained by other branches of the government or by groups in society generally, it might be expected that at the stage of formulation and execution of policies *within his own administration* the President could expect harmonious cooperation and undivided support. That this is not always the case may be demonstrated by an analysis of the President's relations with different sectors of his administration.

*President and Administration.* As nominal head of the administrative branch, the President should be able to draw upon a basic source of control—his power of appointment and removal. It is an old axiom of leadership that finds in the power of hiring and firing an indispensable attribute of management. Yet even this basic prerogative of executive office has been qualified in a number of ways. According to Article II of the Constitution, the President is empowered to appoint all high officers *with* the advice and consent of the Senate. Hence, at the very outset, there is a potential limitation on the presidential appointment power. And although in the vast majority of cases the President exercises this power independently for all practical purposes, the Senate, from time to time, reminds the executive of *its* constitutional prerogative by failing to confirm an appointment. The most recent example of Senate opposition to a high administrative appointment occurred in 1958 when President Eisenhower's choice of Lewis Strauss as his Secretary of Commerce failed of confirmation.

The exact exercise of the President's removal power has been subjected to several judicial determinations, each providing a more restrictive interpretation than the previous. In 1920 President Wilson removed a first-class Postmaster whom he had appointed three years earlier with the consent of the Senate. The Postmaster, Myers, sued in the Court of Claims for back pay, arguing that since the Senate had consented to his appointment, he could only be removed with senatorial approval. When the case reached the Supreme Court in 1926, Chief Justice Taft wrote a Court opinion that interpreted the President's removal power as one of near absolute executive discretion over all administrative officers.[14]

In 1933 William E. Humphrey was serving as a Federal Trade

Commissioner on a seven-year appointment made by President Hoover. Humphrey took a rather conservative view of the government's relations with business and was notably unsympathetic to the views and policies of the new Roosevelt Administration. Hence, the President asked for Humphrey's resignation, stating: "You will, I know, realize that your mind and my mind do not go along together on either the policies or the administering of the Federal Trade Commission, and, frankly, I think it is best for the people of this country that I should have a full confidence."

When Humphrey refused to resign, the President summarily removed him. The Commissioner took his case to court, and this time the majority concluded that the President had removed Humphrey illegally. The Court went into the history and background of the independent regulatory commissions and found that these bodies were established for the purpose of removing the critical regulatory function from politics, including presidential control. The only grounds for removal the justices would admit were inefficiency, neglect of duty, or malfeasance in office. Hence an important aspect of regulatory administration and policy making was excluded from the control of our theoretical "Chief Administrator." [15]

More recently, in 1958 the Supreme Court further clarified—and further restricted—the President's removal power. The office at issue in this case was a quasi-judicial one, the War Claims Commission. In creating the Commission, Congress failed to specify conditions of removal governing the commissioners. When President Eisenhower removed one Myron Wiener "in the national interest," Wiener's contention of illegality was upheld by the Court. The tribunal found that, since Congress had not specifically authorized the President to remove such quasi-judicial officers, it must be assumed that the removal power had been withheld.[16]

The appointment, removal, and use of administrative functionaries by the President as a policy maker are conditioned by other than purely legal considerations. The President's cabinet is usually taken as an instance of the widest discretionary use that could be made of an assemblage of high level bureaucrats. It is a fact that cabinet appointments are almost never questioned seriously (the Eisenhower-Strauss case being one of only three historical exceptions), and the right of removal of cabinet officers for any reason is absolute. The President's use or nonuse of the cabinet is circumscribed usually by nothing more than his own operating style: He may call meetings frequently or rarely; he may meet with some department heads singly, and more often than with others; or he may met regularly and formally with the whole body, as President Eisenhower did. In making policy, the President may take the advice of department heads or ignore them and substitute his own informal sources of intelligence and advice.

On the other hand, certain political and group facts of life limit the exercise of apparent discretion the President has. At the outset, the President may appoint anyone—within limits. He must take account of ethnic, religious, regional, and political factors. President John F. Kennedy's first cabinet appointed in 1960, for example, was unusual in some ways and even established a few precedents. It was the first cabinet to have a brother of the chief executive. It was the youngest cabinet of this century, the average age being 47 years. It was also the first cabinet to include two members of the Jewish faith and one member whose official occupation had been an executive of a research foundation. Underlying all the "firsts," however, were many tried and true principles of cabinet-manship. There was an appropriate mixture of religious backgrounds, including besides Jews, a Catholic, all the major Protestant sects, and a Mormon. The eastern regional "establishment" was balanced off by one southerner (Hodges), two mid-westerners (McNamara and Freeman), and two far-westerners (Day and Udall). A wise President usually appoints at least one member of the opposition party to his cabinet in the hope of appearing to be bipartisan and drawing support from the opposition. Mr. Kennedy appointed two highly regarded Republicans—Douglas Dillon as Secretary of the Treasury and Robert McNamara as Secretary of Defense. It is also useful to appoint a former senator or congressman, or two, in an attempt to pave the way to friendly relations with the legislative branch. Perhaps because President Kennedy himself fell into this category, as a former senator, he felt it necessary to appoint only one congressman (Stewart Udall) to his cabinet. Cabinet appointments are also occasionally made with a view to healing splits in the President's party, or garnering support from various wings of the party. In 1960 there seemed no feasible way of avoiding the appointment of Adlai Stevenson (as the spokesman of an influential part of the Democratic Party), even if the President had sought one. Since Stevenson was not made Secretary of State, he was appointed Ambassador to the United Nations, and the country was assured that the President considered this a cabinet-level position.

Once a cabinet is appointed, however little the President may wish to consult or use it, he cannot ignore the fact of its existence, or—it must be noted—the existence of such subordinates in the departmental hierarchies as undersecretaries, assistant secretaries, and bureau chiefs. These officials are in positions which permit them both to add luster and to do considerable harm to the presidential reputation, thus quickening or inhibiting the march toward goals of executive policy. More than one President has experienced stiff opposition to policies because of a cabinet liability. President Truman had to overcome burdensome opposition to the conduct of his foreign policy that was based partly on congressional disenchantment with his Secretary of State, Dean Acheson. Ezra Taft Benson, President Eisenhower's Secretary of Agriculture, provoked outspoken opposition among congressmen of the President's own party because of Benson's agricultural policies. Recently, Arthur Sylvester, the Assistant Secretary of Defense for Public Affairs, has been a source of vigorous criticism, both in congress and in the press, as a result of rather undiplomatic statements made from time to time. The Assistant Secretary has, *inter alia,* (1) aroused a controversy over executive management of the news by stating that in times of crisis the government uses news as a "weapon," (2) suggested that a congressional committee used "gestapo tactics" in questioning witnesses concerning a government contract, and (3) implied that congressmen might find it difficult to make disinterested judgments about appropriations for military hardware because of constituency interests.[17]

In time of crisis the cabinet may perform a valuable service in symbolizing governmental stability. The smooth transition which followed Lyndon Johnson's sudden accession to the Presidency in the tragic circumstances of President Kennedy's assassination was abetted by the loyal support pledged by the Kennedy cabinet. Some relationships changed, such as the growing stature of Secretary of State Dean Rusk and a degree of estrangement between

Mr. Johnson and the late President's brother, Attorney General Robert Kennedy. Secretary Rusk, operating in the context of a different presidential personality, gradually came to be identified more personally and actively with foreign policy leadership than before. The Attorney General seemed, for a time, to be going through the paces of office without benefit of the close presidential contact he had had before November 23, 1963. Such personal ups and downs aside, there can be no doubt that the cabinet accommodation of the new President was a timely service to the Republic.

Departmental and agency officials are sometimes able to lend status to presidential policies and requests. This is a particular asset to the President in his relations with Congress. Richard Fenno, in a masterly study of cabinet politics, demonstrates how Cordell Hull, Secretary of State to President Franklin Roosevelt, was able to present the President's case with unique force before congressional committees. The Secretary, having been a member of both houses of congress before joining the executive branch, could talk to the legislators in terms that appealed most to them. Hearings at which Mr. Hull appeared as witness took on the aura of a love feast among old comrades. A few lines of cajolerie from one such hearing are suggestive:

> SECRETARY HULL: I have particularly enjoyed this visit here and want to thank you for not asking me any harder questions than you have. But at any rate I want to say that my door is open to any of you people. I will tell you what I would tell any other persons. . . .
> MR. RABAUT: It is my experience that the Secretary himself has never joined the bureaucrats.
> SECRETARY HULL: It is too late in life for me to undertake to do that.[18]

Although the cabinet was the original source from which Presidents were expected to collect advice and to delegate the details of administration, the modern Presidency has called upon supplementary aides for these purposes. Presidents have always utilized noncabinet help in the form of private or personal confidants, whether called informally "advisers to the President" or collectively a "kitchen cabinet." Colonel House, Harry Hopkins, Bernard Baruch, and a host of others are famed as presidential policy advisers. President Eisenhower relied heavily on his Assistant,

Sherman Adams, and occasionally on his brother, Dr. Milton Eisenhower. A landmark of administration was passed in 1939 when President Roosevelt created by executive order the Executive Office of the President and further institutionalized presidential sources of administrative help outside the cabinet. From the time of its creation to the present, the Executive Office has constituted a holding company of vital and changing administrative components. Two of the original agencies assigned to the Office thrive heartily today. The White House Office is a section of immediate presidential aides, including the President's special counsel, his press secretary, and a raft of special assistants. The vast majority of White House Office personnel are clerical and staff aides. Yet among its top members are some of the President's closest advisers. These functionaries often provide a guide to individual presidential preferences, work habits, and predispositions. The first changes in personnel that took place after the short transition period in late 1963 which made way for a Johnson Administration in fact, as well as in name, were shifts among the Special Assistants. The exodus of Arthur Schlesinger, Jr., Theodore Sorensen, and Press Secretary Pierre Salinger signaled the assembling of a more characteristically "Johnson staff."

The other original component of the Executive Office is the Bureau of the Budget which, in addition to being responsible for drawing together the executive budget, is the President's personal clearing house for legislation. It is this body which recommends modification, presidential approval, or a presidential veto for pieces of legislation emanating from Capitol Hill.

The five major remaining offices of the Executive Office represent innovations designed to cope with policy areas that have risen in importance in the last two decades. The Council of Economic Advisers, already mentioned, diagnoses the nation's economic health and reports its findings and recommendations directly to the President. The National Security Council attempts to give the President a broad overview of the military and domestic implications of foreign policy. Included in its staff is the confidential corps of officials making up the Central Intelligence Agency. The sudden advent of a need for policies governing research in space in 1958 brought the creation of the National Aeronautics and Space Council. An Office of Emergency Planning is charged with military and civilian preparedness functions in the era of the cold war. An Office of Science and Technology, created in 1962, signals institutionally the importance of its area of concern to modern America. Finally, as of 1963, an Office of the Special Representative for Trade Negotiations completes the Executive Office.

The sheer magnitude of the administrative establishment and the consequent inability of any President to co-ordinate and control its activities have aroused sentiment in favor of giving the President authority to reorganize and rationalize the far-flung bureaucratic empire. President Roosevelt called together a Committee on Administrative Management in 1937 which made sweeping proposals for executive-authorized reorganization. As a result of this report, Congress first passed a Reorganization Act in 1939. In succeeding years it has passed similar acts as a result of later committee reports, most notably those of the Hoover Commissions. For the most part, Congress has been reluctant to assent to specific presidential reorganization measures, particularly those concerning the independent regulatory commissions which will be considered in greater detail in the next chapter. The reason for congressional reserve in these matters is very simply that most reorganization plans, in one way or another, call for greater executive involvement in and control over policy making. As it stands now, the President has statutory authority to reorganize by means of executive order. However, if within sixty days *either* house of Congress passes a resolution opposed to the reorganization plan it is nullified. President Kennedy had difficulty in persuading the 87th Congress to assent to half of his reorganization plans and was administered a stern senatorial rebuke because of his attempt to create a new cabinet level Department of Urban Affiairs and Housing. The latter proposal was deeply enmeshed in regional and political group interest rivalries. First, the essentially rural and small town outlook that pervades Congress refused to tolerate what it interpreted as solicitude toward big city interests in general. Second, Republicans were overwhelmingly opposed to the plan because many of them viewed it as a partisan sop to urban areas already noted for their heavy Democratic majorities on election day. Finally, the President's announcement that he would appoint Robert Weaver of the Housing and

Home Finance Agency—a Negro—as Secretary of the Department added an additional weight of opposition to the plan among some senators.

Even if the President were given a blank check with which to reorganize the executive branch, seemingly insuperable obstacles to exacting, unqualified presidential policy leadership would persist. The factors of conflicting expert advice, dependence upon subordinates' information, and differing presidential preferences for modes of organization all play a part in the dispersal of executive leadership.

*Bureaucratic Roadblocks.* It must be immediately obvious that rational planning for most of the policies for which Presidents take responsibility depends upon a level of specialized expertise in a multitude of areas far above the capabilities of any one man. Hence the President must rely on the appropriate experts. Yet even within the same administration, different agencies having overlapping spheres of interests often find themselves on a collision course. By what criteria does the President resolve such conflicts? On fiscal and appropriations matters various departments and agencies may disagree with the Bureau of the Budget, or the Bureau of the Budget may disagree with the Treasury Department, or the Treasury Department with the Federal Reserve Board. To cite a recent instance, in 1962 a smoldering conflict between the National Aeronautics and Space Administration and the Office of Science and Technology came into the open. The conflict turned upon alternative approaches to the moon. NASA had for some time been committed to the "lunar orbital rendezvous" technique of sending a manned expedition to the moon. Dr. Jerome Wiesner, the President's Special Assistant on Science and Technology, favored an alternative technique, such as either the "earth orbital" or "direct ascent" method. Failure to resolve this basic conflict meant that a contract could not be let for construction of the appropriate space capsule, and the high priority Project Apollo seemed destined to be delayed in meeting its 1970 target date.[19]

While dissension among bureaucrats can frustrate executive leadership, even in cases where there is a general consensus among the President's advisers, presidential goals may be frustrated by a lack of full information. A classic instance of the

failure of a presidential policy due to faulty intelligence and miscalculation is the Dixon-Yates case. President Eisenhower approached office in 1953 with fixed views on the question of public
power; he saw manifestations of government power projects like
the Tennessee Valley Authority as the most virulent form of
"creeping socialism." His general policy was one of limiting
governmental expansion and retrenchment wherever possible in
economic life. In his first budget message, the President reduced
the TVA appropriation and cut out the proposed steam plant at
Fulton, Tennessee, altogether. Shortly thereafter he directed the
Bureau of the Budget to underwrite a contract between a private
utility company, Dixon-Yates, and the Atomic Energy Commission under which the private utility would build a power plant to
provide power for the AEC which it had previously purchased from
the TVA. The budget director was in full sympathy with the President's objectives as were the AEC, the Federal Power Commission,
and the Securities Exchange Commission; the latter quickly ex-
pedited the contract by approving a special financing arrangement.
There appeared to be no obstacle to the development of the
power site by Dixon-Yates. Then the city of Memphis decided to
construct its own steam plant and not use TVA power resources.
At this point, the chairman of the board of TVA asked that the
Dixon-Yates contract be reconsidered. The President complied
with this request, and a second look at the arrangement revealed
a rather uppleasant situation. It occurred that one Adolphe Wenzell, vice-president of a Boston bank, had acted as consultant to
the Bureau of the Budget and was instrumental in having Dixon-
Yates awarded the contract. The same bank with which Wenzell
was affiliated, the First Boston Company, was to handle the
securities transactions for the Dixon-Yates project. As a result
the Dixon-Yates "deal" became a *cause célèbre,* exploited by
partisans of TVA and public power generally, as well as the opposition party. After further investigation the AEC canceled its
contract with Dixon-Yates on grounds of illegality because of a
conflict of interest resulting from Adolphe Wenzell's dual role
in the negotiating process. Thus the President's attempt in this
case to stimulate free enterprise resulted in frustration.[20]

How does one explain this failure of a presidential policy supported by the major administrative participants engaged in its

implementation? The closest student of the affair, Aaron Wildavsky, concludes that the source of the problem is to be found in a failure of perception on the part of the President resulting from the structure of his advisory machinery. On the surface it might appear that any perceptive official could have detected the potential political dangers created by Wenzell's involvement. Yet, as Wildavsky shows, the advisers surrounding the President, and conditioning his perception of the whole issue, were bankers, businessmen, and lawyers, men of wide financial associations who very likely failed to detect anything unseemly about one of their kind advising the government concerning the financing of a business enterprise. Wildavsky also shows how these advisers to the President, anti-public power men all, framed their reports to the chief executive in terms of the demands of public power advocates, determined to discredit his program to half "creeping socialism." Of the involved financial manipulations and cost computations of the Dixon-Yates project, the President received brief summary reports. Hence he perceived the issue as a struggle between sincere advocates of free enterprise and the nagging claims of socialist-minded opponents. As a result, the President committed himself wholeheartedly to a general principle of policy in ignorance of the important details.[21]

It must be stated finally that, of course, the success of presidential leadership depends in part on the skill of the man and the adequacy of his use of administrative subordinates. The bureaucracy is there and, within limits, functions automatically; it is the President, however, who sets the limits. Techniques vary widely: Franklin Roosevelt was noted for creating a situation of built-in conflict by appointing competing department and agency heads. Out of a debate among experts it was expected that rational policy would materialize. Dwight Eisenhower perfected a highly formal, institutionalized staff system, the motivation for which was his military experience. President Kennedy came to office determined to employ a more direct approach, personally seeking his information on a random basis from a variety of sources.

Each method has its strengths—and its weaknesses. Administrative science has by no means perfected a single technique of leadership suitable to every executive personality and capable of warding off a dispersal of leadership that is endemic in modern bureaucratic government.

## CONGRESS AND POLICY MAKING

Every time Congress passes a law, of course, it legalizes a statement of policy. What is more interesting to the observer is the frequency with which Congress fails to translate policy problems into policies via the legislative process. Furthermore, major pieces of legislation that do achieve passage are often ambiguous compromises which satisfy only partially the needs which called for a policy determination in the beginning. The efficient cause of legislative incapacity is a lack of unified leadership. Congress has been unable to solve a basic functional dilemma: As a representative body in a democratic system, it must serve the interests of a diverse constituency. As a policy making body it must act to create unity out of diversity. Not infrequently, Congress's representative function gets in the way of and eventually absorbs its policy function. The solution to the dilemma appears to lie in reorganization, but reorganization would inevitably blur the fine distinctions to which Congress gives representation. A view of the important features which characterize the legislative body should provide substance for these generalizations.

*Congressional Institutions.* Like any other body of its size, Congress can only hope to conduct its business rationally through a division of labor and a specialization of functions. To do this the 535 legislators organize themselves into standing committees—twenty in the House and sixteen in the Senate—each of which has jurisdiction over a special area of policy. Influence on a committee normally depends upon seniority, the member with the longest service on the committee being its chairman. Again, normally, although there are exceptions, the chairman is sovereign master over the conduct of committee business. He calls the meetings; he appoints subcommittees and their chairmen; he rules on the order of business. If the chairman of a standing committee is unalterably opposed to a bill before his committee there is very little that either the other members of the panel or the whole body can do about it. Thus it is quite conceivable that a committee chairman can impose on any given policy a veto which represents the judgment of a small minority.

In the House of Representatives the existence and traditional importance of the Rules Committee presents an additional obstacle a policy must overcome even to have a chance of adoption. The practice requiring legislation to be cleared for floor action by the Rules Committee has resulted in the summary execution of many policies at that stage. Thus the first item on President Kennedy's legislative agenda in 1961 was his successful attempt to increase the membership of the Rules Committee in order that he might assure a hospitable majority to consider his policies. Though the Committee was reconstituted, the President learned in succeeding months and years that the "new" committee was not always as accommodating as he had hoped. One index of the potency of the committee system in general, where presidential policies are at stake, is the statistic revealing that about 40 per cent of the President's requests received either no consideration or unfavorable consideration at the committee stage in 1962.[22]

In the Senate the tradition of unlimited debate, which can and has often served the purpose of talking a policy to death, is a further brake on the policy making machinery. Likewise, the technique of the filibuster is a tool of minorities since any small, cohesive group of senators determined to reject a policy can be countermanded only by a vote of two-thirds of the senators present and voting. Because of its small size, the Senate is susceptible to a dispersal of leadership along informal lines. The club atmosphere of the chamber assures that all senators are by no means equal. Members of the "club," many but not all of whom are elders and committee chairmen, are granted additional prerogatives and exercise a preponderant influence over the decision making process. Their lesser colleagues accede to the informal influence of the club because they realize their only source of hope for a successful career in the body comes from the indulgences of the established leaders. In a larger sense, it is this general understanding among the legislators which perpetuates the system. Only by working through the system can one hope to take advantage of it. The usual advantages sought are status, power, and a long career.

*Opposition to the President.* The ideal arrangement for the achievement of productive policies would be based upon a working partnership between the President and Congress. Historically, this arrangement has rarely prevailed. Natural antagonisms result from the constitutional position of each of the branches. Fundamentally, President and Congress are responsive to quite different constituencies. The President considers himself and is considered to be the representative of all the people, having been elected by a majority of them. The congressman, on the other hand, represents only a particular segment of the people, or the particular interests of his district. Similarly, the senator represents only one of fifty states. Pious platitudes about legislative representation of the national interest aside, the legislator must give first priority to his district or state or face the possibility of losing his seat. This is a rule to which there have been few exceptions.

The consequence of this state of affairs is that very often the President is committed to one set of policies and Congress is committed to quite another. Since a typical congressman's first loyalty is reserved for the institution in which he serves, presidential assertions of authority over Congress are viewed as alien depredations. Presidents understand this, and are usually discreet in their relations with the legislative body. An occasional loss of temper or miscalculation by the chief executive in this regard can be expected to provoke retribution from the injured lawmakers.

Such an incident was partially responsible for the defeat of President Kennedy's 1962 plan for a Department of Urban Affairs and Housing. Realizing all the sources of group discontent the proposal would arouse, the President concluded that the measure had a better chance of passage in the Senate than in the larger, Lower Chamber. By the middle of February it became apparent to the Administration that the House was nearing a vote on the proposal. Strategically, it was much more helpful to the President if the Senate voted *first,* assuming that body accepted the plan. But the venerable Senator John McClellan, Chairman of the Government Operations Committee, was still holding hearings on the proposal, while in the House, it had already reached the floor. Hence the President instructed his Majority Leader in the Senate to apply a little-used parliamentary technique, a petition to discharge the committee of the proposal and bring it to the floor for a vote. The chamber rang with bipartisan denunciations of executive interference with the business and procedures of the Senate. Senator Mundt saw the move as part of a calculated attempt to reduce the powers of Congress. Senator Dirksen detected a violation of the Senate "club" tradition. But the most mellifluous censure came from Chairman McClellan himself: ". . . The brightness of the legislative skies is clouded, the brilliance of statesmanship is dimmed, and the light of fairness and justice in this chamber is darkened today by this deplorable action." [23]

The motion to discharge was defeated. The next day the House defeated the full proposal.

*Absence of Party Unity.* If party loyalty, enforced by party discipline, existed in the United States, President Kennedy would have gotten his Department of Urban Affairs and Housing and all the other major items of his legislative program because there were solid Democratic majorities in both houses of Congress. However, party unity depends partly upon ideological homogeneity and partly upon structural centralization. Neither component is present in American politics. Conservatives and liberals, moderates and radicals, cosmopolitans and provincials—all shades of philosophy and outlook are welcomed in both parties and confined to neither. It makes a real difference whether one is a Javits-Republican or a Goldwater-Republican; a Humphrey-Democrat or an Eastland-Democrat. While it may be true to say that the Democratic Party has a more liberal orientation and the Republican a more conservative orientation, neither statement must be taken to imply a unified outlook. In consequence, neither programmatic leadership emanating from the White House nor from the congressional party leaders can expect a consistent following among all party members.[24]

Perhaps to confound further those who have been demanding a realignment of our party system, in recent years a subtle, voluntary, *de facto* realignment has occurred in Congress. A conservative coalition has emerged, bringing together essentially southern Democrats and midwestern Republicans who vote rather consistently en bloc on major issues. Although this provides for a certain amount of unity among minority interests, it also constitutes a unified rejection of party leadership. Such a rejection is possible because of the decentralized nature of the party system which is an accurate reflection of our system of representation. For while there are two national political parties, there are a hundred more *state* parties. It is primarily to his state party organization that the legislator owes his nomination, campaign support, and election. Thus if the congressman is found satisfactory to his state party organization and his constituents, there are precious few sanctions the national party leadership can impose upon him.

*Interest Representation in Congress.* The sum of the three characteristics of Congress discussed above make the achievement of access to the legislative process a relatively easy matter for the private interest organization. It should be borne in mind that much of the activity of an interest group in upholding or enhancing shared values takes the form of preventive action. A business corporation opposed to higher taxes, a labor union opposed to greater government regulation, a medical association opposed to public health insurance: each works to block a policy designed to limit or inhibit its interest. In such a situation, the availability of a few, or even one influential congressional ally, is often enough to assure success. Access to a committee chairman or two, or to one of the more powerful members of the Senate Club, is much more attainable than access to a majority of congressmen and senators. Hence the oil industry owes a great debt of gratitude to the late Senator Robert Kerr of Oklahoma who, along with a coterie of other senators from oil producing states, was in large measure instrumental in preventing a reduction in the 27.5 per cent oil depletion allowance benefiting the industry. As chairman of the Judiciary Committee, Senator James Eastland of Mississippi was nearly always able to spike civil rights legislation at the committee stage. The institutions and organization of Congress make soft targets for group pressures.

The common rejection of presidential leadership removes an additional obstacle to special group interests, as does the lack of unified party leadership in Congress. In the absence of central, authoritative direction over legislative policy making a multiplicity of power centers has developed. Only through a temporary coalition of congressional leaders (formal and/or informal) can policy be legislated. Coalitions are created out of the process of bargaining, or logrolling, and the result is often irrational compromise.

Ironically, the conflict-coalition-compromise syndrome that is often characteristic of the legislative process produces an unintended consequence. General legislative acts are passed in order to avoid precise policy declarations offensive to various groups exercising influence on Congress. The executive branch then assumes responsibility for the implementation of broad (and often ambiguous) statutes; at this point bureaucratic discretion in the process of implementation amounts to nothing less than policy making.

Hence a Congress jealous of its policy making function, and critical of bureaucratic "usurpation," contributes to its own subversion.

## THE BUREAUCRATIC SUBSYSTEM

As pluralistic as leadership has become, both within and between the two branches, yet another institutional source of policy remains to be identified and evaluated. I have described the bargaining that takes place between the President and Congress over policy alternatives as a relationship among leaders. The magnitude of the business of government, however, makes it inevitable that most of the bargaining takes place among specialized subordinate leaders in both branches. This pattern of relationships has come to be known as the bureaucratic subsystem.[25] The chief actors in the subsystem are bureau and agency leaders, on the one hand, and congressional committee chairmen, on the other. These leaders particularly relate to one another because they share several common professional characteristics. Both actors in the policy process are endowed with continuity of position. Both are specialists, technicians with wide experience in a particular area of policy questions. Both are relatively autonomous functionaries.

The executive bureaucrat often has a long tenure in his position because if he is appointed by one President, he often carries over into another administration; if he falls within the civil service classification, as many do, he holds his position as a matter of right. A congressional committee chairmanship could be the very definition of continuity. Only after long service on the committee and regular re-election is the position achieved and once achieved, only death, electoral defeat, or personal choice can remove a chairman. Thus typically, the chief actors in the subsystem carry over from one Congress and presidential administration to another. That both actors are specialists is partly a function of the continuity of their offices and partly a function of conscious choice. One joins not the bureaucracy, but a specific sector of it relating to one's interests and talents. Over the years, continuous on-the-job training automatically provides further education. Methods and procedures become familiar, routine; precedents build up and variations teach new lessons. This holds true equally for the congressman. If he is reasonably intelligent and competent, years of reading reports of specialists, of attending hearings and picking the brains of expert witnesses, and of witnessing himself the slow development of policy in his area of interest, make an expert of him.

Both agents of the bureaucratic subsystem enjoy a high degree of autonomy in their spheres of competence. On the executive side this is possible, again, because of the over-all size of bureaucracy, but also because many of the large governmental departments function as holding companies composed of a disparate array of offices performing specialized tasks. Consider the Department of Health, Education, and Welfare. A bureaucrat who nominally works for HEW may be a medical scientist in the Public Health Service, a psychologist in the Office of Education, an actuary in the Social Security Administration, a social worker in the Children's Bureau, or a chemist in the Food and Drug Administration. Each division is relatively insulated from the concerns of the others and relatively autonomous in its policy activities. Likewise, the congressional committee chairman is acknowledged by his peers to be an expert in his field whether it be taxation, foreign policy, or conservation. He and the members of his committee receive deference where matters of committee jurisdiction are at issue. Only rarely is a committee determination radically changed by the whole house. An interesting bit of evidence indicating the greater autonomy of chairmen is provided by Donald Matthews in his study of the Senate. A sample of twenty-seven senators revealed that twenty-one of them scored lower on party unity, i.e., voted less often with their party, *after* they became committee chairmen than before.[26] As in most areas of life, greater independence is a prerogative of high status in the subsystem.

The vagaries of interpersonal relations discussed in the previous chapter are of considerable significance in the environment of the bureaucratic subsystem. Policy is forged in an intimate atmosphere of face-to-face confrontation. And it is not a confrontation of equals. Although there have been cases of mutual respect, consistent co-operation and even high camaraderie between bureau chiefs and committee chairmen, normally the bureaucrat's role is one of persuading the congressman and not the reverse. The administrator may feel intellectually superior to the congressman or senator but, if he is wise, he will remember that *politically* he exists on the indulgences of the legislators. Even considering the commonality of interests that prevails between them, there is a gap to be bridged between the administrator and the legislator. Edward Shils has argued that this gap is the political reflection of a general cleavage in American society: "the tension between intellectuals and politicians." [27] Politicians are by nature primarily men of action—doers, movers, manipulators of environment. Administrators tend to be more reflective, theoretical, and less conscious of wielding power. To the extent that these differences in outlook among the negotiators in the subsystem do exist, they can produce hostile relations if not taken into account. In short, the effective bureaucrat must be a mixture of approximately equal parts technician and diplomat. Not only must he be able to present his case clearly and smoothly to the chairman, but he must gain an awareness of the sensitivity to influential divisions within the whole committee. Some members will be predisposed to favor most of his policy suggestions; others can be counted upon to present an automatic front of resistance. The administrator must be prepared to press his advantages and cut his losses, without giving the appearance of attempting to manipulate committeemen.

In attempting to persuade the congressional committee to accept his policy views, the bureaucrat has at least two potential sources of assistance which, if used carefully, can be powerful levers of argumentation. Depending upon the prestige of the President and the department head in committee circles, the administrator may be able to borrow upon his superior's status for support. During the New Deal period, Commissioner Collier of the Bureau of Indian Affairs was for a long time highly successful in using the strong support of his chief, Secretary of Interior Ickes, to achieve the Commissioner's goals in the congressional committee. Ickes was popular both in the committees and in the President's estimation. In return for support from both the Interior Department and the White House, Commissioner Collier reciprocated by being a fervent supporter of the administration in its campaigns on *other* issues not related to Indian affairs.[28]

A second source of support upon which the administrator may draw from time to time is his *clientele* group. In the federal government many agencies exist to provide services or benefits for a specific category of people who are referred to collectively as the agency's clientele organization. The Bureau of Indian Affairs, mentioned above, is one; the Veterans Administration is another outstanding example of an agency which caters to the interests of a specialized clientele. Cabinet departments of the government, such as Commerce, Agriculture and Labor, are clientele departments. If the bureaucrat is attuned to the clientele organization he serves—and if he is wise he will be—he can enlist its support when negotiating with the congressional committee. Let us assume, for example, that the Administrator of Veterans Affairs is appearing before the House Committee on Veterans Affairs to propose an expanded program of federally financed home loans for veterans. The legislators may be understandingly reluctant to reject out of hand the administrator's proposal, even if "economy in government" is the byword of the day. This is primarily because the administrator's clientele is numerous, widely distributed geographically, and efficiently organized as American Legionnaires or Veterans of Foreign Wars. And they all have votes.

It is important to note that the relationship between the bureaucrat and his clientele organization is a reciprocal one. Just as the administrator uses his clientele, the clientele uses the administrator. Thus we have come full circle, returning to the phenomenon of group participation in the policy process. For it is at the level of the bureaucratic subsystem that private interest groups avidly seek and usually gain access to the leading bargainers in the policy making struggle. An alienated clientele group is capable of ruining an unco-operative administrator by an intensive application of political pressure. More often than not, harassment is unnecessary since the bureaucrat has probably been appointed after executive consultation with the clientele organization and operates in consultation with a clientele advisory group in the agency.

## CONCLUSION

The activity of making public policy has been described broadly as a process of bargaining among leaders of public institutions and private groups. Rather than a formal recitation of the exercise of legal prerogatives, the description has been largely functional and behavioral. A certain amount of depth has been sacrificed in favor of sketching out the broad contours of a vital and complex network. An underlying theme argues that there has been a wide dispersal of leadership in modern American government and one, furthermore, that is characteristic of a society that is both pluralistically and bureaucratically organized. Of the many centers of policy making power that exist in contemporary government, the independent regulatory commissions and public corporations will be analyzed more intensively, as variants of an administrative theme, in the chapter that follows.

### REFERENCES

1. David B. Truman, *The Governmental Process* (New York: Alfred A. Knopf, 1951), pp. 23-24.
2. Arthur F. Bentley, *The Process of Government* [1908] (Bloomington, Ind.: The Principia Press, Inc., reissued, 1949), p. 269.
3. Truman, *op. cit.*, pp. 264-265.
4. Robert A. Dahl and Charles E. Lindblom, *Politics, Economics and Welfare* (New York: Harper and Row, 1953), Chapters 12-13.
5. Representative criticisms of group theory on these and other grounds can be found in Peter H. Odegard, "A Group of Politics: A New Name for an Old Myth," *Western Political Quarterly*, XI (September, 1958), pp. 689-702; and Stanley Rothman, "Systematic Political Theory: Observations on the Group Approach," *American Political Science Review*, LIV (March, 1960), pp. 15-33.
6. James Burnham, *The Managerial Revolution* (New York: Oxford University Press, 1941).
7. C. Wright Mills, *The Power Elite* (New York: Oxford University Press, 1957), p. 28.
8. Dahl and Lindblom, *op. cit.*, p. 336. (Italics in the original.)
9. *Public Law* 87-794.
10. Richard E. Neustadt, *Presidential Power: The Politics of Leadership* (New York: John Wiley & Sons, Inc., 1960).
11. *The New York Times,* April 11-14, 1962, *passim.* For a remarkable journalistic synthesis, see the summary article by ten *Times* correspondents, *The New York Times,* April 23, 1962, p. 1.
12. *Congressional Quarterly Weekly Report,* XX (November 23, 1962), 2196.
13. *Youngstown Sheet and Tube Co.,* v. *Sawyer,* 343 US 579 (1952).
14. *Myers* v. *United States,* 272 US 52 (1926).
15. *Humphrey's Executor* (*Rathbun*) v. *United States,* 295 US 602 (1935).
16. *Wiener* v. *United States,* 357 US 349 (1958).
17. *Congressional Quarterly Weekly Report,* XX (November 2, 1962), p. 2110; *Congressional Quarterly Weekly Report,* XXI (March 29, 1963), p. 449; and *The New York Times,* August 3, 1963, p. 7.
18. House Subcommittee on Committee of Appropriations, *Hearings on Department of State Appropriations Bill for 1945,* 78th Cong., 2nd Sess. (Washington, D.C., 1944), p. 15; quoted in Richard F. Fenno,

Jr., *The President's Cabinet* (Cambridge: Harvard University Press, 1959), p. 205.

19. *The New York Times,* October 14, 1962, p. 46.

20. This is a most abbreviated account of a highly complex case that was a subject of months of speculation, charges and countercharges, and congressional investigations. For a full account, see Aaron Wildavsky, *Dixon-Yates: A Study in Power Politics* (New Haven: Yale University Press, 1962).

21. *Ibid.,* pp. 301-308.

22. *Congressional Quarterly Weekly Report,* XX (November 23, 1962), p. 2187.

23. U.S. Senate, *Congressional Record,* 87th Cong., 2nd Sess. (Washington, D.C., 1962), February 20, 1962, p. 2541.

24. For an anxious view of this state of affairs, see James M. Burns, *The Deadlock of Democracy* (Englewood Cliffs: Prentice-Hall, Inc., 1963); for a less troubled view, read Clinton Rossiter, *Parties and Politics in America* (Ithaca: Cornell University Press, 1960).

25. The best single analysis of the subsystem—and one on which I have drawn in the following discussion—is J. Lieper Freeman, *The Political Process: Executive Bureau—Legislative Committee Relations* (New York: Random House, 1955).

26. Donald R. Matthews, *U.S. Senators and Their World* (New York: Vintage Books, 1960), p. 164.

27. Edward A. Shils, "The Legislator and His Environment," *University of Chicago Law Review,* XVIII (Spring, 1951), p. 579.

28. Freeman, *op. cit.,* pp. 35-37.

# CHAPTER 4

# The Dispersal of Leadership—II

## THE INDEPENDENT REGULATORY COMMISSIONS

In its 1937 *Report,* the President's Committee on Administrative Management made the following judgment about the independent regulatory commissions:

> Congress began 50 years ago to create independent commissions to handle Federal regulatory functions. This movement in the field of national administration is the result of much legislative groping— much reliance upon trial and error. It has developed its own philosophy as it has gone along. Its major principles have never been followed with complete consistency and the commissions set up have varied widely in form and function.[1]

This account of the commissions remains as accurate today as it was in 1937. Furthermore, the appearance of the commissions was, as Robert Cushman has said, much more than a new bud on an old branch of government: "It was a new limb of such major importance that it pointed the whole tree in a new direction." [2] The unique institutional significance of the independent regulatoray commissions is twofold. The generic term given to these bodies, while not self-explanatory, suggests their role. They are independent because they are lodged outside the executive complex of cabinet departments, bureaus, and agencies under presidential control. They are regulatory in that they supervise and control the private conduct of economic affairs and the exercise of property rights. This is the theory upon which the commissions are based and the criterion by which we may identify them.[3]

Attempts to guarantee the independence of the commissions are seen in the limitations placed upon the presidential right of removal, as stated in the Humphrey case, and in the wide discretion the commissioners have been granted to make rules having statutory effect and to adjudicate conflicts between the commission and private parties. The regulatory function is exercised over a disparate array of private facilities. The largest number of commissions regulate all types of common carriers. The Interstate Commerce Commission regulates rail, bus, and truck operations; airlines are governed by the Civil Aeronautics Board, airplanes and pilots by the Federal Aviation Agency; common carriers by water are regulated by the Federal Maritime Commission; interstate and foreign commerce carried on by communications facilities are regulated by the Federal Communications Commission. Another distinct area of IRC regulation concerns banking and finance for which the Federal Reserve Board and the Securities Exchange Commission are responsible. Business practices in general are regulated by the Federal Trade Commission. The affairs of labor fall under the supervision of the National Labor Relations Board. Private power facilities and other utilities have their operations regulated by the Federal Power Commission and the Atomic Energy Commission.

Because of the haphazard development of the various commissions, their modes of operation and membership are marked by a splendid diversity. The average governing board is made up of five commissioners, but memberships vary between two (an Administrator and a Deputy) on the FAA and eleven on the ICC. Similarly, their terms of service vary from five years on many of them to fourteen years for members of the FRB. Special requirements characterize the membership of certain of the IRCs. The FTC has five members, no more than three of whom may belong to the same political party. The five-year terms of the five members of the SEC are staggered so that a new appointment comes due each year. In choosing members of the FRB, the President is required by law to maintain a fair representation among financial, industrial, agricultural, commercial, and geographic interests. The IRCs differ both in the methods of conducting their affairs and in the standards by which they assess their regulatory roles. In short, the commissions collectively form a wide target for attacks based upon their inherent violation of administrative order and consistency. The chief liability of the commissions, however, is not administrative imperfection, but rather the fact that they constitute a brooding omnipresence in the harsh world of political controversy. A consideration of the various problem areas converging on the IRCs sets the agenda for the pages that follow. First, however, an insight into the source of many of the problems affecting the IRCs may be gained by looking briefly at the diverse origins of the commission form.

*Origins of the IRCs.* The root source of the governmental regulatory agency can, of course, be traced to fundamental technical changes that have come about in the nineteenth and twentieth centuries. Just as no one would have conjured up an Atomic Energy Commission before the discovery and use of atomic energy, there would have been no need for an ICC before a complicated system of railroads laced across the nation. Even so, an important change in attitude about the role of government had to take place before the link could be made between physical, technical developments and the *need* for governmental regulation. A gradual disenchantment with the dogma of *laissez faire* accomplished this attitudinal *volte-face*.

Reasons for the choice of the independent regulatory commission as a technique of positive government are more involved and numerous than the plain fact of the acceptance of regulation in principle. One reason was experience. As with many other innovations in American government, the states had experimented with the regulatory commission for some time before the first federal IRC was created. In fact, twenty-five states regulated railroads within their borders by commission before the ICC was established in 1887. A still more substantial cause of Congress's resort to the independent commission was one of rational calculation. It appeared that a rather sharp institutional departure from traditional forms was the only way effectively to provide for the regulatory function. Regulation was a new function which required modern machinery for its performance. James Landis summarizes this reasoning with an apt analogy:

> If in private life we were to organize a unit for the operation of an industry, it would scarcely follow Montesquieu's lines. As yet no organization in private industry either has been conceived along those triadic contours, nor would its normal development, if so conceived, have tended to conform to them.[4]

The granting of a license to operate a television channel by the FCC or the calculation and establishment of fair rates to be charged for electric power by the FPC are activities which demand technical training and an industrial methodology of decision making that traditional government could not readily provide. In order to regulate meaningfully, administration had to have the power to make its own rules, to hold its own investigations, and to impose sanctions upon private parties who failed to conform to its decisions. To do all this, and to do it *quickly*, means had to be found to by-pass Congress and the courts. The obvious solution appeared to be a new, special branch of government endowed with delegated legislative and judicial authority.

While the employment of the commission as a specialized, regulatory functionary seems logical enough, one may well wonder why these bodies had to be withdrawn from the main line of administrative accountability and routed off on a siding clearly marked "independent." The answer to this query may be found in a traditional American mode of thought which dictates that some matters are too important to be left to the politicians. It was an irrational exercise of self-delusion that argued in favor of a substitution of "independent" and "objective" officials for elected policy makers. If only a set of disinterested technicians could be isolated from the strivings and compromises of politics, it was felt that uninhibited calculations of the good, the true, and the beautiful would come to pass. As if the controversial aspects of economic life in which the IRCs would be deeply enmeshed could ever be insulated from politics in the broadest—and truest —sense of that word!

A chronicle of the origins of the IRCs would provide as many individual histories as there are commissions. Since we have neither the time nor the space to relate them in detail, let two generalizations suffice. First, each and every commission was born of political demand and political compromise. Dissatisfaction with the practices of the railroads and widespread demand for regulation led to the Interstate Commerce Act. The demands of workers for bargaining rights and the election of a New Deal Administration pledged to satisfy those demands led to the National Labor Relations Act of 1935—and the NLRB. In each case there were concessions and compromises which decreed, for example, how far the SEC would go in regulating stock margin or to what extent the FCC would govern radio programming.

Second, some of the commissions were created as an act of political expediency. Thus, on those occasions when an issue appeared to Congress to be too controversial to admit of a politically safe legislative determination, the lawmakers solved the problem by creating a commission with a vague mandate. Pendleton Herring notes, for example, that Congress was expected in 1914 to do something about the monopoly problem. There was general dissatisfaction with the ineffectiveness of existing antitrust legislation, and in the political campaign of 1912 all party platforms promised to deal with the trusts. Congress avoided the embarrassment inherent in writing a specific statute and, instead created the FTC to enforce general prohibitions against "unfair methods of competition" and "unfair or deceptive acts or practices" in business.[5] Such ambiguous prescriptions did not augur well for the efficient conduct of regulatory policy by the commissions.

*Legal Problems.* Constitutional challenges based upon the separation of powers have arisen as a result of the creation of IRCs which commonly exercise all three kinds of power—executive, legislative, and judicial. It is obvious that every time the CAB publishes a new rule requiring airplanes to fly at a certain height in a certain path, the commissioners have legislated; it is equally obvious that every time the FTC holds a hearing and decides that a given industry is guilty of price-fixing, the commissioners have put on judicial robes. Yet all these functions have long been justified by the courts through recourse to the curious doctrine of the "quasis." Since the delegation of legislative powers by Congress had always been deemed unconstitutional, the Supreme Court circumvented its own dogmas by applying a new name to what had been delegated. Hence the IRCs exercise "quasi-legislative" and "quasi-judicial" powers, thereby solving the constitutional hiatus over delegation.

What is the rationale of the quasis? It would appear that a rather thin and permeable membrane of limitations surrounds the legislative and judicial functions of the IRCs. That is, the Court has stated on a number of occasions that congressional delegations of power must be made with some standard of specificity in mind. Indeed, in the 1930s important pieces of New Deal legislation were voided on the ground of unconstitutional delegations of legislative authority.[6] In practice, however, since the 1930s the limitations on delegations of these powers to the IRCs have been exceedingly broad, and the courts have consistently upheld them. We are thus left with Cushman's conclusion of nearly a quarter-century ago that, "while the standards limiting the delegations of legislative power may be vague, they may not be too vague, and they certainly must not be wholly lacking." [7]

Because no one could possibly imagine how the multitude of regulatory rules necessary in the modern state could be made without delegations to specialized agencies, the rule making function of the IRCs is no longer productive of heated controversy. The exercise of judicial functions, by the commissions, however, remains a source of dissatisfaction, especially among many members of the legal profession. At the heart of the lawyer's attack lies a fundamental conflict between the common law tradition and the methods of administrative adjudication. Basic to the common law tradition is an independent judiciary made up of professionally trained judges who, acting as disinterested parties, listen to the merits of cases and controversies and reach decisions based upon common law, statutes, and legal precedents. Great emphasis is placed upon procedural due process guarantees, such as the right to counsel, the presentation of evidence, cross-examination, and appeal. Fault is found with administrative adjudication because many of the traditional features of common law courts are absent. At the very outset it is apparent that the commissions must *combine* their judicial work with their policy making function. The commissioners are not only judges but administrators and legislators as well, which means that the tradition of judicial neutrality cannot be serviced. A related fact which arouses legal opposition to administrative adjudication is the fact that the IRC bureaucrats are not in fact judges. This attitude of antagonism was eloquently stated years ago by Professor Max Radin:

> These men are not lawyers. They have not eaten and prayed with us. They do not speak our language. We can follow their reasoning, but, if we disagree with it, we have no intention of accepting the result, if we can possibly avoid doing so. And there is no institutional respect that weighs the balance in their favor. We cannot believe that the totality of their judgment can possibly be law. Every judgment is unique. It will not fuse in our minds with a mass of accepted doctrine, as the Common Law does.[8]

In terms of procedure, the commissions are criticized because they seem at once to perform the roles of prosecutor and judge. Professor Cushman cited the example of the FTC which seeks out and investigates unfair competitive trade practices and holds hearings to decide whether they are unfair; there is a great temptation for the commission to decide that it has in fact proved its case.[9] Dean Roscoe Pound, perhaps the most vociferous critic of the administrative process, has catalogued a long series of adjudicatory shortcomings, including decisions made without hearings, or without hearing one of the parties; decisions based upon private consultations; determinations of fact without sufficient evidential basis; and determinations reached on the basis of preconceptions which accord with policy goals.[10]

As a result of a long campaign by the American Bar Association, Congress passed the Administrative Procedure Act in 1946. The act was designed to accomplish three major categories of reform in administrative adjudication: (1) The procedural rights of private parties appearing before the agencies were specified to include the right to be informed of the organization, procedures, and policies of the agencies; to be made aware of new agency rules and to participate in their formulation; the right to counsel and to be issued legal subpoenas; and the right of private parties to file exceptions to decisions of the agencies. (2) Broader provision was made for a resort to judicial review of formal agency decisions in the courts. (3) The position and activities of the trial examiner—the judicial agent of the IRCs—were made more independent of the commission than had been the case. For example, section 8(a) of the act provides that: "Whenever such officers [examiners] make the initial decision and in the absence of either an appeal to the agency or review upon motion of the agency within time provided by the rule, such decision shall without further proceedings then become the decision of the agency." [11]

In practice, the Administrative Procedure Act—loosely drafted, having inconsistent provisions, and open to broad interpretations—has not removed many of the problems it was designed to cure. Court interpretations of the act's provisions, recognizing the complexity of the administrative process, have tended to grant rather wide discretion to the commissions in their applications of it. One of the key sources of difficulty has been the lack of a consistent definition of the role of the trial examiner. The act attempted to insulate this official from the policy function of the IRCs and yet, as Musolf has phrased it, the examiner must be considered a hybrid official. From the point of view of the commissioners, he is often considered to be an employee of the agency, expected to operate within its particular philosophical frame of reference. From the point of view of the act—and the legal profession—the examiner should act with judicious impartiality. The result of this conundrum is that the commission frequently ignores, reinterprets, or reverses the examiner's determination when it is out of line with commission policy. Moreover, different commissions employ different methods of utilizing the examiners' findings. Some accept his reports as commission decisions; others, such as the FCC, have an opinion writing section which uses the examiner's report as a "testimonial inference" from which it may construct a decision that the commissioners can sign. On the other hand, there are cases where the examiner considers himself an agent furthering the policy goals of the commission. Take the case of the NLRB examiner whose personal view of policy generally supports the aspirations of the Board's clientele—organized labor: his perception of the "facts" is bound to be partially determined by his attitude. And, in the course of writing his opinion, he not uncommonly consults other, nonjudicial employees of the Board, whether in seeking technical information or merely exchanging views concerning the case at hand. In short, the trial examiner very often finds it impossible to isolate himself from the policy process going on inside the commission.

Attempts, such as that inherent in the Administrative Procedure Act, to erect rigid, legalistic fences around administrative adjudication appear even less significant when we consider how large a proportion of IRC determinations are reached by the route of *informal* adjudication.[12] Thousands upon thousands of cases come before the IRCs each year, and the vast majority of them are settled through informal processes. The main difference between formal and informal adjudication is that in the latter case the full paraphernalia of a formal, judicial hearing is not present. Instead, on the basis of correspondence or conferences between the commission and the private party involved, the matter is settled informally. To illustrate some of the different techniques of informal adjudication commonly practiced, let us use the FTC as an example. Suppose the Commission decides, after an investigation, that a business firm is violating the law in some way. It may issue a complaint, presenting its charges and inviting a reply from the respondents. Under formal adjudication, if the respondents contested the Commission charge, a full hearing before trial examiner would take place and the commissioners would issue a final decision. There are several alternatives, however, under the *informal* procedure. If the respondent business admits that it is guilty of the violations named in the complaint (and the violations are relatively unimportant) it may choose to sign a *stipulation* by which it agrees with the Commission's facts and promises to cease and desist. The case is settled. A variation of this technique is the *consent order*. In this situation, after being served with a complaint, the respondent firm does not admit guilt formally, but promises future compliance with Commission rules and may even pay a fine. Under these informal techniques a crude form of justice is achieved which disposes of a case quickly, saves the government the heavy costs of a lengthy prosecution, and saves the violator the embarrassment of a lengthy, public trial.

The frequency of informal proceedings is shown by one study of the NLRB over a six-year period. Between 1947 and 1953 only 8 per cent of the cases initiated reached the Board for formal decision, the remainder being settled by one of the informal methods. Similarly, between 1915 and 1950 only 18 per cent of the cases initiated by the FTC resulted in formal orders.[13] It must be added that, though judicial review on appeal exists in theory, in practice it is rarely resorted to for the simple reason that business affairs cannot afford to await the long process of appeal. Even though some members of the legal fraternity are disturbed by the apparent absence of traditional common law procedures in administrative adjudication, we must conclude with a leading scholar in this area that, because of heavy case-loads, the necessity for technical expertise, and the desirability of quick results, the informal process is "more consonant with administrative procedure in fact-finding and adjudication."[14]

Even a brief summary of the means by which the IRCs attempt to operate effectively and enforce their policies would be deficient if mention were not made of the importance of nonjudicial sanctions. One potential form of sanction available to the commissions is an outgrowth of their authority to license various economic enterprises, such as the SEC's licensing of exchanges and brokers or the FCC's licensing of radio stations and television channels. The power to license is also the power to revoke, suspend, or fail to renew a license. An interesting public declaration of this potential sanction was made by FCC Chairman, Newton Minow, in a May, 1961 speech before the National Association of Broadcasters. The newly appointed Chairman told his clientele that he frankly regarded TV programming as a "vast wasteland" and added the veiled threat that there was "nothing permanent or sacred about a broadcast license." [15]

The commission investigation is another form of sanction. Very often the spotlight of publicity which is a feature of such inquiries is enough to persuade existing or potential wrongdoers to conform to commission policy directives without resort to legal proceedings. In 1963 a study group of the SEC issued three voluminous reports in which it criticized severely the use of mutual fund investment plans and excessively high fees charged by brokerage firms. The final report chided the New York Stock Exchange specifically for failure to require its members to conform to Exchange rules. The report recommended no formal action on the part of the SEC, but admonished the financial community to undertake more effective self-regulation. [16]

*Political Problems.*   Occupying a position midway on the policy battlefield between the executive and legislative branches, the IRCs could not conceivably avoid becoming involved in that historic competition. The lot of the neutralist on belligerent territory is seldom an enviable one. The nominally independent commission, from the time of its creation, is subjected to importunities from both Capitol Hill and the White House. While the IRCs are supposed to be free from executive direction, all Presidents since Theodore Roosevelt have interfered with their work. Franklin Roosevelt refused to consider the IRCs as separate entities immune to his administrative leadership and acted vigorously in the following manner:

> The judicial calm of the Interstate Commerce Commission was left undisturbed, but the most able and aggressive commissioner was created Federal Co-ordinator of Transportation. The United States

Tariff Commission was reduced to a harmless condition through the passage of the Reciprocal Tariff act. The Federal Radio Commission was abolished outright and a New Deal commission took its place. The President secured the resignation of Hoover's chairman of the Federal Power Commission and added two appointees of his own.[17]

If, in the light of the Humphrey dictum, the President cannot summarily remove the commissioners, there is nothing to prevent the application of informal presidential pressures to unwanted officials. Bernard Schwartz reports that when a congressional committee asked Sherman Adams directly in 1958 whether he had ever requested any commissioners to hand in their resignations, President Eisenhower's assistant replied: "If you insist on the question, I should have to answer it in the affirmative." [18]

Moreover, even though the commissioners may refuse to oblige presidential requests by resigning, rapid turnover among IRC personnel often permits the President to staff individual agencies with his men. A recent study of the NLRB relates how President Eisenhower reconstituted that independent body by appointing a majority of the members within the first two years of his administration. The President and his party favored a less accommodating attitude on the part of the Board toward the interests of organized labor and secured a change in approach by appointing men in line with administration views.[19] The President can call upon other, unmistakably executive agencies to help him bring IRC policies into accord with his own philosophy. The important role played by the Bureau of the Budget in legislative clearance and appropriations makes it a mighty force to be reckoned with by the IRCs. A reduction in operating funds can be used as a sanction against uncooperative agencies. Beyond this, the BOB can sometimes even limit or prevent specific IRC investigations and inquiries. Through its authority to withhold clearance for inquiries under certain circumstances according to the Federal Reports Act, the Bureau can prevent investigations that the commissions may feel are necessary to the performance of their regulatory function.

The Congress is no more reluctant than the President to interfere with the IRCs. Its greatest influence derives from its role as parent legislator, the source from which all IRC prerogatives emanate. At any time the legislators may broaden or narrow the jurisdiction of the commissions, reconstitute them, or abolish them altogether. If Congress wishes, under its prerogative of legislative oversight, it can carry investigations beyond the brink of harassment. In some cases the judicial findings and decisions of a commission have virtually been retried in the atmosphere of a congressional hearing and the original decision denounced by the legislators. Regarding legislative interference with the work of the NLRB, one investigator notes that he found only one congressman on a committee that had reservations about the propriety of questioning officials of that IRC. Furthermore, the following remark by one congressman puts the congressional view in perspective: "We never think twice about calling the Board and asking for a little special handling of some cases; not just to speed things up but to look a little differently at the case." [20]

In the policy struggle between President and Congress the IRCs provide an unwilling filter through which congressional adversaries may direct attacks on executive policy making. In the process, the effectiveness of the IRCs is often diminished. This is illustrated with greatest clarity by the attempts of President Kennedy in 1961 to reorganize the commissions to operate more efficiently and rationally. The President's FCC Reorganization Plan called for greater centralization of activities in the Commission with more authority vested in the Chairman. Congressional opponents of the plan raised cries of dictatorship, arguing that the plan constituted a surrender of legislative authority to the President; they contended that there was "no reason why Congress should let the President legislate on agencies that were *supposed to be the arms of Congress*." [21]

It should be noted that the political tug-of-war over the commissions that is conducted by President and Congress has its source in the *legitimate* functions of both branches. The President, as head of the administrative branch, can hardly be blamed for attempting to persuade the IRCs to follow a course he considers to be in the public interest. Furthermore, while the commissions are legally independent, in a popular, political sense the President often finds himself held publicly responsible for commission acts. It should not be surprising, then, that all presidents attempt to exert some managerial authority over the IRCs. Similarly, Congress is expected to exercise legislative oversight over all federal agencies. Indeed, this is one of the few means of making such agencies ultimately accountable to the people. However, the thin line between legitimate oversight and undue interference and perhaps even harassment is a difficult one to determine. The real source of the problem is the unwise act of pretending that agencies which deal with such vital and controversial issues as those over which the IRCs have jurisdiction could ever operate in lofty independence of politics.

*Personnel Problems.* Some of the forces that inhibit successful policy making and administration by the IRCs grow out of factors common to any nonideal bureaucratic organization. Any organization that is collegial in nature is subject to internal strife and dissension. The policies of all the commissions are made and executed by a *body* of officials; though there is a Chairman of each commission, he is usually no more than *primus inter pares.* To make matters worse, the commissioners are appointed at different times by different presidents having different philosophies of regulation. It is natural that ideological conflicts develop within the IRCs. In each commission there are traditional polarities of opinion about the mission of the organization. On the NLRB some of the board members are prolabor, others antilabor; on the FPC divisions develop between propublic power and antipublic power commissioners. Each President attempts to recast the commission (by fixing the majority) in his own philosophical orientation. Since a President can rarely appoint *all* the commissioners, dissent is invariably voiced by holdovers from the previous administration. Often the Chairman of the Commission, whom the President appoints, works in league with the administration, while some of the other members take an anti-administration stance. In 1954 Jerome Kuykendall, FPC Chairman, appealed to President Eisenhower's assistant for legal advice about his powers to control or bypass other members of the Commission in order to get an administration favored bill past opponents within the Commission.[22]

Another means by which chairmen may gain control of the commissions is through the effective control of the Commission's staff. A remarkable use of this technique was reported in an item on the front page of *The New York Times* in 1961. The headline read: A.E.C. RECAPTURES CONTROL OF STAFF. It appears that one-time AEC Commission Chairman, Lewis L. Strauss, established a close liaison with the Commission staff and was successful in stymieing opposition to the Chairman's policy. Because the staff organized the agenda for all meetings, the commissioners found themselves immobilized by lengthy reports on items of priority set by the Chairman and the staff. This situation prevailed until 1961 when the members of the Commission literally revolted against the staff and seized power to set their own agenda.[23]

Since each of the IRCs daily makes policy affecting acutely the interests of far-flung economic enterprises, pressures brought to bear on the people who make the decisions by private interests constitute an abiding problem. The methods of gaining access to and favorable action from commission personnel vary from rare instances of outright corruption to the more common technique of conditioning the perception of issues through propaganda directed at the officials. From time to time whole commissions are "captured" by the interests they regulate. Thurman Arnold has touched the key to this ironic situation:

> One of the things that happens to all administrative tribunals is that it first is opposed by the industry and then it becomes controlled by the principal industry. That does not have anything to do with corruption. That is due to the fact that young men in Government careers want to get the best jobs they can in their specialties and there is this social pressure to be a sound man rather than an unsound man, because if you are an unsound man, you will never get a job in the industry. You cannot remove that.[24]

The implication of the above statement seems to be that many of the commissioners and other personnel working in the IRCs view their position as a kind of internship wherein they may gain experience in the regulatory process in a specific area and thus make themselves attractive candidates for positions in private industry. The rapid turnover rate on the commissions provides evidence to enhance this conclusion. In its 1949 *Task Force Report on Regulatory Commissions,* the Hoover Commission identified the rate of turnover as a fundamental feature detracting from the effectiveness of the IRCs. It was found that on the SEC, incumbents averaged about two years in office; in the CAB, the average was about three years; in the FCC, of the seven incumbents in 1949, one had served fourteen years but the average of the other six members was about one year. Only the ICC and the FTC managed to retain personnel for a length of time appropriate to some measure of stability and continuity.[25]

A rather rapid transference of loyalties from the federal government to a regulated industry by commission officials is frequently observed. Recently an FCC Commissioner provided a typical example. Commissioner John Cross had been appointed in 1958, and, in 1962 when he was about to retire from the Commission, he sent out letters to broadcasting and electronics concerns offering his services at $5000 per year plus $2000 for expenses to each client. Mr. Cross explained: "In return for the retainer, I would undertake to obtain information on such projects as my client might request, including regulatory and legislative projects, and give them the benefit of my advice regarding these projects." [26] There is nothing illegal in this procedure. The question that may be raised is whether an official who works temporarily for an IRC and who plans a private career in the Commission's sphere of regulation can adopt a professional view of regulatory policy that is opposed to the biases of those who are being regulated.

In fact, the IRCs appear to progress through a life cycle from a point of sharp philosophical contrast with the outlook of the regulated instrumentality, to a point of general agreement and even patronage of the interests of the regulated. Marver Bernstein has described this evolution in four phases: gestation, youth, maturity (devitalization), and old age (debility and decline). In a special study, Huntington carefully shows how the ICC was originally opposed by the railroads but now finds its chief support in those same railroads.[27] In terms of policy, a meeting of minds seems to have occurred.

*The Problems of Reform.* Attempts have been made from a variety of sources to solve the problems confronting effective regulatory administration. Proposals for reform have fallen into three general categories: (1) reform of the mixed legislative-judicial-administrative functions; (2) solution of the problem of accountability by placing the regulatory function under presidential control; (3) piecemeal reforms, problem by problem and agency by agency.

The American Bar Association has long called for a strict separation of the judicial function from IRC purview. In a Report of 1936 the ABA called for the establishment of an administrative court which would handle all the judicial work of administrative agencies and apply traditional common law legal standards.[28] There are two principal difficulties with the administrative court proposal. First, it amounts to a sweeping institutional change which, as a practical matter, is difficult to bring about. Second, the problems of regulatory administration are of such a specialized nature that it is questionable whether the common law approach would be most effective in furthering the mission of the IRCs. An alternative means of functional separation was suggested by Professor Cushman. He proposed that, wherever possible, the IRCs be placed in regular executive departments, but within the departments there be two sections—an administrative rule making section and a separate judicial section. Members of the first section would be directly responsible to and removable by the department head; the judicial members, on the other hand, would be removable only for cause.[29] Significantly, when Newton Minow retired as Chairman of the FCC on May 31, 1963, he wrote President Kennedy a letter recommending a split between the administrative and judicial functions. Noting that the multimember agencies find it difficult to resolve differences on policy among themselves, he went on to state: "I do not believe it is possible to be a good judge on Monday and Tuesday, a good legislator on Wednesday and Thursday and a good administrator on Friday." Minow proposed that the FCC be administered by a single official placed directly in the executive branch and that the judicial business be conducted by an administrative court.[30]

The suggestions of the two Hoover Commissions on the organization of the executive branch (1949 and 1955) posed two general kinds of answers to the outstanding problems. The first Commission sought greater centralization and responsibility for the chairmen of the IRCs; the second shifted its emphasis to the isolation of judicial functions which it recommended be conducted by separately appointed "commissioners" on fixed tenure. In practical terms, the most significant result of the Hoover Commissions' recommendations was the continuance of presidential authority to reorganize the IRCs individually by executive order with congressional approval.

Shortly after his election in 1960, President-elect John F. Kennedy appointed a Task Force on IRC problems headed by the eminent authority on the administrative process, James M. Landis.

In December Landis presented his report containing both an analysis of existing problems and recommendations for improvement. The Landis Report avoided prescriptions for change of sweeping and thorough proportions. While the underlying rationale of presidential authority over the administrative process was evident, Landis conceded that such major changes as incorporating all the IRCs into the executive departments would be to plan *in vacuo*. Instead he proposed as a necessary first step, the co-ordination of IRC policies in the Executive Office of the President. Three "Offices of Co-ordination" were suggested, one for Transportation, one for Communications, and one for Energy Policy. In addition, a general "Office of Oversight" over all regulatory agencies was proposed to be placed in the Executive Office.

Further recommendations were made for limited reforms in individual agencies. The general import of these suggestions can be summarized as providing for greater authority for the Chairman of the IRCs, responsibility of the chairmen to the President, and much wider scope for delegation of judicial authority to single agency members, panels of members, hearing examiners, or boards of employees. In the latter instance it was proposed that the full commission would only review judicial determinations when petitioned by the parties in the case. Such proposals were designed to relieve the overburdened commissioners and speed up the adjudicatory process.

The Landis Report did not restrict itself to matters of organization and procedure; it also touched upon personnel problems. Noting that "Good men can make poor laws workable; poor men will wreak havoc with good laws . . ." the report concluded that unqualified personnel and rapid turnover could not be cured by higher salaries alone. Dedicated men and qualified men have long been willing to contribute their services in return for salaries less than their equivalents in business and professions. An administrative ethic of loyal, disinterested service and a degree of social prestige are the compensating factors that have fostered distinguished civil services in Great Britain and continental countries. Landis proposed that one route to these ends in the United States might well be carved out by granting tenure to officials of regulatory agencies similar to that afforded by our universities, and through a small entertainment allowance so that the regulatory official could afford to "pay his own way" on those frequent occasions when his position requires him to deal with representatives of private industry in a social atmosphere.[31]

On entering office, President Kennedy asked for and received an extension of authority to reorganize the executive branch along the lines proposed in the Landis Report. Subsequently, he presented seven reorganization plans to the 87th Congress. Three of the seven plans were rejected (SEC, FCC, and NLRB) and four accepted (CAB, FTC, Maritime Agencies, and Federal Home Loan Bank Board). The most important organizational changes affected the three IRCs which Congress prohibited the President from reorganizing (although Congress later passed its own legislation concerning the FCC). The elements leading to the defeat of the three plans were provisions for increased authority for commission chairmen and discretionary delegation of judicial authority by the chairmen. As was noted above, Congress interpreted these changes as an attribution of greater authority to the President, a step the lawmakers were not inclined to sanction.

The fundamental problems of the IRCs remain with us. Having grown in Topsy-like fashion, they have generated unique versions of universal bureaucratic malfunctions. As nominally independent offshoots of the American institutional triad, they languish in a never-never land of presidential, congressional, and private group pressures.

## A FOOTNOTE ON THE PUBLIC CORPORATIONS

The public corporation is yet another category of institutions that has come to supplement the traditional organs of American government. This novel device of public administration represents an attempt by the government to engage in commercial undertakings according to a pattern which follows the private corporate model. Congress usually establishes a public corporation by passing an enabling act which organizes a corporate facility governed by an independent board of directors appointed by the President. In theory the corporation is an autonomous enterprise which gets its start from a subscription of operating funds by the federal government. Once established, the public corporations bear certain similarities to their counterparts in private economic life. They can sue or be sued. They are authorized to acquire property. They can obtain funds by issuing bonds, borrowing from the Treasury, or using a system of revolving funds rather than the usual annual appropriations source by which other government agencies are supported.

In 1963 there were 84 public enterprises, and net expenditures on public enterprise funds amounted to over $4 billion dollars (that is, the difference between $19.9 billion in gross expenditures and $15.8 billion in receipts from their operations).[32] The greatest number of public enterprises are corporations engaged in lending, financing, and insurance activities. One of the largest is the Commodity Credit Corporation, the agency which handles the price support and stabilization payments to farmers under the agriculture program. The CCC also maintains crop storage facilities and makes loans for the construction and expansion of granaries. Our bank deposits are guaranteed by another public enterprise, the Federal Deposit Insurance Corporation. Until 1954, when it was dissolved, the Reconstruction Finance Corporation was a vast lending agency authorized to underwrite the financing of new business enterprises and the expansion of old.

The few examples cited serve to indicate one of the major reasons for the resort to the corporate form. Many of them were essentially responses to emergency conditions. The great depression and the New Deal were largely responsible for the blossoming forth of the public enterprise technique. Although some of the corporations expired with the passing of the emergency, others lived on and seemingly have taken a place among the permanent institutions of the general welfare state. Indeed, the corporation movement went hand in hand with the progressive acceptance of a larger role by the federal government in the promotion of public welfare. Did the farm economy need a boost from government? A resoundingly positive answer decreed the establishment of a Farm Credit Administration, a Federal Farm Mortgage Corporation, a Federal Surplus Relief Corporation, and many others in the field of farm credit. Encouragement of home ownership was spurred by the Home Owners' Loan Corporation, the US Housing Authority, and the Federal National Mortgage Association. The most famous of all corporations, the Tennessee Valley Authority, was established to foster flood control, area redevelopment, and the production of public power.

The concept upon which the choice of the instrumentality of the public corporation was based is the concept of autonomy. It was felt that the problems for which the public enterprise was a suitable solution were of a nature that required a dedicated, business-like approach. Consequently, the autonomous quality of business enterprise would be imitated publicly. Theory argued that results would come from a declaration of independence which granted to the public corporation freedom from strict legislative control by Congress; freedom from administrative control by the President; freedom from financial controls by the Treasury and the Bureau of the Budget; and freedom from controls over personnel by the Civil Service Commission.

In practice, the public corporations have not been nearly so autonomous as expectations and theory might suggest. The corporation that has exercised the greatest autonomy has been the TVA. It has exercised all the freedoms from political control mentioned above. Yet, over the years, even TVA has been subjected to a degree of financial control, as have the other public corporations. The ideally autonomous funding mechanism is the revolving fund, established by government subscription and used as needed over a period of time by the corporation. Such a system bypasses the delay, red tape, and uncertainty associated with annual congressional appropriations. In reality, because TVA serves a dual purpose, it was for a quarter-century of its short life dependent upon annual appropriations for survival. One purpose of TVA is commercial by virtue of its generation and sale of power and its operation of fertilizer plants. Another purpose, however, is noncommercial; this is TVA's flood control, agricultural experimentation, and general area development tasks. Since TVA's commercial receipts could not cover its noncommercial expenditures, it had to rely upon annual appropriations until 1959. In that year Congress passed a Revenue Bond Act, according to which TVA could sell bonds on the public market. Until 1959 TVA was a pawn in the game of power politics. In Congress, public power advocates supported TVA appropriations each year; opponents of public power sought to pare down the role of the Authority in every way possible—the best way being cuts in TVA appropriations. The Revenue Bond Act itself was a compromise between those who wished to end TVA operations altogether and the regional and congressional advocates of an autonomous Authority.[33]

Because the functions of the public corporations could not be removed from the context of politics—any more than could those of the IRCs—their institutional history has been one of ever increasing restrictions on their independence. In 1935 the President ordered some corporations to submit budgets for "administrative" expenses to the Bureau of the Budget for approval. Shortly thereafter, Congress placed limitations on the amount corporations could spend for administrative expenses, thus continuing the trend toward expanded fiscal oversight. The logical conclusion to this trend appeared in 1945 when the Government Corporation Control Act was passed. Under the new act, all public corporations were required to reincorporate under federal law, and executive power to create new corporations was limited. Beyond this, all corporations were required to submit budgets to be included in the general fiscal budget and to have their accounts audited by the General Accounting Office.[34] With the passage of this act, the public corporations came to resemble other executive departments and agencies more than autonomously operating enterprises.

The brief experience with the public corporations discloses a measure of value different from that available from other administrative agencies. Particularly in times of emergency, the public enterprise is capable of greater dispatch and efficiency in its area of operations than other government institutions. Moreover, the early experience of the TVA shows that the public corporation can mobilize high-level personnel and contribute forcefully to social and economic betterment. On the other hand, the government corporation represents yet a further dispersal of leadership in the making of public policy. In the long run it is doubtful whether the exigencies of an efficient and responsible administrative complex can be reconciled with an autonomous and highly pluralistic set of separate public managers.

## SOME CONCLUSIONS ABOUT THE POLICY PROCESS

In a private organization the theory of policy making is a simple one. The goal of the organization is efficiency, whether it be the efficient production of automobiles, the effective guarantee of the rights of organized workers, or the effective education of students.

The most appropriate means toward efficient goal achievement are usually found in a centralized decision making process wherein authority is exercised by a few expert managers and directives flow down through a hierarchical system. Though for purposes of public relations the private organization may advertise itself as democratic, most often it is not in reality. The efficient achievement of its goals does not readily admit of constant interference in the policy making process by members of its constituency.

Government also attempts to achieve certain goals as efficiently as possible and resembles private organization in its necessary reliance on experts and an authoritative body of administrators. Yet government tends to be more circumscribed in its activities because it operates within an ideological context that demands democracy as well as efficiency. Subscription to a traditional theory of democracy has produced an extreme fractionalization of the policy making function. As we have seen, there are many centers of such power—the Presidency, executive administrators, congressional committees, regulatory commissions, private groups, and so on. In fact, *within* each of these policy centers, organization is hardly democratic; however, since there are many competing centers of power, the sum-total of institutions is neither wholly irresponsible nor elitist in character. An historic American fear of a single sovereign center of power perpetuates institutional pluralism.

The result has been a less efficient system of policy formulation and execution. Most observers would agree that what is needed is a greater measure of centralization and co-ordination of policy making. The difficulty, of course, has been in finding an appropriate institutional location for this policy center. Representative theory would seem to argue for congressional direction. Nonetheless we have seen that Congress is too large and too diverse a body to make effective policy as it is. One approach to a balance between the desire for efficiency and the imperatives of responsible democracy is possible in the twentieth-century administrative state. By granting the chief executive a greater measure of authority to manage, reorganize, and rationalize the jerry-built apparatus of administration, an increment of central leadership and responsibility could be achieved. Realism dictates, however, that a total solution to the problem is not possible in a political environment characterized by both pluralist democracy and functional bureaucracy. As long as we place great value on the one and cannot do without the other, we must settle for somewhat less than perfection in both. In any case, as long as Congress is alert to the function it is able to perform most effectively—administrative oversight—there need be no fear of executive dictatorship, no surrender of democratic values.

## REFERENCES

1. The President's Committee on Administrative Management, *Report of the Committee* (Washington, D.C.: Government Printing Office, 1937), p. 209.

2. Robert E. Cushman, *The Independent Regulatory Commissions* (New York: Oxford University Press, 1941), p. 19.

3. At present I count eleven major independent regulatory commissions (hereafter referred to as IRCs). Listed in order of their creation, these are: Interstate Commerce Commission (1887), Federal Reserve Board (1913), Federal Trade Commission (1914), Federal Power Commission (1930), Federal Communications Commissions (1934), Securities Exchange Commission (1934), National Labor Relations Board (1935), Civil Aeronautics Board (1940), Atomic Energy Commission (1946), Federal Aviation Agency (1958), and Federal Maritime Commission (1961).

4. James M. Landis, *The Administrative Process* (New Haven: Yale University Press, 1938), p. 10.

5. E. Pendleton Herring, *Public Administration and the Public Interest* (New York: McGraw-Hill Book Co., 1936), pp. 110-112.

6. *Schechter* v. *United States*, 295 US 495 (1935); *Panama Refining Company* v. *Ryan*, 293 US 388 (1935).

7. Cushman, *Independent Regulatory Commissions,* p. 431.

8. Quoted in Lloyd D. Musolf, *Federal Examiners and the Conflict of Law and Administration* (Baltimore: The Johns Hopkins Press, 1953), p. 35.

9. Robert E. Cushman, *The Problem of the Independent Regulatory Commissions* (A Study for the President's Committee on Administrative Management). (Washington, D.C.: Government Printing Office, 1937), pp. 16-17.

10. Cited in Walter Gellhorn and Clark Byse, *Administrative Law: Cases and Comments* (Brooklyn: The Foundation Press, Inc., 1954), pp. 27-29.

11. 60 Stat. 237 (1946), 5 USC, Nos. 1001-1011.

12. See Peter Woll, *Administrative Law: The Informal Process* (Berkeley and Los Angeles: University of California Press, 1963).

13. Gellhorn and Byse, *op. cit.,* p. 642; and FTC, *Annual Reports,* 1948, 1949, 1950.

14. Peter Woll, "Administrative Justice: Formal Prescription and Informal Adjudication," *Western Political Quarterly*, XIV (September, 1961), p. 662.

15. *The New York Times,* May 10, 1961, p. 9.

16. *The New York Times,* August 9, 1963, pp. 1, 26.

17. Herring, *op. cit.,* p. 223.

18. Quoted in Bernard Schwartz, *The Professor and the Commissions* (New York: Alfred A. Knopf, 1959), p. 220.

19. Seymour Scher, "Regulatory Agency Control Through Appointment: The Case of the Eisenhower Administration and the NLRB," *Journal of Politics,* XXIII (November, 1961), pp. 667-688.

20. Quoted in Seymour Scher, "Congressional Committee Members as Independent Agency Overseers: A Case Study," *American Political Science Review,* LIV (December, 1960), p. 919.

21. Quoted in *Congressional Quarterly Weekly Report,* XIX (June 16, 1961), p. 975. (Italics supplied.)

22. Schwartz, *op. cit.,* p. 213.

23. *The New York Times,* March 5, 1961, p. 1.

24. Quoted in Gellhorn and Byse, *op. cit.,* p. 40.

25. The Commission on Organization of the Executive Branch of Government, *Task Force Report in Regulatory Commissions* (Appendix N) (Washington, D.C.: Government Printing Office, 1949), p. 24.

26. *The New York Times,* September 29, 1962, p. 6.

27. Marver H. Bernstein, *Regulating Business by Independent Commission* (Princeton: Princeton University Press, 1955), Chapter 3; Samuel P. Huntington, "The Marasmus of the ICC: The Commission, the Railroads, and the Public Interest," *Yale Law Journal,* LXI (April, 1952), pp. 467-509.

28. "Report of the Special Committee on Administrative Law," *Reports of the American Bar Association,* LXI (1936), pp. 720-794.

29. Cushman, *The Problem of the Independent Regulatory Commissions,* pp. 23-25.

30. *The New York Times,* June 5, 1963, p. 1.

31. United States Senate, Committee on the Judiciary, *Report on Regulatory Agencies to the President-Elect,* Committee Print, 86th Cong., 2nd Sess. (Washington, D.C.: Government Printing Office, 1960), pp. 66-68; 83-87.

32. *The Budget of the United States Government for the Fiscal Year Ending June 30, 1963* (Washington, D.C.: Government Printing Office, 1962), p. 358.

33. Aaron Wildavsky, "TVA and Power Politics," *American Political Science Review,* LV (September, 1961), pp. 576-590.

34. Merle Fainsod, *et al., Government and the American Economy,* 3rd ed. (New York: W. W. Norton & Co., Inc., 1959), pp. 762-763.

# PART II

# Areas of Policy

# CHAPTER 5

# The Big Three:
# Business—Agriculture—Labor

## PUBLIC POLICY TOWARD BUSINESS

Political institutions and those who function within them perform a governing role that is shaped in part by the needs, expectations, and activities of men in the process of getting a living. Since the basic institution of man's economic life is the business enterprise, government as the sovereign power in society must concern itself with the affairs of business. It is no more than a surrender to mythology to assume that there ever was a time when private economic life and public political life proceeded independently of one another. In the context of the American experience from Alexander Hamilton's *Report on the Subject of Manufactures* to the most recent report of the Federal Trade Commission, government has stated policies affecting business.

*Promotionalism.* The initial relationship between government and business was one in which government acted as a patron of the interests of business. Following the winning of political independence, early statesmanship wisely addressed itself to the task of assuring American economic independence. By all calculations, the establishment of a tariff on imports was, and continued for a long time to be, the most significant governmental stimulant to American business. The original rationale behind the tariff—the protection of infant industries—was cited in support of ever higher tariff schedules long after it was justified by the circumstances of American economic life. Thus, with a few periodic exceptions, inordinately high tariffs nourished an artificially commodious atmosphere for business down to the 1930s. The reason for this anachronism is that tariff making became an exercise in political manipulation. Business interests which were well organized and financed easily managed to gain access to the legislators who enacted tariff schedules. In Congress the process of log-rolling—by which each congressman stood firm for protection of business facilities in his constituency and was hardly ungracious enough to deny the same stance in his colleagues—was resposible for an over-all high level of protection.[1] Only in the 1930s, with the introduction of the reciprocal trade principle, was the President granted authority to bring about a gradual reduction in tariffs by agreement with other nations.

Another vast source of governmental patronage toward business was the policy of public aid granted for the development of transportation. In the latter half of the nineteenth century both federal and state governments made land grants to the burgeoning railroad industry. One government report estimates that over 183 million acres of public lands were granted to the railroads between 1850 and 1933. This total is equivalent to over 286,000 square miles, or nearly 10 per cent of the area of the continental United States.[2] Additional hundreds of thousands of acres were made available for use to the railroads through grants of right-of-way. The federal government also made loans to the railroads to cover costs of construction on the line running to the Pacific Coast. Some argue that motor transport is publicly subsidized in the United States by virtue of federal highways. The motor carriers contend that the taxes they pay on fuel and fees of other sorts erase any similarity between public roads and subsidies, but it is difficult to interpret the current multibillion dollar federal highways program as devoid of any subsidy to commercial transportation. Of the subsidies to air transportation there can be no doubt. Aside from federal loans and grants for the construction of airports, the federal mail subsidy alone requires (by Act of Congress) that the airlines make a profit from their operations.

Government has for many years stimulated business expansion by acting as a lending agency. From 1932 to 1954 the Reconstruction Finance Corporation loaned billions of dollars for construction in periods of depression, war, and reconversion. It has been succeeded by the Small Business Administration, which was established to encourage growth in smaller enterprises. In 1961 one public response to the economic recession was an Area Redevelopment Administration, which makes loans to business in depressed areas.

An indirect form of government subsidy to business is found in a variety of tax allowances which grant special financial advantages to commercial firms. Among these, second-class mail privileges, depreciation allowances, and tax write-offs save business billions of dollars every year. An outstanding example of such favoritism is the 27.5 per cent depletion allowance granted to the oil industry. Under this system the oil industry may deduct a fixed 27.5 per cent from its gross income regardless of what actual depletion may amount to. As a stimulus to business in general in 1962, President Kennedy, by executive act, liberalized the prevailing schedule of depreciation allowances for machinery and equipment that businesses could claim. The Secretary of the Treasury predicted that this act would constitute a gain of about $1.5 billion for business through tax savings in the first year of its operation.[3]

The era of the cold war has brought still another indirect benefit to business by government policy. In a calculated attempt to create a stockpile of strategic materials available in time of emergency, the government has over the past years amassed stores of some twelve major items (largely metals, such as aluminum, cobalt, copper, and lead) worth $7.7 billion. In 1962 President Kennedy called for a congressional investigation of the stockpile, stating that he feared such a massive store was "a potential source of excessive and unconscionable profit."[4] A side effect of the stockpile is to maintain higher prices for such metals by keeping surpluses off the world market.

These are but a few of the mechanisms used by the federal government to promote successful business enterprise in the United States. The list could be extended at length to include such public policies as the awarding of government contracts to private firms for research and development of military and defense hardware; the maintenance of a patent office to protect inventions of commercial use; the heavy subsidization of the Merchant Marine; and the promotional activities of various agencies of the Department of Commerce. Each of these and other policies have contributed significantly to the welfare of business enterprises. The long history of government promotionalism has demonstrated one fact clearly: once the state begins to contribute a part of its largess to the private sector, it is very difficult to discontinue the practice.

*Approaches to Regulation.*   The explosion of technological innovation that occurred in the post-Civil War period was in large part responsible for a rapid increase in business activity. As we have seen, the first reaction to what was described at the time as "cut-throat" competition was a resort to various forms of combination. The first and simplest form of combination was the "pool" by which the production of several firms was lumped together and income divided according to fixed proportions not necessarily related to actual, individual plant production. The result was to fix prices and regulate total output. A more sophisticated, legal device was the trust, by which several companies joined the organization, transferred policy making power to a board of trustees, and received income in the form of trust certificate shares. The object of trust building was the same as that for which pools were formed. The result was the growth of giant monopolies, such as the Standard Oil trust, which, through centralized control of the major oil producing companies, controlled over 90 per cent of the oil refining output in the United States.

In response to adverse public reaction to the trusts, particularly in the West and the South, Congress in 1890 passed the Sherman Antitrust Act. The two major provisions of the act forbade (1) contracts, combinations, and conspiracies in restraint of trade and (2) monopolization or attempts at monopolization. In the first years of its existence the act was of little practical use since presidents expressed little enthusiasm in enforcing it. Also the courts interpreted its provisions so narrowly that in 1895 the Sugar Trust, which controlled 98 per cent of the domestic refineries, was found *not* to violate the Sherman Act.[5]

Theodore Roosevelt's accidental succession to the Presidency in 1901 marked a new era in antitrust prosecutions. Roosevelt's determination to enforce the Sherman Act vigorously was crowned with at least symbolic success when the Supreme Court upheld his prosecution of the Northern Securities Company—a railroad holding company—in 1904.[6] After Northern Securities, Roosevelt initiated several prosecutions, none of which were sustained during his term of office. When in 1911 the Supreme Court did ultimately uphold the cases against Standard Oil and the American Tobacco Company, it did so in a way that was to hobble future attempts to use the Sherman Act. In both cases a "rule of reason" was enunciated which held that only where a combination was considered by the Court to be "unreasonable" or "unreasonably restrictive" would the Sherman Act apply.[7]

The trust issue was a major one in the presidential campaign of 1912, and in its course two opposing philosophies of regulation emerged. Roosevelt, the candidate who preached a New Nationalism, called for a return to vigorous, central government based upon Hamiltonian principles. The Sherman Act was declared to be useless, and a resort to the prosecutions of "bad trusts" by an administrative commission was recommended. In expounding the doctrines of the "New Freedom," candidate Woodrow Wilson called for the dissolution of all forms of monopoly. Relying on Louis Brandeis's conception that size is the index of culpability, Wilson advocated the fractionalization of the community of business interests by careful, persistent applications of antitrust legal proceedings. Wilson won the election, but, ironically, his administration introduced not only statutory amplification through the Clayton Antitrust Act, but also the Federal Trade Commission, which was given responsibilities in the area of antitrust prosecutions. Henceforth, regulatory policy was conducted both by the Antitrust Division of the Justice Department and the FTC. Neither, it must be said, has been notably successful in its overlapping sphere of operations.

In the period between the end of the first Wilson administration and the New Deal, antitrust enforcement was sporadic and ineffective. A succession of Republican presidents, for the most part philosophically opposed to restrictions on business, made little use of antitrust legislation and severely limited the effectiveness of the FTC by appointing commissioners who viewed their function as one of guardianship of the interests of business.

The legacy of the New Deal in regulatory affairs has been to grant a new lease on the life of vigorous antitrust policy. Initially, the national economic emergency, with which the new administration had to contend, in effect placed a moratorium on antitrust activity. The Administration's National Industrial Recovery Act, which authorized the voluntary making of codes of fair competition, had, for a time, the consequence of encouraging cartelization of industries and suspending antitrust legislation. However, with the outlawing of the NIRA in 1935 and a subsequent shift in regulatory policy, antitrust action became the keystone of business regulation. The appointment of Thurman Arnold as Assistant Attorney-General in charge of the Antitrust Division and the reports of the Temporary National Economic Committee signaled a new era of antitrust prosecutions. In the years that followed, there was no shortage of litigation, and the development of policy depended in large measure on how broadly the Supreme Court interpreted existing antitrust law. In general, the Court considerably expanded the area of prosecution, finding in one case after another that a variety of monopolistic techniques—basing point systems, price-fixing agreements, patent monopolies, and so on—was prohibited by the Sherman and Clayton Acts. The "rule of reason" was finally abrogated by judicial determination, and the laws were found to deny oligopoly (the control of a whole industry by a *few* competitors) under certain circumstances as well.

In recent years the revival of antitrust activity has continued apace. In 1960 the Justice Department announced that more cases were initiated in that year than in any other since antitrust legislation had been on the statute books, and in 1961 one of the most celebrated cases was concluded. Seven vice-presidents of the General Electric Company and the Westinghoue Electric Company were given jail sentences. Fines amounting to nearly one million dollars were imposed against the price-fixing electrical companies in what was termed the largest criminal antitrust case in history.[8] Still, the exact future of policy in this complex area of political and economic relations remains to be plotted out in the courts. An eminent economist has stated the current judicial tendency:

What the courts appear to be reaching for, above and beyond the range of traditional Sherman Act violations, is a doctrine of permissible power. Some power there has to be, both because of inescapable limitations to the process of atomization and because power is needed to do the job the American public expects of its industrial machine. There is no reason, however, to tolerate positions of market power that can be lessened by appropriate antitrust action unless it can be shown that this lessening substantially interferes with the job to be done.[9]

*Challenges to Traditional Regulation.* In recent years critics of American antitrust policy have sought to bring about a clarification of the goals of regulatory policy. A conviction has grown among these critics that the principle of antitrust has been elevated to the level of a dogma and thereby suffers from the irrationality that is often characteristic of dogmatic thinking. Too often the target of antitrust policy has been pure size. The reasoning—which in our own history can be traced back to Jefferson—which concludes that big business is bad business should be subjected to a more critical evaluation. One may well identify business practices, such as price-fixing, patent monopolies, and other forms of unfair competition that result in damage to the interests of consumers, without concluding that all industry must be dissected into charming little packages of equal size, weight, and content. And yet there has been, from time to time, a prepossessing tendency among regulatory officials and the courts to view size itself as incompatible with the public interest.

Such attitudes have found favor in Congress, and a body of "fair trade" legislation supporting the claims of small business has resulted. The Robinson-Patman Act of 1936 amounted to a legislative denial of the advantages of large-scale business by outlawing discounts and special allowances for large order buying. A similar aspect of this policy is the statutory enactment of resale price maintenance (RPM). In brief, RPM means that distributors of certain goods are prohibited by contract from selling below a certain agreed-upon price. Thus, if a large chain store wishes to sell an item falling under fair trade legislation for 15 per cent less than the corner drugstore, it is prohibited by legislation from so doing. According to the McGuire Fair Trade Enabling Act of 1952, in states which have RPM laws, even those distributors who have not signed RPM contracts are required to abide by RPM price levels. In the same act, fair-trade contracts were exempted from the antitrust laws. Hence in a move to restrict competition in favor of the small producer, Congress assured that the consumer must pay a higher price on certain items. One wonders about this formulation of the "public interest."

In an intriguing analysis published in 1952, John Kenneth Galbraith carries the criticism of traditional patterns of thought about regulation a step further. The Harvard economist argues that, whereas the substance of public policy is grounded on the notion of competition as the automatic, impersonal regulator of the economy, in fact competition among producers is no longer the key dynamic in the process. Rather, the active check on the policies and activities of business enterprise in our times comes from the *countervailing* power exercised by strong buyers, organized laborers, and retail sellers. An example is in order. Galbraith relates how the mail-order house, Sears, Roebuck & Co., was able to exert enough market power to force down the price it paid for Goodyear tires. In buying tires for retail sale, Sears confronted an oligopoly of four leading tire manufacturers; yet, since Sears was such an indispensable customer, it could force the wholesale price down by threatening either to produce its own tires, or to deal with another manufacturer who would offer a better price. Thus Sears got its tires for from 29 to 40 per cent less than the going market price and retailed them to consumers at a price from one-fifth to one-quarter less than the buyer would have paid to Goodyear directly.[10] It was not competition among tire producers that achieved this benefit for the consumer (and Sears), but the market power of the retail organization. The example could be repeated for other products simply by substituting company names, such as the Great A & P Tea Company, Montgomery Ward, or Woolworth's and Kresge's.

If countervailing power is the vital private regulatory factor that Galbraith claims it is, it follows logically that the policy of breaking up large-scale businesses merely places restraints on socially beneficial countervailance. This is the case since it is only against the large, economically efficient enterprises—which have a margin that affords concessions to the other side of the market—that countervailing power operates most effectively. In fact, as Galbraith himself notes, in periods of inflation the large enterpriser can bow to the pressures of the retailers and labor organizations and still avoid profit losses by raising prices. And it must be admitted that, in past years, inflation was the rule rather than the exception. Still, a policy of economic wisdom does not encourage inefficient enterprise (for which the consumer ultimately pays) merely to deny success to big business. One may surely expect government to prohibit collusive and coercive business practices without assenting to economic atomization on the questionable ground that a maximum level of competition is always in the public interest. Antitrust prosecutions against such enterprises as A & P appear to do precisely that.

*The Emergent Corporate Leviathan.* The challenges posed by big business in the past, baffling as they may have been to the maker of public policy, appeared to be essentially of an economic order. At times the hand of government may have been unsteady, and occasionally the right hand has not known what the left hand was doing. Yet the development of the modern corporation in recent years has been marked by broader social and political trends whose implications produce nothing so much as a wariness of the unknown. The changes that have been taking place in American economic life may produce the most demanding test to date of the viability and imagination of our domestic politics.

What are the dimensions of corporate gigantism? In crude but revealing terms it may be said that about 130 of the largest manufacturing corporations in the United States account for half of the manufacturing output and that the 500 largest corporations conduct nearly two-thirds of all nonagricultural business. Carl Kaysen notes that in 1960 438 firms employed about 28 per cent of the corporate labor market; that the 202 largest corporations owned 40 percent of all nonfinancial corporate assets; and that in a six-year survey period (1950-1956) the 100 companies receiving the largest defense contracts accounted for two-thirds of the total value of all defense contracts.[11] Furthermore, because of the prevalence of monopoly, oligopoly, and other forms of concentration, the critical range of operating choices open to the corporate managers is a wide one. Yet this concentration of economic *power* (produced out of size plus relative lack of market restraints) is not new to American economic life. A half-century of sporadic antitrust and regulatory activity have managed to dilute economic power only at the margins, and competent observers maintain that there is little reason to believe the well-established trend toward concentration is likely to be reversed.[12]

The cause of concern about corporate power is grounded in the belief that it has spilled over economic boundary lines and has been transformed into social and political power. That is, the decisions made by the corporate elite, separately and collectively, cannot avoid affecting society in its extraoccupational context.

The role of the corporation as a social model—partly via the mass media of communications at the national level, but more revealingly at the state and community levels—cannot be gainsaid. The stereotyped image of the "organization man" may seem to have exaggerated consequences attributed to it until we pause to consider the key leadership roles assumed by these articulate, educated, style-setting types in our new middle class communities. The materially beneficial, but nonetheless socially aggrandizing, practices of the modern corporation—the country clubs, nurseries, insurance and adult education programs, and so on—mark a social system that has become so pervasive in some areas as to provoke discussion about *corporate citizenship*. Some political scientists have expressed the fear that the corporate life distracts private man from the public duties upon which a democratic society is based. Thus Andrew Hacker concludes a thoughtful study of the problem with this judgment: "The corporation has certainly not set out to weaken the foundations of democratic politics, but its growth as the characteristic institution of our time is having this consequence." [13]

That corporate decisions can affect political as well as social affairs can be seen on a moment's reflection. The basic decision, for example, to locate in or move out of a community can change the whole character of that community. Such questions as the building of new roads, sewers, and schools; of changing the tax base or rates; and of regulating labor relations at the state level are all influenced by corporate presence or absence, or the prospect of either, in the community. A few years ago when the state of Michigan was reconsidering its tax system, one of the large automobile manufacturers publicly declared its intention of "moving out" if a corporate profits tax were legislated.

The term "corporate citizenship" noted above is realistic in another sense: the modern corporation is an eminently *political* institution. In its sphere of activities it functions politically as a user of authority, and administrator of functions bureaucratically, and a dispensor of corporate justice through a system of rewards, punishments, and enforcement machinery. For its legitimacy, it rests on the symbolically democratic electorate of its stockholders.[14] A notable feature of the corporation, as a political body within the body politic, is that it is an irresponsible one. The characteristic separation of ownership from control in the modern corporation means simply that the owner-constituents (stockholders) have practically no control over the decisions made by the controlling managers. The latter function as a hired bureaucracy, and, though their decisions are ratified officially by their nominal employers, in fact only on the rarest occasions do the owners have any alternative but to give their stamp of approval to *faits accomplis*. The current trend appears to lead to the loss of even this symbolic function in cases where corporations are no longer owned by shareholders but by trustees of pension funds, mutual funds, or directors of insurance companies. Berle reports on how this diffusion of property has been carried to its logical extreme in at least one exceptional case. A pension fund now claims title to the largest share of Sears, Roebuck & Company stock. In terms of effective ownership Sears is dominated by a pension trust.[15]

To summarize briefly, the modern corporation is an institutional embodiment of great economic power. Such economic power automatically involves the use of social and political power—and in ways that are neither democratic nor accountable. Finally, the decisions made and the power exercised by the corporations are so momentous as to challenge the vitality of the institutions of representative government. A number of alternative arrangements have been suggested. At the extreme, socialization, or government ownership of productive facilities, presents a traditional answer. Aside from the fact that this is politically unacceptable in the American context, the experience of the British suggests that it does not erase the problems we have considered here. A second, and hardly more fruitful response, has been the atomization formula which declares that political conquest can be achieved through economic division by route of antitrust action. Again, some of the economic consequences of this method are unfortunate at best. It has been argued finally that self-restraint in the use of corporate power may provide the solution, and that this will emerge from the dictates of a "corporate conscience" or the felt-imperatives of a "public consensus" which sets the outer limits of corporate activity informally and extralegally.[16] Whatever direction the ultimate resolution of these forces takes, it is certain that they pose problems with which politics must ultimately come to grips.

## PUBLIC POLICY TOWARD AGRICULTURE

The combination of urban and technological revolutions of which we have become so conscious in the middle years of the twentieth century has brought governmental activity in the agricultural sector into sharper focus. Indeed, it is ironic that, as our farming population has steadily decreased, public perception of a "farm problem" and government's attempts to solve it have increased. On the other hand, the promotional activities of government in the agricultural domain have roots which extend far back into the nineteenth century. Seeds were distributed and governmental research in agronomy undertaken in the 1830s. In 1862 the Homestead Act was passed and an agriculture bureau established which would later achieve departmental status. The Morrill Act of 1862 fostered the establishment of land grant colleges for the teaching of agricultural and the mechanic arts, a course of action that was to have profound effects on the development of American agriculture. Funds were made available for agricultural experiment stations which came to be associated with the state agricultural colleges. At the turn of the century the advent of the county agent was instrumental in bringing the fruits of scientific research to the attention of farmers through demonstrations in the local farm community. By World War I government became involved in extending credit to farmers through the Federal Land Banks. Hence the massive federal involvement in agriculture that came on the heels of the Great Depression was not a total innovation in political economy.

*Sources of Public Involvement.* Of the many reasons for the need for a public policy concerning agriculture, the fundamental one is that, as society has grown more complex, a part of government's mandate to promote the general welfare consists in its duty to assure the availability of an adequate food supply. In an age of heavy surpluses of farm production this may appear unimportant, and yet the ability to guarantee a food supply could be crucial in an emergency. In making provision for the maintenance of agriculture, government must direct its attention to the peculiar problems with which the farmer must contend. The individual farmer is subjected to a greater range of intervening variables which affect his calling than is the businessman or the professional.

Factors which cannot be anticipated with precision, such as weather, climatic changes, and natural disasters, can destroy at one blow a flourishing agrarian enterprise. A concomitant of the uncertainties of production is the relatively fixed nature of consumption. That is, the demand for farm products is relatively inelastic. There is a limit to how much food can be consumed by any family or any society. If one should posit a sudden increase in prosperity and family income, perhaps a small measure of the new-found wealth would be spent on food, but this would be marginal; most of the windfall would command new luxury items or a greater variety of existing luxuries. In sum, society wants from the farmer a stable, *gradually* increasing supply of his products—an accommodation which he cannot guarantee with certainty. Farmer and nonfarmer alike need help from government in constructing the "ever-normal granary."

Science and technology have inhibited the achievement of this goal. By making it possible for farmers to produce more than they can sell, except in times of emergency, our knowledge has fashioned an economic vise within which the average farmer can exercise little maneuverability. The results of the application of scientific principles to farming, new farm machinery, and new and improved fertilizers can be seen dramatically in sharp rises in productivity. Table 5-1 indicates the yield per acre of six basic crops for two periods separated by a quarter of a century in American agriculture.[17]

TABLE 5-1     *Yield per Acre of Six Basic Crops*

|         | 1931-1935 Average | 1960 |
|---------|-------------------|------|
| Wheat   | 13.1 bushels      | 26.2 bushels |
| Rice    | 2135 pounds       | 3423 pounds |
| Corn    | 23.3 bushels      | 54.5 bushels |
| Cotton  | 191 pounds        | 446 pounds |
| Peanuts | 695.2 pounds      | 1266 pounds |
| Tobacco | 808 pounds        | 1702 pounds |

Hence we have reached a stage of agricultural supply where far fewer farmers can produce far more commodities on the same land than can be absorbed by the consumer market. When the market for a certain skill shrinks, the normal expectation is that the affected parties will pursue other occupations for which there is economic demand. Yet the desired outward mobility from the farms has not been nearly sufficient to compensate for reduced needs. The reasons for this are fairly clear. Because farm families are generally larger than others and are relatively more isolated in a rural environment, sons of farmers find the vocation of farming to be the only appropriate one. Educational opportunities and educational attainment on the farm are less than in an urban environment; thus farm youths are characteristically prepared by their schools for nothing other than farming. To make matters more critical, the great proportion of higher educational opportunities available to the sons of farmers is oriented toward vocational training in agriculture, typically through the agricultural colleges. Moreover, there appear to be certain psychic ties to the land felt by those who have grown up on it. Finally, if the young, unprosperous farmer can wrench himself from his environment and move to the city in the hope of finding work in an unskilled industrial capacity, he is more than likely to find himself excluded from even this opportunity because of substantial rates of unemployment in these areas. Thus the harsh fact of occupational imbalance which works so inequitably against our farmers cries for governmental action to right the balance.

*Forms of Public Involvement.* While the initial character of government involvement in agriculture took the form of promotionalism almost exclusively, as the plight of the farmer became more critical due to conditions of general depression throughout the world in the 1930s, bloated surpluses, and depressed farm income, steps were taken to foster a degree of regulation in the agricultural sector. The various types of public control inaugurated in the early years of the New Deal are important, not merely historically, but because many of the general formulas devised in the 1930s remain operative in the 1960s.

To meet the related problems of heavy surpluses and low prices, Congress passed the first Agricultural Adjustment Act in 1933, which provided for payments to farmers in return for a voluntary reduction in output. In 1936 the Supreme Court found the section of the act which levied a tax on processors unconstitutional.[18] In 1938 a more comprehensive program, the second AAA, provided for acreage allotments, marketing quotas and agreements, and nonrecourse loans to be made to farmers when prices fell below a specified level. Variations of each of these mechanisms have been applied at different periods and for different crops over the years to the present.

Acreage allotments and marketing quotas operate toward the same end, though by slightly different routes. In both cases, the Secretary of Agriculture calculates ahead of time the probable yields for certain crops and thus determines the appropriate acreage to be planted for the desired supply. The acreage allotments are then broken down to determine the individual farm's quota, and overplanting incurs a penalty in the form of a denial of price supports to the farmer. When marketing quotas are in force, penalties for overproduction are increased. Not only are price supports withheld, but also a fine is imposed on excess production. This formula operates when two-thirds of the concerned farmers vote in advance through referendum to accept the Agriculture Department's marketing quotas. A somewhat similar attempt by government to encourage limited production was the mechanism of the "soil bank" instituted in 1958. Under this system farmers growing certain surplus crops were paid to withdraw acreage from cultivation and plant trees or other vegetation instead. Payments by a system of contracts were designed to equal the income the farmers would have drawn if crops had been grown on the acreage.

The price support or subsidy system is a program designed to supplement the various crop reduction mechanisms by the construction of a suitably high scaffolding to support farm prices and income. Under this program the government makes loans to the farmer in compensation for the produce he withholds from the market. The collateral for these loans which the Commodity Credit Corporation accepts is the produce the farmer does not market. If the farmer does not take back his produce from government storage, it is accepted as payment for the loan. The exact loan price which the government pays is determined by a calculation of parity. That is, a base-period (of high farm prosperity) is adopted as the standard for farm prices. At exact parity (100 per cent), farm production would grant to the farmer purchasing power exactly equivalent to that in the base period. For example, if the monetary equivalent of a bushel of wheat could have been exchanged for a pair of shoes in the marketplace in the base period, adherence to full parity would preserve the same relationship today. Government policy establishes from time to time the degree, or per cent, of parity-pricing it will underwrite. If the farmer cannot command the artificially determined "fair price" in the marketplace, he can thus "sell" his produce to the government at the guaranteed price. A recurring domestic, group political controversy over the last thirty years has been the fight over the per cent of parity to be fixed in farm legislation. On the whole, Democrats have favored high parity and the Republicans, lower or flexible parity guarantees. However, the divisions are not merely partisan, for different regions and different types of crop producers can find different advantages and disadvantages in the parity system.

Government has also responded to the plight of the farmer with policies directed toward the improvement of his credit sources. The New Deal Farm Credit Administration provided greater borrowing facilities, and the Emergency Farm Mortgage Act of 1933 allowed for the refinancing of farm debt. An attempt was made to encourage wider farm ownership, particularly among the poorer tenant farmers. The Farm Tenant Act of 1937 made possible the long-term purchase of farm land by the most disadvantaged class in the agricultural world. Finally, such publicly supported projects as rural electrification sought to raise the standard of life on the farm to a level closer to that of the urban citizen.

*The Results of Public Involvement.* While it is true that public policy related to agriculture has not been a total failure, seldom have the labors of political decision makers been so ungenerously rewarded. For although it is true that sound sources of farm credit have been created, farm foreclosures diminished, the retention of the family farm made possible, and successful conservation of resources brought about, it is equally apparent that farm income continues to decline, government spending increases steadily, and price support policies produce waste, contradictions and inequities. To speak of declining farm income requires careful interpretation. It is true that net return to farmers has been declining since boom years. Yet gross statistics mask the fact that over-all decline is really an average, and that large, efficient farms do very well economically while small, "nonindustrialized" farms (making up the vast majority of all farms) are, to be sure, caught in a cost-price squeeze which diminishes their net incomes steadily. Furthermore, farm price support policy accelerates this tendency. Those who profit most heavily from the subsidy payments are the gigantic, industrialized enterprises while the small, under-ten-acre farms find barely marginal support from the price subsidy system. At the same time, overproduction is encouraged among those who are most capable of accomplishing it. In the end, the urban taxpayer picks up an annual check amounting in recent years to $6 and $7 billions to support a program which encourages surpluses and helps the vast majority of farmers very little.[19]

*Alternatives.* The fundamental problem of American agriculture may be stated simply: In an era of monumental technological advancement, America has far too many citizens engaged in farming. If two-thirds of the small, marginal farms went out of business tomorrow, in a productive, economic sense, they would not be missed. Yet it would be inadmissible to condemn millions of our citizens to a *laissez-faire* struggle for the survival of the fittest with little chance of survival. On the other hand, it is also clear that the current farm policy is neither rational nor notably humane. Hence the only feasible alternative is one such as that suggested by the Committee for Economic Development.[20] A *comprehensive,* well-integrated program directed toward the removal of human resources out of agriculture and providing for the absorption of these resources by the labor market is the single rational goal to which policy makers must dedicate their energies. Such a program implies transitional public aid to those leaving the farms and a thoroughgoing manpower retraining and vocational rehabilitation enterprise. There can be no doubt that the transition would be a costly one, but it would also be one which gives promise of greater long-run savings by solving the existing occupational imbalance and removing the pretext for heavy governmental subsidization of agriculture.

## PUBLIC POLICY TOWARD LABOR

On the field of competition among major economic groups, seeking either the favors of government or relief from public regulation, labor was a latecomer. A major historical reason for the lateness of direct governmental involvement in the affairs of work-ingmen is the long and tenaciously held assumption that workers constituted one side of a private and inviolable relationship—that of employer to employee. Though this attitude was granted the nearly unquestioned sanctity of an immutable law of nature by many public spokesmen, writers, and scholars, there are no sources that proclaim the orthodoxy better than the words found in major Supreme Court decisions. It was the High Court that formally and finally bestowed the public seal of approval on *laissez faire* in the workplace.

In 1905 the Supreme Court decided a controversy between a citizen and the state of New York. The citizen, one Lochner, had violated a New York labor law which limited the hours of work in any "biscuit, bread or cake bakery or confectionery establishment." The limit of ten hours a day or sixty hours a week was legislated by the state on the premise that longer hours were detrimental to the health and welfare of employees. Finding the act unconstitutional, the Court declared:

> . . . The statute necessarily interferes with the right of contract between the employer and employees, concerning the number of hours in which the latter may labor in the bakery of the employer. . . . It seems to us that the real object and purpose were simply to regulate the hours of labor between the master and his employees (all being men, sui juris), in a private business, not dangerous in any degree to morals, or in any real and substantial degree to the health of the employees. Under such circumstances the freedom of master and employee to contract with each other in relation to their employment, and in defining the same, cannot be prohibited or interfered with, without violating the federal Constitution. . . .[21]

Furthermore, if the sanctity of contract had not prevented public regulation of the affairs of employees and employers, the limits on the commerce power imposed by federalism could be called upon to plug the unconscionable gap. In 1916 Congress prohibited, by the Child Labor Act, the interstate shipment of goods produced by child labor. As late as 1918 the Court found the legislature had acted unconstitutionally when it sought to prohibit indirectly the employment of children under age fourteen. In fact, it would appear that such a humane act was seen as the opening gambit in an eventual legislative *coup d'état:*

The far reaching result of upholding the act cannot be more plainly indicated than by pointing out that if Congress can thus regulate matters entrusted to local authority . . . all freedom of commerce will be at an end, and the power of the States over local matters may be eliminated, and thus our system of government be practically destroyed.[22]

Expressions of judicial disfavor were not destined to prevent the ultimate sanctioning of governmental intervention in the affairs of labor. The gradual development of group consciousness among laborers and the subsequent organizations of trades unions created pressures that made it impossible for government to avoid the issue. Demands for the eight-hour day, equal pay for women, the abolition of child labor, and other reforms constituted the platform of the Knights of Labor in the 1870s. In succeeding years further demands for higher wages and improved working conditions, together with jurisdictional fights among the Knights and other craft unions, brought about the formation of the American Federation of Labor in 1886. Thus was initiated a large-scale union organization pledged ultimately to achieve collective bargaining with employers, if necessary through the use of the strike. The closing years of the nineteenth century brought with them widespread violence and bloodshed on the labor front. At the same time union membership continued to grow and, with it, the political influence of organized labor. At McKinley's first inauguration the AFL had only about a quarter million members, but by 1904 the federation could boast of nearly one and three-quarter million adherents.

Employer reaction to organized labor's demands assumed two general forms. To protect their interests, companies employed private armed police forces and Pinkerton detectives to undermine union activity; they used such devices as "yellow-dog" contracts by which workers promised, as a condition of employment, not to join unions. Beyond these and other direct acts, employers sought the aid of the judiciary in blocking union bargaining activities. The judges proved faithful allies to the employers, freely granting injunctions to prevent strikes well iinto the 1920s and early 1930s. In the decades beginning 1890, 1900, 1910, and 1920, the number of injunctions granted were 122, 328, 446, and 921 respectively.[23]

*Promotionalism and Regulation.* Increased union membership and the election of representatives more sympathetic to labor's cause inaugurated a trend toward promotion of the interests of labor through public policy in the years before World War I. The Clayton Antitrust Act of 1914 exempted unions from antitrust prosecutions and attempted to limit the use of injunctions in labor controversies by federal courts. In fact, however, the Clayton Act was subsequently interpreted in a light which gave little comfort to the unions. By 1928 the platform of both major parties contained provisions which, if somewhat equivocal, opposed the injunction. In 1932 the passage of the Norris-LaGuardia Act signaled the most significantly sympathetic thrust of prolabor sentiment up to that time. Yellow-dog conracts were made unenforceable in federal courts; the use of injunctions was strictly limited; and the right to organize and participate in union activities was firmly guaranteed.

Public labor policy received full patronage as a result of the Great Depression. The National Industrial Recovery Act was the key feature of the New Deal's attempt to meet the crisis of economic dislocation, and Section 7a of that act enunciated a momentous principle of labor policy: Henceforth, the right of workers to organize and bargain collectively, free of restraint and through representatives of their own choosing, was recognized. Furthermore, even before the NIRA had been declared unconstitutional, Congress was considering a specific National Labor Relations Act. This measure, the Wagner Act, when passed in 1935 went well beyond Section 7a of the NIRA. Unfair labor practices on the part of employers were defined and prohibited. Interference or coercion of employees, interference with union administration, company pressures designed to discourage union membership, discrimination against employees giving testimony under the act, and refusal to bargain collectively with union representatives were all proscribed by the act.[24] Finally, it was the Wagner Act which established the NLRB as the regulatory agency charged with the enforcement of its provisions.

Because the Wagner Act so clearly granted special favors to labor unions and because it was felt union prerogatives had been too often abused, dissatisfaction with the act grew over the years and came to a head in the first postwar Congress. By 1946 the closed shop (in which only union members can obtain employment), featherbedding (payment for work not done), and coercion of union members by union officials were cited in support of demands that the time had come to restrain union power. In 1947 the Taft-Hartley Act was passed and sustained by well over the two-thirds majority in both houses of Congress needed to countermand President Truman's veto. Now the closed shop was prohibited, though the union shop (in which new workers must join the union) was permitted under certain circumstances. Restrictions were imposed on union administration, especially on the dues-collecting system. And finally, unfair union practices were defined and proscribed. Coercion of union members, issuing ultimatums in bargaining sessions, jurisdictional strikes, secondary boycotts, and featherbedding are examples of practices now declared illegal.

What has happened over the last quarter-century is that labor organizations, after a slow and gradual development followed by vigorous governmental promotionalism, have achieved full status in American life as a functioning and competitive economic power. In the process this power has from time to time been abused and public policies have emerged to curtail such abuses. As a result of Senate investigations in 1957-1958, a new measure of regulation was imposed. The Management Reporting and Disclosure (Landrum-Griffin) Act of 1959 enforces greater financial accountability on the unions and sets criminal penalties for false statements, conflict of interest payments, and embezzlement of union welfare and pension funds. In the 1960s, Big Labor faces still further challenges to its integrity as a major economic force, and some of the most critical problems arise from circumstances not of labor's own making.

*The Future of Labor Policy.* Government labor policy in recent decades has addressed itself largely to the encouragement and maintenance of free collective bargaining among workers and employers. The private bargaining principle was induced by a vigorous and expanding *organized* labor movement. The economic and social gains of working men may be traced to the vitality and effectiveness of organizational power. It is thus of no little concern to both labor and government to note that the very context of labor policy is changing in the 1960s. For a number of years now labor organizational membership has remained rather static and even shown some indications of decline. The great surge of organization developed during the war years. In 1940 union membership was under 9 million; by 1950 it had grown to 15 million. Thereafter, however, it has hovered between 17.7 million (1955) and 18.1 million (1960). Moreover, the per cent of the total labor force that is unionized has actually been dropping each year since 1955.[25] Decreasing membership is only one measure of change in organized labor; there have been important indications of a weakening in the union loyalties of working men who are already organized. For example, the number of organizational elections that unions have lost has been on the increase since the end of the war. Recently, labor leadership was so shocked at a series of negative votes among workers against the union shop in the aircraft industry that a polling organization was employed to study the sources of labor dissatisfaction. The results, discussed openly by several UAW leaders, show that many workers "felt that they were being encompassed by bigness within the unions as they have been by bigness in the corporations." [26]

A feeling of disenchantment with big labor bureaucracy accounts for part of the decline of strong unionism, but other regional, economic, and social facts of life have come to plague the labor organizer in recent years. The psychology of organization itself has been steadily weakened by the growing assumption that the major battles have been won. The initial reforms for which the unions provided an organizational weapon have long since been granted and legitimated. One of the results of this attitude among workers has been that in newly industrializing areas, notably in the South, the unions have been especially unsuccessful as missionaries. Furthermore, a technologically based change in the structure of the labor force, over which the unions have had no control, augurs poorly for organizational growth. This is the increasing appearance of the white collar in the labor force. During the decade, 1950-1960, the white collar sector of the labor force grew by 35 per cent, and its members contributed 73 per cent of the total union *potential*. On the other hand, while nearly one out of three members of the national work force are of white collar status, they contribute only 15 per cent to the total of organized labor.[27] For a variety of reasons, white collar workers have traditionally avoided the union commitment. Particularly in the professional and semiprofessional categories feelings of identification with profession or trade have blocked competitive claims for identification made by labor organizations. In an age when even the blue collar worker's identification with his union has been strained, it seems unlikely that the white collar sector will merge with the union sector.

A source of general disenchantment with labor organization has been the recurring disclosures of corruption and lack of democracy within the unions. Antiunion feeling has produced in fully twenty states of the nation constitutional or statutory provisions which bar union membership as a condition for holding a job. These politically controversial "right to work" laws have now won judicial acceptance since the Supreme Court has found that such matters are legally within the jurisdiction of the states.[28] The decision, coming at the end of 1963, aroused speculation that the "right to work" cause would now be taken up with renewed vigor in additional states.

In more than one way 1963 appeared to be a turning point in the relations between government and labor. A series of long strikes in transportation, in the newspaper industry, and shorter strikes or threats of strikes in industries servicing national security production prompted more serious discussion of compulsory arbitration, a step that would seriously undermine the principle of collective bargaining. The precedent-setting act of Congress of August 1963 which imposed compulsory arbitration and banned a strike in the railroad industry for 180 days was unfortunate— though perhaps unavoidable—for at least two reasons. First, statistics demonstrate clearly that the number of work stoppages and percentage of man-days lost due to strikes have declined sharply since the end of World War II.[29] Low statistics, however, have been obscured by a few strikes which have affected many people and been subjects of wide publicity. Second, it is acknowledged by nearly all experts in this area of policy that compulsory arbitration merely *postpones* the problem; the *solution* lies deeply imbedded in the substance of economic and technological change.

The new and dramatic word "automation" has come to represent a major domestic source of challenge and concern to government and the varied sectors of the American economy. The interest of perspective is served if we remember that, in reality, automation represents no more than the acceleration of technological trends that were set in motion long ago. Yet acceleration itself—the quickened pace at which men are being replaced by machines—seems to require that government play a still larger role in economic life. At the present stage, even the full dimensions and consequences of automation are not precisely understood. Congressional committees, the Bureau of Labor Statistics, and private economic research groups project widely varying estimates of the toll of workers taken by mechanization. The range of estimated job losses per year caused by technological advances runs from 200,000 projected by the Labor Department to over 2 million forecast by John I. Snyder, Jr., Chairman and President of US Industries, Inc.[30] And while automation is often assumed to be a burden born most heavily by the unskilled factory worker, it becomes increasingly apparent that the skills of thousands of white collar workers are being made obsolete annually by IBM machines.[31]

What role remains to be played by collective bargaining under these circumstances? One indication is given by the demands of some labor leaders for a shorter work week as a means of spreading employment around. Yet government is inclined to oppose this course on the grounds that only through increased productivity and steady economic growth is there a hope of continuing prosperity. On the other hand, government has made some limited approaches to a rational policy of avoiding the consequences of automation through worker restraining programs. For the most part, it is the unskilled and semiskilled routine tasks (clerking, filing, and other "paperwork") that machines have taken over. Workers in these categories must be re-educated and retrained for more complex productive and service occupations, and the Manpower Development and Training Act of 1962 constitutes a beginning. Even so, the benefits of this limited beginning have been only marginal. Studies have shown that the retraining that has been done has benefited those in the already higher educated and prime working-age groups far more than the hard core of low-educated and young and old workers. This merely illustrates what might have been expected: The big job of retraining must be undertaken among the millions of young and poorly educated entering the labor force and the over-forty-five group of unskilled and uneducated workers.

Should the fear of automation encourage the labor organizations, in Luddite fashion, to fight the machine with featherbedding practices and strikes (as seems to have been the case in the railroad industry), government may be expected to narrow the scope of collective bargaining rights again as it has in the recent compulsory arbitration act. Furthermore, as government becomes more committed to fighting inflation and maintaining production in those ever-increasing areas of government-sponsored industry, a further narrowing of the private sector covered by collective bargaining may be anticipated. The conclusion of an authority in the area of labor problems sums up our view:

> The days are also past when the government's role in labor-management relations was merely as a referee. Today, whether union leaders and management spokesmen like it or not, government is entering directly and increasingly into these relations. Both the courts and the legislature have begun to involve themselves in areas that were once considered inviolate.[32]

CONCLUSIONS

The foregoing pages of this chapter were written for the purpose of pointing out in a cursory way some of the complexities of government involvement in the economic life of the nation. Doubtlessly many lessons could be drawn from the raw data of policy questions raised and policy acts committed by government in its relations with business, agriculture, and labor. By way of conclusion, two general ideas will be suggested here: First, the extent and manner of government's involvement in the economy grows and becomes more complex as time passes. Second, this quantitative and qualitative growth of the policy function is conditioned by the imperatives of broad social change.

In the three areas of economic life considered, the policy making function seems to proceed through a life cycle of three reasonably identifiable stages. Government approaches the economy first as an interested patron. Thus the state promotes business, stimulates agricultural progress, and encourages labor organization. Soon the nutriment of public patronage, added to the vitality of private ingenuity, produces flourishing empires of organized economic power.

Next, government attempts to fulfill the role of an impartial referee of conflicts among its economic clients, regulating their activities to a certain extent. Antitrust laws are passed, acreage allotments and marketing quotas enacted, and unfair labor practices prohibited. The Federal Trade Commission, the Commodity Credit Corporation, and the National Labor Relations Board become the institutional symbols of this phase.

Finally, the general policy of regulation assumes such expansive proportions that government can no longer be considered a mere referee, but has, in fact, become a full-fledged participant. It is this stage that characterizes the political economy of the nation in our times. Government's multitudinous roles as major investor in the economy, as indirect allocator of resources, as financial stabilizer, as guardian of employment and promoter of prosperity—all these and more—mean that the makers of public policy participate intimately in all major economic policy decisions.

And inevitably, this means a greater role for the bureaucracy in policy making. Recalling references in earlier chapters to the various means by which bureaucracy influences policy, we may now pause to consider the administrative role evident in some of the areas under discussion in this chapter. But first, a word of caution is in order: The process of policy making is so obviously complex, the convergence of actors in producing policy outcomes so variable, that exact calculations of the measure of influence exerted by any one office or individual in major policy decisions are usually impossible. Even so, we know that administrators give shape to the policy process in two ways. As advisors, they influence policy determinations, and, as implementors, they become decision makers in routine but, nevertheless, extremely important matters.

Thus Thurman Arnold, as head of the Antitrust Division of the Justice Department in the New Deal Era, was instrumental both in the decision to make a long-term principle of antitrust action and in the implementation of that principle by vigorous prosecutions. Later, the philosophy of the Employment Act of 1946, which committed government to greater economic planning, resulted from a long incubation period in the minds of economic bureaucrats in two administrations.[33] In agriculture, the description "Benson Administration" could accurately characterize farm policy in the Eisenhower years. The Secretary of Agriculture, along with a corps of like-minded administrators (popularly referred to as the "Cornell crowd"), conducted an ambitious campaign against high price supports. Finally, presidential appointments during the early years of the Eisenhower Administration refashioned the NLRB into an instrument far less accommodating to the interests of organized labor. NLRB decisions during this period may well have had greater effect in reorienting government labor policy than did the existence of the Taft-Hartley Act itself.

A second major conclusion suggests that the nature of change we have experienced in political-economic relations has been shaped by factors of organizational change in our society. Among these changes are the gross quantitative aspects considered in Chapter 2; the triumph of technology; the progressive dispersion of property and even greater dilution of the claims made in the name of property; the emergence of a new middle class; and the development of a categorical imperative which ordains that government shall be responsible for channeling these forces along paths that will insure viability to society. In the process, momentum itself helps to insure that the greater role government plays, the still greater role it is expected to play.

The same phenomena exist in connection with political responsibility for the general welfare of all the people, a subject to which we address ourselves in the chapter which follows.

### REFERENCES

1. See E. E. Schattschneider, *Politics, Pressures and the Tariff* (New York: Prentice-Hall, Inc., 1935).

2. Federal Co-ordinator of Transportation, *Public Aids to Transportation,* 4 vols. (Washington, D.C.: Government Printing Office, 1940), vol. I, p. 13.

3. *Congressional Quarterly Weekly Report,* XX (July 13, 1962), p. 1167.

4. *Congressional Quarterly Weekly Report,* XX (April 6, 1962), p. 551.

5. *United States* v. *E. C. Knight Co.,* 156 US 1 (1895).

6. *Northern Securities Company* v. *United States,* 193 US 197 (1904). The holding company device is a variation of the trust concept whereby one corporation controls several others through the ownership of a controlling share of their common stock.

7. *United States* v. *Standard Oil Company of New Jersey,* 221 US 1 (1911); *United States* v. *American Tobacco Company,* 221 US 106 (1911).

8. *The New York Times,* February 6, 1961, p. 1.

9. Edward S. Mason, *Economic Concentration and the Monopoly Problem* (Cambridge: Harvard University Press, 1957), p. 387.

10. John Kenneth Galbraith, *American Capitalism: The Concept of Countervailing Power* (Boston: Houghton Mifflin Co., 1952), Chapter 9.

11. Edward S. Mason (ed.), *The Corporation in Modern Society* (Cambridge: Harvard University Press, 1960), p. 86.

12. See, for example, Adolf A. Berle, Jr., *The American Economic Republic* (New York: Harcourt, Brace & World, Inc., 1963), p. 154.

13. Andrew Hacker, *Politics and the Corporation* (Fund for the Republic: An Occasional Paper, 1958), p. 13. See also Hacker, "Liberal Democracy and Social Control," *American Political Science Review* LI (December, 1957), pp. 1009-1026.

14. See the essay by Earl Latham, "The Body Politic," in Mason (ed.), *The Corporation in Modern Society,* pp. 220-236.

15. Adolf A. Berle, Jr., *Power Without Property* (New York: Harvest Books, 1959), p. 54.

16. See Adolf A. Berle, Jr., *The Twentieth Century Capitalist Revolution* (New York: Harvest Books, 1954), Chapter 3; and Berle, *Power Without Property,* Chapter 3.

17. US Bureau of the Census, *Statistical Abstract of the United States: 1962* (83rd ed.), Washington, D.C., 1962, pp. 651-652.

18. *United States* v. *Butler,* 397 US 1 (1936).

19. See Edward Higbee, *Farms and Farmers in an Urban Age* (New York: Twentieth Century Fund, 1963), and an excellent report in the *Congressional Quarterly Weekly Report,* XX (June 11, 1962), pp. 1017-1023.

20. Committee for Economic Development, *An Adaptive Program for Agriculture* (New York, 1962).

21. *Lochner* v. *New York,* 198 US 45 (1905).

22. *Hammer* v. *Dagenhart,* 247 US 251 (1918).

23. Edwin E. Witte, *The Government in Labor Disputes* (New York: McGraw-Hill Book Co., 1932), p. 84.

24. Harry A. Millis and Emily Clark Brown, *From the Wagner Act to Taft-Hartley* (Chicago: University of Chicago Press, 1950), p. 31.

25. US Bureau of the Census, *Statistical Abstract of the United States: 1962* (83rd ed.), Washington, D.C., 1962, p. 241.

26. *Labor Looks at Labor: Some Members of the United Auto Workers Undertake a Self-Examination* (Santa Barbara, Calif.: Center for the Study of Democratic Institutions, 1963), pp. 1-32.

27. Benjamin Solomon and Robert K. Burns, "Unionization of White-Collar Employees: Extent, Potential, and Implications," *The Journal of Business,* XXXVI (April, 1963), pp. 143, 147.

28. *Retail Clerks, Local 1625* v. *Schermerhorn,* 375 US 96 (1963).

29. Committee for Economic Development, *The Public Interest in National Labor Policy* (New York, 1961), Table IV, p. 57.

30. *The New York Times,* October 4, 1961, p. 1.

31. See, for example, Thomas O'Toole, "White Collar Automation," *The Reporter,* XXIX (December 5, 1963), pp. 24-27.

32. Paul Jacobs, *Old Before Its Time: Collective Bargaining at Twenty-Eight* (Santa Barbara, Calif.: Center for the Study of Democratic Institutions, 1963), p. 42.

33. See Stephen K. Bailey, *Congress Makes a Law: The Story of the Employment Act of 1946* (New York: Vintage Books, 1964), Chapter 2.

# CHAPTER 6

# The Welfare State

## THE EVOLUTION OF A CONCEPT

The term "welfare" in its simplest dictionary definition means no more than well-being and encompasses such conditions as happiness, health, and prosperity. Somewhat greater precision results when we apply descriptive adjectives to the term and speak of "public welfare" or "general welfare" (the well-being of all or most of society), "social welfare," or "economic welfare." Whether or not, or the degree to which government *should* promote the general welfare of the people is a subject of contention at least as old as the earliest recorded political theories. Another way of stating the (false) alternatives of the argument is to ask whether government exists to promote the Good Society or should confine itself merely to the maintenance of order. Obviously, all governments attempt to do both things.

The fundamental American statement of political principles appears to leave no doubt in its response to this question. The Preamble of the Constitution declares that one of the purposes for which the charter was formed was to promote the general welfare. And Article I, Section 8, which lists among Congress's powers taxing and spending, cites as the reason for the provision, promotion of the common defense and general welfare. Yet grammatical shifts can both symbolize and provoke political controversy. By using the term "welfare" as an adjective to modify the term "state," a once attractive concept is surrounded by fears and forebodings. A whole new connotation emerges which suggests to some that the state has arrogated to itself *exclusive* responsibility for the welfare of the people. In fact, of course, the popular term "welfare state" should be taken as no more than a shorthand form, indicating the greater role modern government has been asked to play in promoting the general welfare. In its popular, emotional sense, "welfare state" has an equally inaptly baptized companion in the "garrison state." The latter phrase summons up images of a barbed-wire compound filled with a citizen body in military uniform. Manifestly, the modern state can no more be *characterized* as a military state than it can an economic benefactor, although elements of both exist.

That there has been a progressively greater acceptance of governmental activity by means of specific programs in the area of public welfare cannot be gainsaid. In its broadest sense the public welfare sector encompasses many of the activities discussed in Chapter 5 which severally sought to promote the well-being of businessmen, farmers, and laborers. In the more limited context which we are considering at this point, public welfare activity includes, typically, government assistance to individuals through insurance programs, loans, direct grants, and indirect redistribution of wealth through the tax structure. Individually and in combination these techniques have been applied particularly in the areas of employment, retirement, health, education, housing, and public works. In 1960 over $50 billion was spent by government (federal, state, and local) for welfare services. This amounted to over one-third of all government expenditures and somewhat more than 10 per cent of the total value of all goods and services produced (GNP).[1]

If we pause to ask why government has been called upon to formulate ever more expansive and inclusive welfare policies, our answer must, in large part, repeat the determining social and economic factors discussed with reference to the growth of Big Government in general. Industrialization, urbanization, concentration of economic activity, specialization, and the division of labor have all worked together to produce a society in which individual self-sufficiency and the efficacy of individual effort have become increasingly limited. The typical citizen, working in a specialized capacity for a large enterprise and raising a family in a highly concentrated urban environment, is overwhelmingly dependent upon the services of his government at all levels. Public sanitation and health services support his physical well-being; public schools and recreation centers educate and occupy his children; perhaps his income is such that he can only afford to live in public housing; he must depend upon public transportation to take him back and forth to work. If there is general unemployment and he is unable to find work, he must survive on unemployment compensation. Industrialization has probably left him unfit for all but a very few occupations, and it is logistically impossible simply to pack up and move to the country in hopes of living off the land. When he retires—voluntarily or involuntarily—it is unlikely that he can live out his lengthened life expectancy without income from social insurance. In short, Horatio Alger can no longer be a meaningful hero to the vast majority of Americans.

Modern industrialism and all the consequences which flow from it have set the stage for the welfare state, but it was the prompting of economic crisis that brought increased public welfare activity out of the wings. Panics, recessions, depressions, and other "hard times" that fell upon the nation in the generations before 1930 were usually accepted as unfortunate, but necessarily inevitable, downturns in the business cycle. Like a storm, the hard years had to be ridden out; government was expected to do little, and the citizen was resigned to the prospect of muddling through alone, perhaps with a little help from private charity. But 1932 was different; the massiveness of economic dislocation demanded public action. National income had more than halved. Twelve million workers (nearly one out of four) were unemployed. From the bread lines to the soup kitchens, from the city reliefers to the dust bowl farmers, anguished cries for help resounded. The universal negative answer given to the popular lyrical question of the Thirties—"Brother, Can You Spare a Dime?"—bespoke the realization that private charity could no longer do the job.

A broad change in philosophical outlook supplemented the necessary public adjustment to hard economic facts of life. In the context of the 1930s the intellectual market for *laissez-faire* and Social Darwinist responses had shrunk to meager proportions, and few upheld the God-given right to starve. The lessons of the Great Depression, however, taught more than the mere need for government activity in times of crisis; they reinforced the attitude that modern government has a *general* responsibility for the welfare of citizens in a highly complex society. Furthermore—and this is terribly important—minimum standards of public welfare have been raised, which have resulted in expectations of public aid to guarantee an existence on par with these higher standards. Getting a living now means not just a subsistence living, but a healthy living, an educated living—in short, a living which translates former luxuries into present necessities. A fabulous industrial machine has developed which is capable of producing both great prosperity and, when the machine breaks down, great suffering. Government responsibility for the continuation of the former and the prevention, or at least the treatment, of the latter has come to have supreme political validity. Another way to view what has come to pass is to recognize that in the twentieth century the democratic-egalitarian strain in our national fabric has taken precedence over the puritan-individualistic strain.

In the pages that follow we shall spell out some of the more important policies of government which give substance and content to the idea of the general welfare state.

## THE ANATOMY OF THE WELFARE STATE

The immediate reaction of the Hoover Administration in 1930 to the implacable facts of general economic disaster was to depend upon private charity and limited governmental assistance at the state and local levels to assuage human suffering. Such federal emergency assistance programs as were passed before 1933 came at the initiative of an aroused Congress. The inauguration of the New Deal Administration signaled a momentous change in attitude whereby the executive assumed leadership in welfare policy making.

*Public Assistance and Social Insurance.* Initial public assistance through federal relief grants in the early 1930s was looked upon as an emergency measure, soon to be supplemented, and later to be replaced by a comprehensive *insurance* system. The focus of this transition was to be the Social Security Act of 1935. Both forms of aid, however, seem to have been permanently engrafted onto the welfare structure. In the early New Deal years relief and public works projects flourished in alphabetical profusion. A Civilian Conservation Corps gave jobs to hundreds of thousands of youths in work camps and provided a subsistence level wage. Matching funds, usually in a ratio of $1 (federal) to $3 (state) for public relief projects were provided under the Federal Emergency Relief Act of 1933. A giant public works project under the Public Works Administration was inaugurated with a budget of over $3 billion in 1933 further to stimulate employment.

Since 1935 both the volume and varieties of public assistance have grown. Originally provided in the Social Security Act and, since 1953, administered by the Department of Health, Education, and Welfare, the key assistance programs provide aid for the needy aged, dependent children, the blind, the partially and totally disabled, and the families of dependent children. In 1962 these programs (including payments for medical assistance to the aged) accounted for expenditures of $4.3 billion. In that year slightly over $2 billion in old age assistance was distributed to 2.2 million people; 944,000 families received nearly $1.5 billion in aid for 2.8 million dependent children; $100 million was dispersed to 100,000 blind persons; and $373 million in grants were made available to over 400,000 permanently disabled persons.[2]

In order to create a useful place in society for the mentally retarded, the deaf, the blind, disabled workers, and older people who are otherwise limited in the kinds of jobs they can perform, the Office of Vocational Rehabilitation of HEW makes grants to the states to encourage them to establish appropriate training facilities. In 1962 over $57 million in grants went to all the states, Puerto Rico, and the Virgin Islands, and over 100,000 disabled persons were successfully rehabilitated.[3] Additional millions of dollars every year are made available in grants to the states to improve maternal and child health, to provide services for crippled children, and to support child welfare services throughout the nation. These and other assistance programs account annually for about 6 per cent of federal budgetary expenditures.

On the other hand, a large part of the public welfare system is, since 1935, based upon the insurance principle. Hence this form of welfare should not be thought of as governmental expenditure on a charity principle. It is, rather, a kind of forced savings built up during working years and reimbursed in pension form at retirement. In fact, many economists look upon the social security insurance system as a real increase in wages and salaries, with the difference that payment is deferred until retirement.[4] The mechanics of the Old Age and Survivors Insurance program, as established in 1935 and subsequently developed, are as follows:

A federal tax is imposed upon both employers and employees. The initial tax rate was one per cent but has been raised periodically to the point where at present employers and employees each pay 3⅝ per cent of earnings up to $4800 into a special trust fund in the Treasury Department. The rate of contributions is periodically increased and is designed to level off in 1973 at 4.95 per cent. At present over 90 per cent of the American work force is covered by social security; self-employed workers pay a special, higher tax since there is no matching payment made by an employer. For male workers, full benefit payments begin at age sixty-five and partial benefits are available to the worker who chooses to retire at age sixty-two. Wives of workers receive benefits at age sixty-two and dependent children up to age eighteen. Widows and children of workers who have died also receive payments. By 1963 about 13.5 million persons over age sixty-two were sharing $13 billion in old age and survivors benefits, and the number is increasing each year as life expectancy increases and the number of eligible persons grows. At the end of fiscal year 1962, average monthly benefits paid were $79.90 for a retired worker, $135.20 for an aged couple, $212.70 for a widowed mother with two children, and $76.50 for an aged widow alone. Since 1956 when Congress added the permanently disabled to the categories of those eligible for social security benefits, those over fifty years of age are eligible for payments on the same basis as that for retired people over sixty-two. Thus in 1962 the average payment made to a disabled worker, his wife, and one or more children was $200.70 per month.[5]

After the nearly thirty years of its existence, there is no real controversy over the social security insurance principle. Yet there are real administrative problems to tax the imagination of the policy makers of the welfare state. One basic concern is the maintenance of the actuarial soundness of the system. Reduced to its simplest terms, the question is whether and how the principal trust fund can maintain a rate of growth sufficient to cover the steady increase of eligible pensioners and to permit increases in the size of the payments in order to make them meaningful sources of income. Over the past decades, Congress has been reluctant to raise the amount of employer-employee contributions to the fund sufficiently to meet the needs of the future. That the average benefits are not presently adequate is indicated by the number of beneficiaries of the program who must also depend upon old age assistance, medical assistance, and other forms of *grants* from government. Hence the original aim of the insurance scheme—to remove the need for extensive public charity—has not been achieved. Furthermore, technological advances, economic evolution, and even medical progress work together to test some of the assumptions of the social security system. For example, as wage and salary levels continue to rise, how realistic is it to retain the tax rate only on the first $4800 earned? Clearly, the more money earned by an individual, the smaller is the proportion of his income paid into the system. Or, to consider another problem, if the tax rate percentage should be increased quite substantially in order that benefit payments could justifiably be increased, might this not be just the marginal incentive sufficient to encourage more people to retire earlier and thus place a still heavier burden on the trust fund? Moreover, it is quite likely that older people, who have but a few years of employment left to them, would favor tax increases (and pension increases), while younger people who have thirty or forty years of employment ahead of them would be less than enthusiastic about additional taxes obligated for the remainder of their work lives. Questions of equity and balance of interests which must be considered by the policy maker are no better illustrated than by the alternatives of policy posed concerning social insurance.

*Unemployment Insurance.* Since the ultimate threat to personal and family security is unemployment, a major policy goal of the welfare state, beyond promoting maximum employment, is the maintenance of a source of income for those members of the labor force temporarily unemployed. The most satisfactory means to this end has been found in the insurance principle. The Social Security Act of 1935 contained provisions for financing and operating an unemployment compensation system. The object of the system is to provide temporary subsistence for workers who become unemployed through seasonal factors or while changing from one job to another, the assumption always being that such idleness will be of brief duration. About 47 million of the roughly 70 million-man labor force is covered by unemployment insurance. The program is financed by a government payroll tax on employers who, in general, have four or more employees for twenty or more weeks a year. To encourage state administration of the compensation system, the federal government offers to relieve employers of up to 90 per cent of the tax if they will instead contribute to a state unemployment insurance system. In practice, each state operates its own compensation agency and sets its own tax rate on employers; the small proportion of the tax collected by the federal government is returned in the form of grants to the various states to finance the administration of the system. Though the federal government sets the basic tax rate at 3 per cent of a worker's wage, not to exceed $300 per worker per year, most of the tax is credited to the state which may charge some employers more than others, depending upon the history of unemployment in a given enterprise.

Since each state administers its own compensation system, subject to certain standards laid down by the national government, the amount of weekly unemployment payments and the duration for which payments are made varies somewhat from state to state. Normally, compensation is granted for a period up to twenty weeks as long as the idled worker is unable to find a job comparable to his former employment. In 1961—a year beset with widespread recession unemployment—8.1 million unemployed insured workers received one or more compensation checks; total compensation paid reached $3.7 billion, and the average weekly tax-free check amounted to $33.80.[6] At this time the period of coverage was temporarily extended to twenty-six weeks due to the serious and long-term unemployment conditions.

The persistence of long-term, high unemployment rates raises some basic questions about the adequacy of the present unemployment compensation system. A system devised to cope with temporary and seasonal unemployment is not adequately capable of meeting the challenge of structural unemployment. The latter form of idleness arises from a fundamental lack of adaptation of workers' skills to available jobs and results from technological advances and shifting patterns of demand. As the President's economic advisers pointed out in their 1963 *Economic Report,* since 1957 unemployment has averaged 6 per cent of the labor force and in some years has risen well above that figure; it has fallen below 5 per cent for only one month in the last five years.[7] Naturally, structural unemployment, being but one aspect of the larger problem of industrial change taking place at mid-century, cannot be removed merely by a few changes in the unemployment insurance system. Yet, it would appear that certain reforms in the system could help to alleviate the effects of such continued unemployment.

Some economists and labor union leaders, among others, have advocated the "nationalization" of the insurance system. Since there is a variation in the benefits available from state to state, and since structural unemployment often burdens certain states, or even parts of states, more than others, it is argued that only a nationally operated system can produce equitable benefits for all idle workers. Beyond this there is the question of the fair rate and extent of unemployment compensation. Clearly, in individual cases and in particularly depressed areas where unemployment continues for months and perhaps even years, limited and subsistence level payments are inadequate to alleviate the inevitable human suffering.

John Kenneth Galbraith has suggested an intriguing line of attack on the unemployment compensation problem in his call for a program of cyclically graduated compensation (CGC). The essence of the proposal consists of a plan for relating the amount of compensation to size of the unemployment figure. In relatively stable times, an unemployment rate of 2 million is to be expected, and compensation should remain low and temporary in order not to encourage voluntary idleness on the part of the unemployed. As unemployment rises, however, to 4, 5, and 6 millions, compensation should rise proportionately until it approaches equivalence to lost wages. This is proposed on the not unrealistic premise that high unemployment is indeed involuntary and not a product of sudden and general human indolence. In other words, Galbraith argues that the state has an obligation to its citizens when, because of trends and conditions not remotely controllable by them, workers are deprived of their livelihood for long periods of time. For financing, CGC would depend upon federal government contributions which would presumably bring returns in the form of economic growth since a high compensation level would create high purchasing power exercisable by unemployed workers.[8] The suggestion surely merits consideration, but, as Galbraith admits, it should not be taken as a substitute for more comprehensive measures involving fiscal management, education, and worker retraining.

*The Nation's Health.* The health aspect of the general welfare in America is a bundle of paradoxes. We have all been impressed by the near-miraculous advances in medicine in recent generations, and the development of drugs, vaccines, and other immunizing and preventive measures has granted today's children a life expectancy of seventy years. Yet we are appalled, on the one hand, that the cost of the medical services necessary to maintain a modern health index has placed them out of the reach of a large proportion of our citizens and, on the other hand, that such a large proportion of our young men have been rejected in recent years from the armed services for physical and mental health reasons. Government's duty to support the health needs of the nation has long been accepted in principle. In our times the extent and means of governmental involvement have been a source of controversy. At the noncontroversial end of the spectrum of public involvement, the Public Health Service performs a wide variety of indispensable functions. With a total of $1.63 billion in funds expended in 1962, the Service conducted dozens of medical surveys, assembled statistics, and conducted hundreds of medical experiments. Actually 72 per cent of the PHS budget was allocated to state and local agencies through grants as well as to private institutions, universities, and hospitals across the nation. National Institutes of Health surveyed such specialized areas as child health, allergies, and cancer research. The Bureau of Medical Services of the PHS operates hospitals, clinics, and health centers which employed 13,000 staff members in 1962, processed 50,000 hospital admissions, and provided 1.3 million outpatient visits by PHS physicians. In addition, in the same year, millions of doses of vaccines for polio and other diseases were administered by the PHS and were responsible for preventing numerous epidemics.[9]

As necessary and valuable as all this activity is, great unfulfilled needs still remain. Nowhere are America's health needs more critically concentrated than among the aged. In 1900 only one person out of twenty was sixty-five years and older; today nearly one out of ten are in that age group, and it is estimated that this aged population will more than double in the forty years between 1960 and 2000.[10] The rate of chronic illness (for example, heart disease, cancer, diabetes, arthritis) in this age group is more than double that of those under forty-five years; less than 10 per cent of the population, this age group constitutes more than 55 per cent of persons with physical disabilities; and the proportion of aged hospitalized is nearly 60 per cent greater than the proportion for the rest of the population. Finally, on a per capita basis, medical expenses for the aged were 88 per cent greater than for the general population.[11]

At the same time, costs of medical care have been advancing rapidly. The index of medical care prices assembled by the Bureau of Labor Statistics, given in Table 6-1, shows a substantial rise (1947-1949 as the base period of 100).[12]

TABLE 6-1   *Index of Medical Care Prices, 1955 and 1961*

|                       | 1955  | 1961  |
|-----------------------|-------|-------|
| Total medical care    | 128.0 | 160.9 |
| Physicians' fees      | 123.3 | 148.9 |
| Hospital room rates   | 164.4 | 240.3 |
| Hospital insurance    | 115.5 | 187.4 |
| Prescription drugs    | 111.2 | 121.3 |

The only way middle and lower income groups can pay the costs of modern medical services is through adequate insurance coverage. Yet hospital and medical insurance are, themselves, not inexpensive. For younger, working persons *group* health plans are quite feasible and have been increasing in popular subscription for some time. At present, over two-thirds of the general population has some form of private medical insurance. For the older, retired person living on social security and perhaps some savings, private medical insurance is a real burden. Once again, statistics tell an important part of the story: In 1959, among the retired age over sixty-five, only 42.3 per cent had hospital insurance, only 32.8 per cent had surgical insurance, and only 8.3 per cent had doctor visit insurance.[13] Thus that sector of our population which has the poorest medical record and the greatest need for insurance has the least coverage.

Policies proposed to provide public medical insurance, particularly for the aged, over the past years have been objects of keen political controversy. While the American Medical Association and an alliance of private insurance companies have vigorously denounced various forms of public medical insurance as "socialized medicine," increasingly, presidents and large numbers of congressmen have been pressing for some form of medical aid for the aged. As an alternative to compulsory medical insurance, Congress in 1960 passed the Kerr-Mills Act. This measure was designed to provide medical assistance to the aged (MAA) financed by grants made by the national government and matched in part by the states. The MAA program was related to the existing and expanded old age assistance program (OAA) in that benefits for medical needs could be made by the states to individuals whose incomes were too high to qualify for OAA but not high enough to support their medical expenses. In practice many of the participating states fixed a maximum income level for potential beneficiaries of MAA which limited the scope of the program considerably. On the basis of the limited nature of the Kerr-Mills program, both the Kennedy and Johnson Administrations have continued to call for a "medicare" program which is compulsory in that it would be financed by additional taxes under the social security insurance program. By 1964 Congress was thus asked to act as broker, weighing the interests of increasingly politically conscious "senior citizens" and those who either opposed increased payroll tax deductions or argued against compulsory medical insurance in principle.*

*Education as an Aspect of Welfare.* The idea that a high level of education is a legitimate subject of governmental encouragement is not novel. The famous passage from the Northwest Ordinance of 1787 still has a meaningful ring: "Religion, morality and justice, being necessary to good government and the happiness of mankind, schools and the means of education shall ever be encouraged." In the mid-1960s Americans might well expand the religion-morality-justice triad to include social and economic stability. For it is becoming abundantly clear that in our technologically advanced, service oriented society, the demand for skills and services obtainable only through extensive education increases every year. In many ways, education appears to be the key variable in the process of reallocating human resources in a way that will contribute to the general welfare.

* See Epilogue.

The great difficulty in providing the facilities for an enormously and rapidly expanding educational plant is partly a financial one and partly a logistical one: What is to be the source of sustaining funds and how is the supply of qualified teachers to be obtained? Historically in America, public education has been the province of the local community and the state. For the most part, local taxes supported and local school boards governed public education. At the state level, support and governance were largely limited to institutions of higher learning. In our own times there is powerful evidence available to suggest that the resources of local and state government are no longer capable of meeting increased educational needs. Thus, more and more, Americans look upon federal aid as the only possible vehicle for the survival and growth of mass education.

The educational crisis has its roots in the present disproportionate growth in the numbers of our children of school age. The post-World War II boom in babies began to be felt strongly in the 1950s. One way to gauge the problem is to note that from 1930 to 1950 there was practically no growth in school enrollments (29.6 million to 30.2 million); by 1955, however, the school population had jumped to 37.4 million and by 1960, to 46.2 million. Moreover, projections forecast a continuing student explosion. The most conservative estimate of enrollments for 1980 is 62 million, but the more probable forecast of the student population of 1980 is 75 million. Although the bulge in student population is now moving up through the primary and secondary grades, it is already reaching, and will further expand, the ranks of the college population in the Sixties and Seventies. In 1960 college enrollment was up to 3.6 million, and some forecasts project a 1980 enrollment as high as 9 million.[14] The critical nature of this educational explosion becomes apparent when we consider the high cost of college level education and problem of obtaining enough adequately trained educators to meet the rising numbers of students. Finally, this is predominantly a *public* problem since the great expansion in enrollments, facilities, and faculties has and will continue to take place in the large state universities, municipal colleges, and junior and community colleges. By the 1960s the small, private colleges and universities were clearly giving way to the large public institutions.

All of these trends point to sharply increasing burdens of public expenditure and taxation. Between 1951 and 1961 total expenditures for education in the United States grew from $11.3 billion to $28.9 billion, and in the same period the per cent of the gross national product spent on education increased from 3.4 to 5.6.[15] Yet even this rate of increased support failed to meet educational needs. In 1961 there were 1.7 million pupils enrolled in schools in excess of the normal capacity of facilities. Shortages of classrooms and teachers made half-day sessions and uncertified or part-time teachers a more common occurrence than ever. Furthermore, the Committee for Economic Development estimated that, if resources per pupil were held constant, the costs of public schools would increase by 47 per cent in the period from 1958-1959 to 1969-1970.[16]

Since the end of World War II many proposals have been made for a massive federal assault on the education problem but until very recently only rather piecemeal sorties have been conducted. The most substantial federal program of the 1950s was the enactment of the National Defense Education Act which finances federally the construction of dormitories and similar facilities and makes fellowships, loans and other assistance available to qualified and needy students at the college level. In 1963 the greatest increase in federal support to education to date was recorded. A medical school aid bill was passed which authorized $200 million in grants over a three-year period for the construction and rehabilitation of medical and dental schools and for loans to medical, dental, and osteopathy students. A $1.2 billion vocational aid bill was enacted which inaugurated a four-year program to expand vocational training and extend the loan making authority granted under the National Defense Education Act. Finally, at the end of 1963 a $1.2 billion general college aid measure was signed into law.[17] This act provided for a three-year program of grants for the improvement of graduate, undergraduate, and two-year community colleges. Funds were made available to both public and private institutions but could not be spent for sectarian use.

Thus an important beginning has been made in federal educational support, but many conflicting religious, regional, and ideological interests remain to be appeased before fully adequate federal support at all levels of education can be made a reality. Each proposal including federal aid for sectarian-based or related schools arouses the opposition of those who define strictly the boundaries separating church and state. General school aid proposals tend to receive less sympathy among citizens in states which already have good school systems because these citizens see themselves as taxed to support not only "their own" schools, but also those of distant states which need much heavier support even to approach a satisfactory level of education. Finally, large-scale federal aid to education is opposed by those who argue that federal aid must eventually bring centralized federal control over all American education. Proponents of expanded federal aid argue that education is the key to continued prosperity and economic development, that education is a *national* community responsibility, and that national support need not at all result in tyranny over the minds of the educated.

## THE PROBLEM OF POVERTY

In a society that has been variously described as affluent and classless—and apparently likes to think of itself in those terms—it comes as a shock to some to learn that substantial numbers of our people live in conditions of poverty. The recessions of the middle and late 1950s and the identification of depressed areas in the early Sixties have stimulated investigations and discussions about the plight of what one writer has called "The Other America." By 1964 the problem of poverty assumed a high position on the national policy agenda. In his first Economic Report to Congress, President Lyndon Johnson fired the opening guns in his war on poverty:

> Americans today enjoy the highest standard of living in the history of mankind. But for nearly a fifth of our fellow citizens, this is a hollow achievement. They often live without hope, below minimum standards of decency.
>
> The per capita money income of these 35 million men, women, and children was only $590 in 1962—against $1900 per capita for the nation as a whole.
>
> We cannot and need not wait for the gradual growth of the economy to lift this forgotten fifth of our nation above the poverty line.[18]

Since poverty describes the condition of those in our society who need the help of the welfare state most of all, the programs of assistance and insurance discussed above should be of greatest benefit to this underprivileged class. Commonly the poorest among us have the least education, the lowest paid jobs, and the worst health record. The prevailing expectation has been that with a healthy, growing economy, plus such assistance as is afforded by the existing welfare structure, our impoverished class will gradually shrink until it passes from existence. Unfortunately, however, as the President's Council of Economic Advisers reported in 1964, the passage is slow indeed. One reason for the slow rate of progress is that poverty tends to be *concentrated* in areas, the total environments of which tend to perpetuate the desperate causal components which produce it. Thus, typically, a major historic industry providing employment for a whole region dies out and is not replaced by a new employment and income-producing facility. Whole areas of such distress symbolized by Appalachia and Northland (Northern Michigan, Wisconsin, and Minnesota) suffer from the debilities of general depression. Unemployment in such basic industries as coal mining or textiles is reflected in a shrinking market for consumer goods, lower tax revenues, and thus poorer public services, such as health and education. Other factors also come into play: For example, the decline in defense industry employment combined with a more competitive automotive industry and consequent plant relocations brought about a precipitous downturn in the general economy of the Detroit area in the Fifties and Sixties.

Great concentrations of poverty have meant that the usual welfare aids provide only marginal relief. In the 1960s a meaningful concept of government welfare activity must include programs to redevelop whole regions. The Area Redevelopment Act of 1961 constituted a modest beginning in this area of policy. Under its terms the Departments of Commerce, Labor, Interior, and Health, Education, and Welfare—along with the Housing and Home Finance Agency and the Small Business Administration—have pooled their resources to offer technical assistance and economic development information to depressed areas. Moreover, the staff of field workers of the Area Development Administration provides assistance to state and local agencies charged with economic development. Redevelopment activities take the form both of manpower retraining projects and the acceleration of public works projects to utilize the services of unemployed laborers.

Even poverty that is highly concentrated is often not readily apparent to the unstudied eye in the affluent society. Low levels of education and literacy, chronic, unmet health needs, and the personal tragedy of psychic frustration that results may go unnoticed. But there is one unmistakable physical manifestation of poverty that is not lost on the most casual observer, and this is the eyesore of run-down housing and property. A short walk along the other sides of the railroad tracks in nearly any city in America dramatically telescopes the problem by focusing on our urban slums. Sometimes, however, the shock of recognition distorts our view of poverty by making it appear a wholly urban phenomenon. Yet, while the greater part of our impoverished are concentrated in the cities, there exists widespread rural poverty as well. The city slum tenement has its counterpart in the rural shack, often hidden from our eyes by the surrounding pastoral landscape.

Like all the other interlocking characteristics of American poverty, poor housing is both an effect and a contributing cause. Hence public housing developments do not in themselves cure poverty but rather treat one of its notable symptoms. At the same time, squalid housing conditions and an unhealthy community environment may act as a deterrent to general improvement. That this is a real problem is suggested by 1960 census figures which indicate that fully 26 per cent of our 58 million housing units are unsound. Some 16 million homes lack full plumbing facilities; over 8 million homes are described as deteriorating; and over 3 million (of which the slum tenement is typical) are dilapidated.[19]

The Great Depression saw the beginnings of federal involvement in housing, primarily through the underwriting of government mortgage insurance. Subsequently, the Housing Act of 1949 represented a more ambitious and comprehensive approach to the housing problem. A Public Housing Administrator was authorized to assist local governments in clearing slums and constructing low-cost public housing. Since 1949 loans and grants have been made to local communities to finance planning and studies of blighted areas as well as the relocation of dispossessed inhabitants of razed slums. The Housing and Home Finance Agency, under the 1961 Housing Act, has made loans for local water, gas, and sewage plant improvement as well as for housing, hospital, and college construction. One of President Johnson's first special messages in 1964 was devoted to proposals for the construction of 200,000 new public housing units in the next four years and extended federal promotion of urban renewal, community development, and urban mass transportation. He also renewed President Kennedy's ungranted request for a cabinet-level department of Housing and Community Development.[20]

While improved housing—as well as improved health and improved education—will create a better climate within which our lowest economic stratum can attempt to lift itself upward, the essential long-run goal must be greater employment opportunities. Likewise, it is the formulation and implementation of policies leading toward this goal that present the most difficult challenges. As we have seen, retraining is absolutely indispensable; but retraining is not a short-run solution. If we are determined to raise the level of welfare among our poorest citizens quickly and measurably, still greater public stimulus must be applied. Through its fiscal management responsibilities, the federal government is capable of stimulating the economy by a number of different devices. The most direct of these devices is the vigorous pumping of money into the economy by heavy government expenditures for public works. This is *politically* perhaps the least feasible means of stimulating the economy and is normally reserved for times and situations of direct emergency. (Having said this, one must acknowledge the continuing and generally accepted high level of government spending on defense and armament projects which constitutes a heavy contribution to economic activity.)

A less direct form of economic stimulus comes into play when government alters the tax rate or base. It is obvious, for example, that a progressive income tax is an equalizing force in the economy; on the other hand, a sales tax represents a greater burden to the poor and boon to the rich in relative terms. The policy of both the Kennedy and Johnson Administrations of lowering income tax rates was based, in part, on welfare considerations. The 11 billion tax cut was designed to put additional money in the pockets of taxpayers, who as consumers would demand more goods, thus stimulating production, plant expansion, and growth of employment. The Council of Economic Advisers was so committed to this theory of stimulating economic growth that it forth-rightly took a controversial stand on the budget question, proposing a planned deficit in its *Report* of 1963.[21]

Some sense of the complexities of public policy may be gained through a brief consideration of some of the facets of the tax reduction scheme. Through stimulation of economic growth, new employment sources are anticipated, which should provide opportunities for our poorer citizens to help themselves. But will our underprivileged be *capable,* by training, of availing themselves of such new jobs as do appear? (Moreover, if they *can,* will they be permitted to if they are Negroes—which a large portion of them are?) Furthermore, what if—as some critics have predicted—the increase in spending power made available through tax reduction results in inflation? Such an increase in the consumer price index could cruelly check the upward mobility initiated among our poor. Finally, the hopeful cycle of development could be breached if consumer dollars demanded imported goods and increased imports damaged our international balance of payments. Such a consummation would encourage the Federal Reserve Board to raise interest rates on borrowing, and this would bring a partial halt to desired productive expansion.

No policy is without its gambles or even its perils. Yet a recognition has grown in mid-century that a part of the American dream which calls for equality of opportunity has been imperfectly fulfilled. The organizational revolution has brought great affluence to a large part of our society; at the same time it has bypassed smaller but significant numbers of our people, leaving them mired in an economic and social trough that has long been overlooked. But the word has gotten abroad, and new demands for new policies to raise the level of American welfare will be a major concern of government in the decades ahead.

## CONTROVERSIES SURROUNDING THE WELFARE STATE

Lest I close this chapter leaving the impression that the American attitude toward the welfare state is an unqualified vote for continuation "onward and ever upward," mention should be made of the controversies which still brew—if they no longer rage—over the role of government in relation to social welfare. It seems to me that arguments about the welfare state are carried on a three levels: the moral and ideological, the political, and the institutional. These bases of argumentation are not mutually exclusive in relevance or application; in the course of any discussion, protagonists usually leap from one level to another and back again. Yet these levels of discourse are distinctive enough to bring some clarity to an analytical assessment of the controversy.

(1) THE IDEOLOGICAL QUESTION. Principled opposition to expanding public welfare activity is usually based upon a moral commitment to extreme individualism. This form of individualism is grounded on a theory of human nature which dictates that men are likely to become shiftless and indolent if given half a chance. Society is thus making a mistake when it accepts responsibility for individual welfare; for, although there are some unfortunate cases of nonself-imposed hardship, an institutionalized program of public aid is bound to encourage the worst tendencies in human nature. Moreover, the reasoning continues, the prudent, diligent, and farsighted members of society are unfairly penalized when the fruits of their industry are taxed away to support the nonindustrious.

Those who oppose the individualistic conception contend that, while there are undoubtedly slackers in any society, the major burdens of poverty are borne either by those who have not had sufficient opportunity to help themselves, or have been visited by catastrophes beyond their ability to surmount. It is thus the responsibility of those in society who are able, to help expand the horizons of the disabled. The philosophical supports of the welfare state grow out of an angle of vision directed toward the community rather than the individual. Finally, the advocate of a generous public welfare program is quick to point out that the state has always supported munificently the interests of large, organized enterprises through taxes, subsidies, and other forms of aid. This being the case, it is suggested that elementary fairness requires government to give some attention to the needs of the unorganized poor.

(2) THE POLITICAL QUESTION. "Political" is used here in that broad sense that connotes conflict and bargaining over alternative courses of action. The political arguments concerning welfare turn on the question of who gets what, when, and how. Since the various forms of welfare aid may justifiably be expected to inspire gratitude among the recipients, political brokers of welfare

interests have not infrequently been accused of purchasing public favor with tax money. To be sure, the famous recipe, "tax and tax; spend and spend; elect and elect," represents a queasy morality at best. To watch any session of Congress devoted to debate over the kinds, form, and amounts of welfare aid proposed is to witness a contest among representatives of the various classes, and groups in American society. Moreover, since one of the major American political parties has been historically identified with the growth of public welfare, differences of opinion about welfare needs sometimes reduce to partisan differences.

In any case, that the politics of welfare can in a very true sense be equated with the politics of democracy is suggested by an historical phenomenon: In middle class America the preponderant weight of public aid has been distributed to the middle class. Thus in the past three decades, while there has been material improvement in the welfare of all strata of society, it is the middle level that has reaped the greatest advantages from government programs. In a pluralistic democracy this is hardly surprising since it is the middle class whose quests are fortified with greater education, more substantially vested interests, and much keener political participation and influence. The decades of the Sixties and Seventies will disclose the extent to which representatives of the "affluent" middle class are willing to speak for the needs and aspirations of the lower stratum in American society.

(3) THE INSTITUTIONAL QUESTION. A third kind of controversy about the welfare state relates to institutional changes in American government that are attributed in large part to public welfare activity. The criticisms are usually directed to the growth of bureaucracy and the erosion of states' rights and responsibilities. In some cases, the institutional basis of criticism appears to be rationalization which masks a deeper antipathy to the *substance* of public welfare rather than to the means by which it is administered. Nonetheless, the institutional criticism is commonly expressed and must be considered a part of the controversy.

Strictures about the growth of bureaucracy related to the administration of welfare activities are part of a generalized fear of bureaucratic aggrandizement in government. Again, it is inevitable that welfare bureaucrats influence policy. For example, reports on the nation's health made by the Federal Security Administrator in the late 1940s, as well as those drafted by the HEW in recent years, serve as spurs to expanded public medical insurance programs. Yet the specter of a welfare Leviathan is somewhat exaggerated. The most recent, thorough tabulation of executive employees in government suggests that of the 2,462,262 civilian employees of the executive branch, some 264,787, or somewhat over 10 per cent, are occupied primarily with the welfare function. This figure includes the totals for the Department of Health, Education, and Welfare, the Housing and Home Finance Agency, and the Veterans Administration which alone accounts for 173,-000. Furthermore, this number of welfare bureaucrats may be compared to over one million Defense Department administrators and the 588,000 Post Office Department employees.[22] In any case, overemphasis of crude numerical totals is a preoccupation with trivialities. It seems only reasonable to expect that if government is to minister to the welfare needs of its constituents, there will be a significant number of civil servants performing such ministrations.

A second institutional source of concern about the growth of the welfare function is addressed to the changing nature of federalism. It is sometimes implied that proponents of expanded public welfare are engaged in a plot to bring about total centralization of the governing function in America. This argument was used most recently by congressional opponents of President Kennedy's proposed Department of Urban Affairs and Housing. Moreover, no objective student of political trends in twentieth-century America would deny that federal programs involving grants-in-aid to the states do carry with them a measure of federal supervision and control. Whether this is necessarily wrong or even dangerous is certainly questionable. Finally, if we may resort once more to statistics, it can be shown that the states are far from being submerged by a national appropriation of the welfare function. While it is often pointed out that the federal government spends an increasing amount on welfare services, it is less often noted that the states and local governments always spend absolutely and proportionally *more*. Thus, to take the most recent year for which we have complete figures, the federal government spent in 1960 nearly $24 billion on welfare which amounted to 26 per cent of expenditure for all purposes. In the same year, state and local expenditures amounted to almost $28 billion and this was 59.3 per cent of all expenditures.[23] It could thus reasonably be argued that the states are partners with the federal government in dispensing the welfare function rather than minions of a federal monolith.

Much of the controversy which surrounds the growth of public welfare activity in the United States is based upon suppositions: assumptions about the nature of man and his relationship to his fellow men; assumptions about the proper role of government; and assumptions about the ideal relationships among political institutions. In closing, it may be instructive to consider the mode of life in modern, industrial, mass society as it would be *without* the existence of a public welfare structure. Indeed, to do this we need not rely exclusively on our imagination. We have at least a modicum of empirical evidence. In 1961 Clermont County, Ohio, canceled all public welfare because of financial difficulties. Subsequently, the Community Health and Welfare Council made a study of the effects of this act. The general finding reported indicates, not surprisingly, that welfare needs did not disappear; the responsibility for them was simply shifted. In short, what the county government gained was lost to landlords, physicians, churches, schools, and civic groups. Bills went unpaid, debts owed to doctors, hospitals, stores, and landlords rose by 54 per cent in fifteen months. Smallpox, diphtheria, polio, and other vaccinations for school children were almost totally ended, resulting in serious dangers to community health. Adults were reluctant to seek medical services for which they could not pay. Needless to say, personal anxiety and general unhappiness characterized life in a portion of the community.[24]

One is led to conclude that the practical imperatives of life in modern, democratic America leave no room for meaningful debate about whether there should or should not be a national public welfare responsibility. The real questions turn on the nature, form, and extent of the welfare state in the latter half of the twentieth century. In the process of providing answers to these questions, policy makers must acknowledge, assess, and finally attempt to balance the interests of the rich and the poor, the young and the old, the urban masses and the rural minorities, the nation and the states, and domestic needs in relation to international responsibilities.*

### REFERENCES

1. US Bureau of the Census, *Statistical Abstract of the United States: 1962* (83rd ed.), Washington, D.C., 1962, p. 274.
2. US Department of Health, Education, and Welfare, *Annual Report, 1962* (Washington, D.C.: Government Printing Office, 1962), pp. 130-133.
3. *Ibid.,* pp. 363, 393.
4. See, for example, Adolf A. Berle, *The American Economic Republic* (New York: Harcourt, Brace and World, 1963), p. 179.
5. HEW, *Annual Report, 1962,* p. 38.
6. US Department of Labor, *Annual Report, 1961* (Washington, D.C.: Government Printing Office, 1961), p. 98.
7. *Economic Report of the President Together with the Annual Report of the Council of Economic Advisers,* 1963 (Washington, D.C.: Government Printing Office, 1963), p. 23.
8. The scheme is presented fully in John K. Galbraith, *The Affluent Society* (Boston: Houghton Mifflin Company, 1958), Chapter 21.
9. HEW, *Annual Report,* 1962, pp. 139-234.
10. US Senate, *A Staff Report to the Special Committee on Aging.* Committee Print, 87th Cong., 1st Sess., May 24, 1961, p. 1.
11. US Senate, Committee on Labor and Public Welfare, *Report: Action for the Aged and Aging.* Report No. 128, 87th Cong., 1st Sess., March 28, 1961, pp. 42, 46.
12. *Statistical Abstract, 1962,* p. 77.
13. *Action for the Aged and Aging,* Senate Report No. 128, p. 49.
14. *Statistical Abstract, 1962,* p. 115.
15. HEW, *Annual Report,* 1962, p. 258.
16. Committee for Economic Development, *Paying for Better Public Schools* (New York, 1963), p. 20.
17. *Congressional Quarterly Weekly Report,* XXII (January 3, 1964), p. 10.
18. *The New York Times,* January 21, 1964, p. 16.
19. *Statistical Abstract, 1962,* pp. 759-760.
20. *The New York Times,* January 28, 1964, p. 16.
21. Council of Economic Advisers, *Annual Report, 1963* (Washington, D.C.: Government Printing Office, 1963), pp. 52, 66.
22. US Senate, Committee on Government Operations, *Organization of Federal Executive Departments and Agencies.* Report No. 23, 88th Cong., 1st Sess., April 1, 1963, Table VII, pp. 79-80.
23. *Statistical Abstract,* 1962, p. 274.
24. *The New York Times,* November 10, 1963, p. 82.

* See Epilogue.

CHAPTER 7

# National Security: Problems of Organization and Administration

## THE PRIMACY OF SECURITY

Whether or not Americans have become widely preoccupied with personal security, as has been alleged, is open to question. There seems little doubt, however, that since the end of World War II Americans collectively have never for long been able to escape from an atmosphere of concern and anxiety about national security. Before the era of atomic superpowers, threats to national security were limited, sporadic, and never taken quite seriously in the ultimate sense of danger to national survival. The events of the postwar period have changed all this—permanently. Now a continuous potential threat to national survival has been acknowledged intellectually and emotionally by all literate citizens. And though the threat may be symbolized by antagonist nation states and their policies, its essential nature consists in the very existence of lethal weapons of mass destruction such as the world has never known.

In the days before the atomic bomb, maintenance of national security was really quite a simple matter. Splendid isolation—a phrase and an idea borrowed from our British cousins—was our guiding principle. The fundamental defenses needed were little more than well-fortified boundaries; policies that took us to war on foreign continents were justified as acts of American generosity directed toward peoples we liked who represented moral and political principles we favored. By 1945, however, all but the most unreconstructed isolationist minority had come to accept permanent American involvement in world affairs. The great hope of the early postwar period was that this involvement would be a co-operative and peaceful one. To this end, Americans grasped, perhaps too enthusiastically, for the peace keeping promise of the United Nations. The immediate impulse for demobilization was satisfied in 1945, and President Harry Truman would later complain that, as headlong and frenzied as demobilization was in the weeks following the surrender of Germany and Japan, he was under heavy pressures to "bring the boys home" even faster.[1]

The closing years of the 1940s brought hardened Soviet intransigence over Germany and Eastern Europe, explosion by the Soviets of the atomic bomb, and the triumph of communism in China. American reactions took the form of diplomatic talks, foreign aid, and debate over universal military training. It was the shock of direct conflict in Korea from 1950 to 1953 which set the pattern for future national security activity. Henceforth, huge defense budgets, a military draft producing large standing armies, and increased emphasis on technological sophistication in weaponry would characterize the American commitment to national security. The gross dimensions of this commitment are revealed by the most recent Defense Department statistics:[2]

In numbers of active duty servicemen as of June 30, 1962

| | | | |
|---|---|---|---|
| Total | 2,807,819 | | |
| Army | 1,066,404 | deployed in 16 | divisions |
| Navy | 857,390 | 900 | commissioned ships |
| Air force | 834,025 | 97 | combat wings |

As a measure of financial investment, the defense budget (which accounted for 63 per cent of the total national budget) for fiscal year 1963 (in billions) [3]—

| | |
|---|---|
| Total | $50.365 |
| Army | 12.196 |
| Navy | 15.527 |
| Air force | 19.828 |
| Defense agencies | 2.120 |
| Civilian defense | .695 |

Even these broad indexes of commitment to national security in manpower and financial resources merely highlight the basic concern. The depth of national security involvement is more fully appreciated by noting that, in addition to the nearly 3 million active duty servicemen, as of June 30, 1962, there were 2.9 million men in the reserves not on active duty. Still additional millions who have had military experience and since been discharged from the reserves round out the proportion of our population with military connections or experience. Finally, at the end of fiscal year 1962, the Defense Department employed 1.24 million civilian workers in the three services.[4]

The most striking innovation in national security policy, however, has been the shift away from such limited concerns as the size of the military establishment, the number of ships, tanks, guns, and planes, or the effectiveness of combat readiness training, to still more complex concerns of technological preparedness. Startling advances in the mechanical versatility available for the conduct of war—both offensive and defensive—have altered the very orientation of our national security planners. Making atomic energy operational for warfare purposes constituted, of course, the climactic breakthrough in the technique of destruction. Yet the orbiting of space satellites, first the Soviet Sputniks, then the series of American flights, added a still greater dimension of capability and complexity to considerations of national security. These changes in the very nature of warfare forced the security planners into a position of quite considerable dependence upon the findings of basic scientific research. Increasing emphasis in this area has made R & D (research and development) a commonplace designation in government circles. The dramatic growth of government's patronage of this function may be seen in the increased proportion of the federal budget allocated for it from the first postwar year to the present (Table 7-1).

Since 1953-1954, federal expenditures for research and development have been increasing at a rate faster than over-all budgetary expenditures; for example, it can be seen that R & D doubled between 1959 and 1963. Moreover, this government-sponsored research is almost entirely related to defense and security projects. During the fiscal years 1961-1963, 90 per cent of total federal outlays for R & D went to three agencies: Department of Defense, National Aeronautics and Space Administration, and Atomic Energy Commission. In 1963 the R & D expenditure was divided as follows: Defense—$7.4 billion; NASA—$2.8 billion; AEC—$1.1 billion.[6]

TABLE 7-1    *Federal Expenditures for Science*[5]

| Year | Total Budget Expenditures (billions) | R & D Expenditures (billions) |
|------|--------------------------------------|-------------------------------|
| 1946 | $60.448 | $  .918 |
| 1950 | 39.544 | 1.083 |
| 1955 | 64.389 | 3.308 |
| 1957 | 68.996 | 4.462 |
| 1959 | 80.342 | 5.803 |
| 1960 | 76.539 | 7.738 |
| 1961 | 81.515 | 9.278 |
| 1962 | 89.075 | 10.195 |
| 1963 | 92.537 | 12.337 |

Two considerations, thus, prompt an inquiry into the apparatus of our national security establishment: First, the apparently permanent allocation of more manpower, brain-power, time, and funds to defense concerns in their broadest sense have made national security considerations paramount in all postwar administrations. Second, the changed context of national security policy making—from the exploitation of essentially military strategy to science and technology—has created new kinds of problems for the midcentury administrator. The pages which follow are devoted to an examination of some key organizational, political, and intellectual challenges attending national security decision making.

ORGANIZING A MODERN SECURITY ESTABLISHMENT

*Defense Reorganization.* The history of defense reorganization over the last two decades is a history of ever-narrowing centralization of authority over military and defense policy making. Interservice competition and rivalry as well as a lack of service coordination prompted congressmen and other responsible public officials to press for military unification as World War II wore on. By the end of the war, there could be no doubt that reorganization would take place, and the Army supported a quite thorough unification of the three services. While the Air Force supported the Army's call for unification, the Navy was, on the whole, opposed. Having been advised that stubborn naval opposition to unification must give way to "constructive alternatives," Secretary Forrestal asked his friend, Ferdinand Eberstadt, to draw up an alternative to proposed unification.[7] The resulting Eberstadt Report is important at this stage because it contained the main principles eventually adopted in the National Security Act of 1947. This compromise act created a National Military Establishment in which the previous three cabinet service secretaries were subordinated to a single cabinet-level Secretary of Defense.

It must be noted that the NSA was *not* a unification act; rather, it permitted the Secretary to coordinate the functions of the three services by wielding the power of "general authority, direction, and control." None of the services was deprived of its existing roles and functions, and the first Defense Secretary, James Forrestal, sought to coordinate, through conferences and the development of interservice, consensuses on the major problems. Gradually, Forrestal, who had originally opposed unification, came to recognize the necessity for greater central control in creating service unity and cooperation. Similarly, President Truman became discouraged at the limited nature of defense coordination and in 1949 sent to Congress requests for three revisions in the National Security Act.[8]

Three major revisions concerning the authority of the Department of Defense, certain other organizational changes, and the position of the Joint Chiefs of Staff were passed in 1949 as amendments to the NSA. Henceforth, the National Military Establishment would become the Department of Defense, and the three services would be "military departments" clearly subordinate to the Secretary and deprived of their "reserved" powers under the 1947 act. Moreover, the hobbling modifier "general" was removed from the Defense Secretary's grant of "authority, direction, and control." A Chairman was created for the Joint Chiefs of Staff—a most significant change since, in practice, the Chairman has come to speak for the Joint Staff and to work very closely with the Secretary as well as the President, Congress and the NSC. Perhaps the most momentous yet subtle revision was the passage of a new Title IV which effectively tightened up the purse strings of the defense establishment. Comptrollers were added to the Department and to each of the service subdepartments. Some measure of the importance of these budgetary officials may be gleaned from the description of the office of Assistant Secretary of Defense (Comptroller) found in the *Goverment Organization Manual:*

> [He] establishes and supervises the execution of principles, policies, and procedures to be followed in connection with organizational and administrative matters relating to: (1) the preparation and execution of the budgets, (2) fiscal, cost, operating, and capital property accounting, (3) progress and statistical reporting, (4) internal audit, and (5) the expenditure and collection of funds administered by the Department of Defense; and established uniform terminologies, classification, and procedures in all such matters. . . . [He] is authorized to issue instructions appropriate to carrying out policies approved by the Secretary of Defense for his assigned fields of responsibility.[9]

Even the 1949 amendments, however, did not remove all the major obstacles to authoritative, central civilian control over the defense establishment. In 1953 the Rockefeller Committee on Defense Organization proposed a plan to President Eisenhower which was embodied that year in Reorganization Plan #6 and was eventually accepted by Congress. In two ways the defense structure was further centralized: Greater authority was given to the Secretary through the creation of six new Assistant Secretaries capable of providing needed staff aids and the Joint Chiefs of Staff were brought further under the general managerial authority of the Chairman.

Continued public rivalry among the various services throughout the Eisenhower Administration blocked the former General's campaign for unification of military responsibilities. Development of such new weapons systems as missiles aggravated the interservice competition for the performance of new roles and allocation of new funds. At the height of the controversy in 1958 General James Gavin resigned from the service to carry his protests to Congress and the public, partly through signed articles for *Life* magazine. If various degrees of insubordination within the services were not enough to galvanize the President in reorganization pursuits, the alarming prospects outlined in the Gaither Report gave needed impetus to further rationalizations in the national security network. The prestigious committee lead by Rowan Gaither and supported by the Rockefeller Brothers Fund warned in 1958 that the United States must take drastic steps if the balance of international power were not to tip finally in the direction of the Soviet Union.

Thus it was that President Eisenhower called upon Congress to enact an ambitious reorganization program.[10] At the heart of the program was the authority sought for the Secretary of Defense to establish unified commands and to transfer, abolish, reassign, or consolidate combatant functions. Further, research and development contracts were to be assigned by the Secretary; appropriations were to be allocated to the Department of Defense and parceled out to the services therefrom; and authorization was sought for the Secretary to prohibit any service secretary or JCS member from making recommendations to Congress on his own initiative.

Ultimately, presidential requests were quite generously fulfilled. General authority over the separate services was clarified, and the Secretary was authorized to assign new weapons systems to the various services, to consolidate common service functions into a single agency, and to transfer officers from one department to another if the individuals agreed. As for the control and reassignment of service functions, Congress went only a part of the way: the legislators gave themselves the right to veto any such transfers, on the recommendation of the congressional Armed Services Committees. Finally, Congress was determined not to permit thorough control either by the President or the Defense Secretary over the speech of military leaders and thus invited any member of the JCS to make recommendations to Congress providing he first informs the Secretary of Defense.

The most recent contribution to the process of centralization in defense is Secretary McNamara's budgetary consolidation schemes carried out in the first years of the Kennedy Administration. McNamara has approached the organizational problem in terms of the rational allocation of resources and facilities by means of tying military plans, programs, and budgets together into a single system. The Secretary argues that such over-all planning has four major advantages for Defense Department management: (1) Long-range planning is permitted which gets beyond the

reached often outside and sometimes in spite of NSC recommendations. For example, if, as we are led to believe, the doctrine of "massive retaliation" emerged from deliberations of the NSC, it was nevertheless a doctrine which became clearly inapplicable in specific situations, such as the Indochina crisis of 1954. This is true, in part, because the NSC at the stage of policy formulation had failed to take account of congressional reaction possible in given situations. Congressional opposition to an American troop commitment in 1954 was a fact of life that even strategic purists could not remove. In the end the President decided against intervention on the basis of advice other than that proffered by the NSC. Similarly, in 1958 when President Eisenhower decided to send troops to Lebanon, "the National Security Council did not loom any larger in the sequence of events preceding action than it had under Truman." [13]

When President Kennedy came to office he immediately abolished the Planning Board and Operations Co-ordinating Board in favor of a more integrated plans and operations function. The key to this integration was specificity. That is, in specific situations the President would call upon *certain* sources of advice deemed most appropriate at the time rather than resorting to a standby council preoccupied with long-term policy making. This attitude implied a weakened link between President and NSC in general—and one that was demonstrated in actuality more than once by Kennedy foreign policy. The fact that the Bay of Pigs enterprise was a notable failure has sometimes been attributed to the President's failure to meet regularly with the NSC before-hand. On the other hand, the apparently successful policy adopted by the administration in the Cuban missile crisis of 1962 depended not on an NSC recommendation as such, but rather on the plurality of opinions offered by an *ad hoc* group of about fifteen foreign policy leaders. The point of these two incidents is simply that the exact use or nonuse of the NSC—or any other permanent council—is probably largely irrelevant to policy outcomes. Presidents must have expert advice and each president will seek advice in his own way; hence it is unrealistic to expect that the sources of advice can be completely institutionalized. And in the end, as President Kennedy himself concluded: "No matter how many advisers you have . . . the President must finally choose." [14]

Among the many presidential advisers who must be heard, those who make up the intelligence community have been among the more controversial in recent years. The Central Intelligence Agency was established in Title 102 of the National Security Act of 1947 to provide the NSC with intelligence gathered from within its own organization and to co-ordinate the intelligence activities of such other agencies as the State and Defense Departments, the FBI, and the AEC. In addition to the traditionally bureaucratic function of information gathering (whether provided by domestic researchers and analysis or espionage agents abroad), the CIA performs highly secret *operating* functions, such as the intelligence-gathering high altitude reconnaissance air flights which provoked the U-2 affair, or the training of Cuban refugees to be used in the Bay of Pigs invasion.

In order to accomplish such functions under cover of adequate secrecy, the CIA has been granted certain privileges uncommon to governmental agencies. It is not required to publish personnel data in the *Federal Register;* it is exempted from certain congressional and Bureau of the Budget oversight requirements; and it can bring up to 100 aliens into the country annually outside the normal immigration channels. Finally, very few public officials even know what the CIA's budget is since it is effectively concealed within the budgets of a number of other agencies.

The CIA has been subjected to considerable criticism because the uneasy feeling has grown that, in its operating functions, the Agency could hardly be held precisely responsible to the NSC or even the President. Yet there is no evidence to indicate that in the Bay of Pigs incident President Kennedy was unaware of CIA activities, and President Eisenhower has stated that he was personally aware, not merely of the program of U-2 overflights, but also had given the order for the particular mission in 1960 which resulted in an international incident of critical proportions.[15] That the CIA has at times been mis- or uninformed is obvious, but this is a hazard common to all government agencies; to suggest that the CIA should be abolished, or even closely scrutinized by the normal governmental agencies, is to deprive ourselves of an unpleasant necessity in an era of cold war.

*Emergency Planning and Mobilization.* On entering office in 1961, President Kennedy was impressed by the multitude of eruptions on the international scene and their implications for American security. With the Congo in ferment, crisis in the United Nations, and presidential conviction that the nation's defenses lagged due to a "missle gap" (which later proved illusory), hard-headed planning and security reorganization seemed the challenge of the hour. One reaction to the challenge was to give the Defense Department a broadened role in civilian defense mobilization, and another was to create an Office of Emergency Planning, which is lodged in the Executive Office and represented on the NSC. The administrative lineage of the OEP traces back to the Office of Defense Mobilization, which had been created at the end of World War II. The ODM supervised the organization of manpower, production, stabilization, and telecommunications. Largely a co-ordinating and fact-finding body, it advised the President on security needs in its areas of competence. An example of the results of one of its studies is the Armed Forces Reserve Act of 1955, which established the present pattern of short-term active duty and long-term military reserve service. In 1958 President Eisenhower transferred the civilian defense function to the agency, thus creating an Office of Civilian and Defense Mobilization.

President Kennedy's thinking in the security area led him to place increased emphasis on civilian defense and particularly on the construction of fallout shelters. This function he felt could be better implemented by the Secretary of Defense, and thus all federal civil defense authority was transferred to the Department by executive order in 1961. Deprived of its civil defense function, the old OCDM became the OEP and was charged with the problem of planning and co-ordinating the functions of government at all levels in order to preserve civil authority in time of emergency. This mandate involves the Office in plans for emergency use of resources, manpower, industrial capacity, economic stabilization, and rehabilitation activities after an enemy attack. It is the Director of the Office of Emergency Planning who determines which materials are of strategic value and the quantity in which they are to be stockpiled; he determines the rate of importation of certain commodities which satisfy the national security interest; and he develops plans for emergency transportation and communications maintenance and control.

The effects of this most recent reorganization, separating civil defense and emergency planning functions, cannot yet be determined. Two criticisms of the reorganization might be considered, however. Some students fear that the transfer of civilian defense functions to the Defense Department might result in the subordination of civilian defense to military considerations and requirements. Others have argued that the placement of emergency planning functions in the executive office may permit the rather sweeping authority of the OEP to be exercised under cover of executive privilege and secrecy and thus deny Congress the right of oversight in this important area.[16]

The cycles of organization and reorganization through which the national security apparatus has developed in the course of the cold war illustrate the complexity of the problem involved at a topographical level. More revealing than the twists and turns of the organizational fabric, the fusion and fission of administrative compartments, is the identification of underlying trends and social demands made and satisfied in the name of the preservation of national security. It is to this more analytical exercise that we now direct our attention.

## THE STRATEGIES OF CONFLICTING INTERESTS

*Civil-Military Relations.* Throughout American history the relationship between the civilian and military branches has been one characterized by the subordination of the latter to the former. Fears of military dominance—whether they take the form of *praetorianism* (government by the military) or *caesarism* (government by an autocrat, through manipulation of the military)—have always haunted the American political mind. In consequence, institutional hedges have been erected to contain potential military aggrandizement. Presidential appointment and removal powers, presidential authority as commander-in-chief, congressional oversight, and congressional control of appropriations are all traditional constitutional means of controlling the military.

Presidents and administrations have likewise always sought to maintain a strict separation of general policy making authority over the conduct of war (or foreign relations affected by military considerations) and precisely military activities. Our history abounds with notable "military" decisions which were made by civilian authority because they involved consequences far beyond the winning or losing of a battle. Most recently, the basic decisions in World War II to fight a European war first and a Far Eastern war secondarily, to invade the Normandy coast in 1944, and to hold back the forward thrust of American troops in Germany in 1945 were politico-military decisions made by civilian authority and carred out as orders by military commanders. The rationale governing this system is that the military commander is a specialist in the strategic and tactical uses of violence and little more; hence, military acts which have a larger foreign policy consequence must be removed from the control of the limited military technicians and lodged in the more broadly trained and publicly accountable civilian governors. Whenever the principle has been challenged, civilian authority has reasserted itself, sometimes dramatically as when President Harry Truman removed General MacArthur from Supreme Command of UN Forces in Korea because the General had publicly criticized civilian authority over the operation of the Korean campaign. More recently, Major General Edwin Walker was reprimanded and transferred as a result of his political criticism and apparent attempts to indoctrinate troops under his command.

At mid-century such fears of the military as are expressed from time to time from knowledgeable sources are not prompted primarily by concerns about American caesarism or a possible military coup such as that dramatized in the best-selling novel, *Seven Days in May*. Rather, fears of military influence in America are grounded on more subtle trends in society. There seems to have been, in the course of the past decade, a gradual acceptance of the permanence of the military service obligation by the American people. Similarly, the high military budget seems to have been granted a legitimacy—both popularly and in Congress—that is unusual in American politics. Finally, the cold war has made the acceptance, indeed the indispensability, of military advice paramount in the policy deliberations of responsible congressional committees. Occasionally, a military or service interest representative uses the tactic of aligning himself on one side or the other of the ever-present executive-legislative contest. The debate over the RS-70 bomber program in 1962 provides an instructive example. Defense Secretary McNamara had decided to discontinue the costly manned bomber program in favor of an emphasis on missile development. Not unexpectedly, the Air Force was displeased at the decision, and the Chief of Staff, General Curtis LeMay, publicy opposed it. Representative Carl Vinson, the powerful Chairman of the House Armed Services Committee supported the Air Force view, and the appropriation for the bomber was forced upon the Department of Defense against its own wishes. In this as in other such cases, however, the Secretary simply avoided spending the money appropriated.

Military influence on policy making sometimes exerts itself through the use of clientele organizations which may inform or sway opinion through their publications and other representations. Veterans' organizations play this role prominently, and in 1963 the Air Force Association—which describes itself as a nonpolitical organization, one-third of whose membership includes active Air Force officers—injected itself into a crucial policy decision made by civilian authority. In its annual convention, the Association published a manifesto highly critical of administration policy and denouncing, *inter alia,* the nuclear test ban treaty, an alleged administration pursuit of a nuclear stalemate, and alleged government practice of "tactical disengagement." In protesting the Association's criticism, the civilian Air Force Secretary, Eugene Zuckert, refused to attend a reception held in his honor, but Air Force Chief of Staff LeMay did attend the festivities and made a speech lauding the Association.[17]

While it is essential to recognize military influences on civilian policy and on society generally in a cold war environment, the picture is distorted unless we consider the reciprocal influence of civilian imperitives on the military. That is, in an age of technology and "push-button warfare," some of the skills most highly prized in the military world are typically *civilian* skills. What one writer has called the "civilization of the military" makes the traditional identification of military versus civilian interests and outlooks appear simplistic.[18] Today, the young officer who hopes to move ahead as a military careerist is well advised to develop administrative, scientific (pure and applied), and diplomatic skills in addition to (and eventually, possibly in place of) the traditional skills of loyalty, bravery, obedience, and leadership. Evidence for this trend is to be found in changes in the academic curriculum of the service academies and in the greater emphasis placed upon studies in law, politics, and diplomacy in the war colleges and staff schools.[19] Moreover, with the huge expenditures devoted to research and development by the several services, scientific and technical skills have come to be as much appreciated within the services as without. Interestingly enough, a 1959 directive of the Secretary of Defense requires that officers who seek promotion to general or flag officer rank "will serve a normal tour of duty with a Joint, Combined, Allied or OSD [Office of Secretary of Defense] Staff before being considered qualified. . . ." A significant exception is made for Army and Air Force Officers "whose proposed advancement and qualifications for promotion are based primarily upon their scientific and technical achievement and proposed utilization in that specialty." [20]

The trends identified here appear to indicate that, while there are indeed persistent conflicts between civilian and military attitudes and aspirations, the context of these differences has changed sharply. Once again, technology seems to have been responsible for an attitudinal merger, the military becoming less identified with its vocational traditions and more associated with technical skill values. As this progresses, it is possible that the contest of wills will be less identifiable as civil-military and more properly described as one set of technicians competing with another for funds, social approval, and policy making power. It may be cause for concern that, just as military leadership has absorbed civilian values, a certain degree of the military posture has become a part of civilian existence.

*Military-Industrial Relations.* On January 17, 1961, three days before he left office, President Eisenhower delivered a farewell address which has been quoted more often than anything the President said in the previous eight years of his incumbency. Counseling against the "acquisition of unwarranted influence" by a "military-industrial complex," the President saw in such a trend the gravest dangers to the republic. To the extent that such a powerful complex exists, calculations of policy concerning national security may be influenced not only by rational evaluations of the requirements of the national interest, but also by the competing claims of organized selfish interests.

The basic structure of the military-industrial complex is quite simple and its elements readily identifiable. Given the multibillion dollar expenditures for military procurement and research and development activities noted in the opening pages of this chapter, large industrial contractors are faced with a lucrative market for their services. Like any large, attractive market, the national defense customer stimulates keen competition among potential industrial sellers. Moreover, the commercial aspects of defense industry are not unlike those in any other industry: cost, quality, reputation, and dependability are not the only assets of a strong competitor. Advertising and public relations are important factors in getting the contract. It is in this area that the miliary can perform a service in a number of ways. Major defense industries commonly employ retired Army, Navy, and Air Force officers in executive positions, on their boards of directors, and as consultants. It is good public relations to have a retired Air Force general on the board of an aircraft corporation. Whether the "influence" of these ex-military personnel is within the spirit and the letter of the law as they seek contracts for their companies is difficult to determine. That there *is* influence, however, cannot be doubted.

Some interesting correlations have been revealed as a result of the investigations of a House Armed Services Subcommittee in 1959. To begin, there is heavy concentration in the defense industry as in others, to the extent that in 1960, 25 per cent of the dollar volume of government contracts were let to five leading companies, and the top twenty-one companies accounted for 50 per cent of the defense dollars spent. Furthermore, there seemed to be a correlation between size of contracts and number of retired officers employed by a corporation. The 100 largest corporations employed more than 1400 ex-officers, of which 261 were of general or flag rank. General Dynamics Corporation was tops in government contracts in 1961, receiving more than $1 billion in work orders. Also, General Dynamics employed 187 former officers and was headed by former Army Secretary Frank Pace for good measure.[21] Without even suggesting that "improper" influence is exercised over the Defense Department and other agencies by defense industries, it seems obvious (as it seemed obvious to Vice Admiral Rickover in direct testimony) that high-level officers who retire and represent defense plants are often succeeded in military position by close associates, perhaps even men whose promotion they at one time have influenced. Is it unnatural, then, that the advice of old comrades-in-arms should be considered?

Although the military branches of government often work at close quarters with industry in planning, building, and outfitting weapons systems, ultimately, military-industrial relations are really but two sides of a triangular relationship, with the third part of this liaison being performed by Congress. Since it is Congress that finally appropriates the funds, the legislators could not avoid being concerned with the purposes for which the funds are spent—and *where* they are spent. Congress approaches national defense expenditures in the same manner as other expenditures: The individual congressman is concerned to see that his district derives some benefit—in terms of profit and employment—from such projects. Each of the fifty states has defense installations or large production facilities which are benefited by defense spending. *Congressional Quarterly* made a survey in 1961 which indicated that fully 282 of the nation's 437 congressional districts had at least one installation operated by the Defense Department, AEC, or NASA.[22] Thus, for example, the large California aircraft industry finds allies in its search for government contracts both in its corporate military brass and the local congressman, not to mention reserve Air Force officers in Congress and, more than likely, the Air Force itself along with its clientele organizations, such as the Air Force Association. It should come as no surprise that the Defense Department award of a TFX fighter plane contract to General Dynamics and the Grumman Aircraft Corporation in 1962 should have provoked a call for an investigation by Senator Henry Jackson of Washington. The chief competitor of General Dynamics was Boeing Aircraft, located in the state of Washington.

In a pluralistic society, governed ultimately by competing interests, the kinds of competition engendered by defense and national security activities are natural enough. What gives genuine cause for concern is the *concentration* of political power capable of being wielded by the military in association with big industry. To consider a hypothetical—but surely not unrealistic—situation, if a sudden breakthrough at the diplomatic level gave real promise of wide-scale disarmament, would the executive or any given administration have sufficient fortitude to overcome the deep-seated inertia of the military-industrial status quo? Some appreciation of the pressures involved can be seen on a much smaller scale by noting the congressional outcry that arose when Secretary McNamara announced the closing of certain military installations in several states in 1963.

*Domestic-Diplomatic-Military Relations: Ugly Americanism.* The calculations which must be made in developing policies to protect national security are based upon additional sources of information other than those we have considered thus far. The domestic officials of the NSC, the CIA, the Defense establishment, and other organs are equipped by experience and training to provide many of the answers to security questions; but a large measure of American security depends upon the other nations of the world—allied, opposed, and uncommitted. This means that rational policy planners must be kept informed by overseas representatives, and that these representatives, in turn, must be skilled at interpreting and applying the policies developed by the White House, the Pentagon, and the State Department in the foreign countries with which we have relations. This has come by mid-century to be pre-eminently a problem of administrative organization.

Traditionally, the functions noted above were carried out by the American ambassador. Since World War II, however, the overseas establishment representing the American government has flowered in such exotic varieties as to create real doubts about who is in charge. Typically the modern American diplomatic mission is composed of the following elements: State Department, Agency for International Development (AID), United States Information Service (USIS), military attachés of the three services, military assistance advisory groups (MAAGS), and the CIA. Quite often, in addition, an area military commander plays an important role on the local scene. Presidents Truman and Eisenhower repeatedly expressed their confidence in the abilities of ambassadors to fulfill the role of supreme representative of the United States at their stations. Early in his administration President Kennedy sent a letter to all American ambassadors in which he stated his conviction that they should be the chief co-ordinating authorities on the scene, having jurisdiction over all government agencies with the exception of the military. Yet, the "country team" concept, by which the ambassador holds a position of primacy, remains a polite fiction.[23]

The extent to which the ambassador is practically able to control the activities of each of the operating agencies of the team is limited for a number of reasons. Often the ambassador is more misled than helped by the babble of tongues advising him. Each agency views the problems of the country in the context of its own specialized preconceptions. The USIS agent stumps for the primacy of propaganda; the AID man gives preference to economic development schemes; for the MAAGS it is a military problem; and for the CIA it is a security question. Moreover, each agency is so involved in its own day-to-day operations that little time is left for reflection and planning and—most needed of all—co-ordination of its activities with other team-members. The result is that sometimes there is not a single, unified, consistent American policy toward a country but rather several independent, perhaps inconsistent or even contradictory courses of action being pursued, all under the authority of the United States. The effects of such an administrative hiatus at the Yugoslav mission are recorded in a frank memorandum delivered to the Senate Subcommittee on National Security Staffing and Operations by the veteran foreign service officer and a former ambassador, George F. Kennan:

> The difficulties were greatest, it seemed to me, when the matters in question were ones considered to lie within the primary competence of AID, of the Pentagon, of the Budgetary or fiscal authorities, or of those authorities . . . which backstop the Department of State in, and in some respects control, such matters as the issuance of passports, visas, reentry permits, etc.
>
> With these latter, in particular, I felt the lack of any effective liaison. They included, I suppose, people in the Immigration Service, and in the FBI. I was never sure that they *understood, or shared, or respected* the policy determinations of the Department of State with relation to Yugoslavia. I had the impression, perhaps erroneous, that many of these people were going on the assumption that Yugoslavia was a member of the Soviet bloc, a thesis contrary to our own observations and to the established analysis of the Department. This hampered our operations and had, in a number of instances, what I considered to be adverse effects on our operations in the field.
>
> In budgetary and fiscal matters, again, the Ambassador was sadly powerless. In general, he simply took what he got. . . .[24]

More recently—and more critically—the unsettled situation in South Vietnam illustrated boldly the aspects of administrative disharmony leading to dissension over the proper course of American policy. The matter came to a head when the newly appointed Ambassador, Henry Cabot Lodge, requested that his authority over the CIA chief in Saigon and his relationship with the military commander, General Harkins, be clarified. The basic problem at hand was how most effectively to combat the Communist Vietcong. Whereas Ambassador Lodge favored greater pressure against the ruling family of South Vietnam in order to extract reforms in the government, the CIA had long established itself as a partial spokesman for the Diem regime and opposed such pressures. Moreover, General Harkins continued to send reports back to Washington suggesting that the war against the Vietcong was progressing much more satisfactorily than the Ambassador and other observers were inclined to credit.[25]

Conflicting interests based upon convictions formed out of differing institutional, occupational, and educational backgrounds create obstacles to the rational development and consistent administration of national security policies. These conflicts have been described as polarizations of institutional entities—civilian versus military, the State Department versus the Pentagon, the CIA versus the foreign service, and so on. However, an additional dimension of the policy making complex in a highly technological age remains to be considered. The quest for rationality, though transcending all the other organizational challenges, has itself produced a further complication in the process of formulating and executing national security policy.

THE TYRANNY OF EXPERTISE: SCIENCE AND STRATEGY

*A New Function of Government.* The growing prominence given to scientific and technical intelligence in considerations of national security suggested by the rapidly increasing government expenditures on R & D have required a corresponding growth of government agencies designed to assemble this intelligence. The proliferation of advisory machinery since World War II constitutes what some have described as a novel relationship of interdependence between government and private institutions.[26] Government agencies established in the past two decades to promote publicly sponsored scientific research function in two ways: by awarding contracts and making direct grants for research. The first major postwar agency established for this purpose was the Atomic Energy Commission, created in 1946 and governed by a five-man board which is authorized to award contracts to private industries, universities, and individuals to operate its laboratories and other research facilities.

In 1950 Congress created the National Science Foundation charged with the task of promoting basic research and coordinating all the scientific activities within the federal government. The NSF operates by awarding scholarships, fellowships, and other grants for mathematical, physical, biological, engineering, and other research projects. In 1963 the NSF employed more than 1200 aides and disbursed some $229 million in research grants.[27] Following the orbit of the first Russian Sputnik, Congress created NASA to put America into space. The Space Agency operates fourteen major installations across the country, the most well known of which is the Launch Operations Center at Cape Kennedy, Florida. Although the space flight program has aroused some controversy—particularly at budget time—it apparently has produced a new breed of pioneer-hero in the astronauts. Consequently, as pressures have built up in favor of shaving the space budget, NASA has usually been able to produce a space spectacular sufficient to capture the imagination of the American people and counteract such pressures. Even the astronauts themselves have not been reluctant on occasion to protest publicly against proposed limitations on the manned space flight program, thereby indicating that lessons of politics as well as science have not been lost on them.

The proliferation of science projects and science agencies supported by government moved President Eisenhower to appoint James Killian of MIT as the first Special Assistant for Science and Technology in 1957 to serve as Chairman of the President's Science Advisory Committee. In 1962 President Kennedy further institutionalized the executive machinery of scientific advice by creating the Office of Science and Technology which is lodged in the high-status Executive Office. OST, aside from serving as the President's closest source of information in this area, has been given the herculean task of reviewing, integrating, and co-ordinating federal science activities.

A large proportion of government science work is contracted out to extramural sources, such as the great universities which have extensive scientific research establishments of their own. Among these, Harvard, MIT, Chicago, the Los Alamos Laboratory of the University of California, and the Applied Physics Laboratory of the Johns Hopkins University are leading protégés of government agencies. The competition among universities and academicians for government contracts sometimes becomes so keen as to bring the scientists into the political lists. The cancellation by the AEC in 1963 of a proposed atom smasher to be built for the Midwestern Universities Research Association aroused a storm of protest from the federation of midwestern universities. They argued that the Midwest was being slighted by government in favor of the large established recipients on the East and West coasts and succeeded in getting pressure applied by midwestern congressmen.[28]

*The Think Tanks.* Not all of government's sponsorship of R & D is directed toward the universities, and the age of the cold war has seen the rise to prominence of private professional institutes which exist in order to sell their advice to various government agencies. The oldest and most well known of the so-called "Think Tanks" is the RAND Corporation. RAND is associated with the Air Force and was originally created in 1946 with the help of the Ford Foundation and Douglas Aircraft. This Santa Monica, California, institute which has a staff of over 800 and a multimillion dollar annual budget ranges far afield from pure physical scientific research; it is rather the prototype of the strategy advice organization and deals with such matters as disarmament, political and economic analysis, as well as military strategy and tactics. Its members and consultants are unquestionably among the science and strategy elite of the nation; some of the RAND alumni operate as part of Secretary McNamara's corps of "defense intellectuals" and include Charles Hitch, Defense Comptroller; Alain Enthoven, Systems Analysis; and nine other ex-RAND men at Defense.

The conventional bureaucratic demand for parity ordains that if the Air Force is to have its RAND Corporation, the other services must have their own intellectual strategy hatcheries. Thus, a Research Analysis Corporation (RAC) is associated with Army; an Operations Evaluation Group (OEG) is supported by Navy; and the Weapons System Evaluation Group (WSEG) operates out of the Defense Department itself. Other private organizations which carry on defense strategy studies are the Aerospace Corporation, the Institute of Defense Analyses, and various centers for international and peace studies at such university bases as Harvard, MIT, Columbia, and Princeton. These institutes together publish hundreds of thousands of pages of reports, plans, analyses, and recommendations annually which have a varying impact on the deliberations of public policy makers. To cite just one contribution to the strategy debate Herman Kahn's *On Thermonuclear War* was an influential and provocative contribution to the ferment of ideas concerning the possibilities in all-out nuclear conflict.

There can be no doubt that the growth of the idea factories constitutes a great mobilization of intelligence and talents available to government policy makers. To the extent that this phenomenon lends greater rationality to national security policy—in an age when mistakes, miscalculations, and emotional responses could have disastrous consequences—it is to be applauded. Unfortunately, each trend has its questionable by-products. One problem may be a surfeit of advice. The indispensability of expertise can result ironically in greater confusion and indecision when battalions of competing experts serve up conflicting expert advice. This becomes increasingly dangerous a prospect when different agencies of government, such as the military services, underwrite their own funds of expertise. It can hardly be doubted that the research and strategy organizations must think in terms of the interests of their sponsors at least part of the time. In some instances the ideas and studies become weapons of a new sort in the combat between the various services and agencies. Furthermore, there is evidence that the strategy planning business has spawned a new species of entrepreneurs who market expert advice. When this comes about there often develops an intellectually inhibiting progression of fads in ideas as in other products. Correspondingly, studies pour out analyzing, justifying, and promoting arms control today; "second-strike counterforce capability" tomorrow;

and the concept of "overkill" the next day. The basic rationality of a system which produces such confusing and contradictory prescriptions is at least open to question. In the end, the policy maker is faced with the unenviable task of deciding which of the assorted sets of experts is likely to be *most* expert. Needless to say, there are no technical experts on *this* question, and the high-level decision maker must finally rely on his own experience, logical processes, and judgment of men.

*The Scientist as Strategist.* The newest elite body to spring forth on the American social landscape is the community of scientists. Indeed, it would probably be more accurate to say that this elite was *called* forth because its appearance was occasioned by the growing predominance of technical considerations in our times. In a vague and remote sense one often heard of science's "service" to society in the uncomplicated years before 1945; today that concept of service has come to have a very direct and immediate meaning. Thus according to Lee DuBridge, by 1955, nearly 50 per cent of America's engineers and 25 per cent of her scientists were employed either directly or under contract by the federal government.[29] Presumably these figures would be considerably higher today. On the whole, the scientist has not sought after this relationship; it just happened.

Certain characteristics of the scientist as a member of a very particular skill group help to explain some of the organizational problems occasioned by his involvement in policy making.[30] Traditionally, the scientist has tended to hold himself—and to be held —incommunicado from the rest of the intellectual community and society generally, a point well made some years ago by C. P. Snow in his discussion of the "two cultures." [31] The scientist has always spoken an alien tongue and practiced an occult profession in the eyes of the humanist, the statesman, and the businessman. Personally, the scientist normally feels a confidence about the importance, even pre-eminence, of his kind of work; in an age of scientific revolution he is riding the wave of the future. Unlike most of his nonscientific counterparts, the scientist is antiorganizational in temperament; his self-image is the individual following his own inspirational drives, guided only by the scientific method. Finally, the scientist in America has traditionally been apolitical, knowing and caring little about what goes on in bureaucratic offices and legislative halls.

Now that events have brought the scientist of necessity into close relationship with the nonscientific interests he is asked to serve, his inbred occupational traits make of him a special case among civil servants. He is far more independent than his non-scientific co-workers. He can always leave government and return to his university or industrial research laboratory with no loss in status or income. Consequently, he is, in a very fundamental sense, less responsible to considerations other than his own professional precepts. As a functionary in government the scientist often expresses disdain for many of its operating imperatives. Warner Schilling has catalogued a number of approaches that scientists often take to their work which run against the grain of those professional, political men with whom they must cohabit. Among the work habits of the scientists is what Schilling calls the "whole-problem approach." That is, the scientist is unwilling to apply himself to a single, narrow aspect of a problem, to fit into a bureaucratic niche. He more often prefers to analyze the whole problem and freely gives his advice about matters which his political co-workers consider the exclusive specialty of other experts. A typical case might be of the sort that finds the highly specialized bacteriologist determined to make foreign policy proposals.

A second scientific characteristic that sometimes evidences itself is a preference for drastic innovations rather than incremental improvements. Thus, the scientist sometimes becomes impatient with the military for thinking in terms of weapons improvements when the technologist might prefer to make the great leap ahead to develop an entirely new system. Another difficulty Schilling perceives in the scientific stance is summed up in the attitude which likes "technology for its own sweet sake." [32] This is a way of stating the scientist's penchant for tinkering, for seeking improvements through ever more sophisticated apparatus or more elaborate experimental devices. The conflict that can arise between this attitude and the choices which might be taken by the political branch of government in an area where both scientist and politician are involved in some degree is no more aptly illustrated than in the case of the nuclear test ban treaty of 1963. Opponents of the treaty within the scientific community were led by Dr. Edward Teller who argued that the banning of further tests would deprive the United States of potentially vital data. In his press conference of August 20, 1963, President Kennedy was forced to defend the test ban on the grounds that enough tests had already been made to satisfy American security interests:

> . . . And we, in fact, did more tests—several more tests—than we had originally planned six months before. So I don't think that the charge is valid. But, obviously, we didn't test unnecessarily. Quite obviously, there may have been tests that Dr. Teller would like to have run. I don't know about that. . . . There may have been, as I say, several tests that different scientists wanted to run on one point or another, but I think we did the major tests. And I think they were an impressive series. But it would be very difficult, I think, to satisfy Dr. Teller in this field.[33]

As this incident implies—and it could be multiplied a hundred-fold—the scientist who has achieved high status in his profession and qualifies for membership in that elite of the scientific community which is called upon to consult on the scientific aspects of national security policy cannot avoid becoming involved in questions of a nonscientific nature. At an extreme the scientific community is polarized on the major policy questions of the day. These scientists have, in other words, become "politicized." They are willy-nilly defense strategists who are expected to have an opinion on the great *political* issues. When Hans Bethe, the eminent Cornell nuclear physicist, attends a conference on disarmament in Geneva he is acting in a capacity which transcends his primary skill orientation.

Finally, however, the politician—or statesman, if there is a difference—must reign supreme. As indispensable as the intelligent advice of the technician is, and as difficult as it may be to weigh conflicting recommendations of different technicians, this is a job that can only be accomplished by the political class in a democracy. As one specialist pointed out years ago, there are at least three good reasons why the politician must have the final word. First, some questions must be answered immediately and cannot await the results of prolonged researches. Second, a point is reached where a halt must be called to a self-feeding progression of researches, researches into the research, and so on. Finally politics is a profession too, and it is only the mature, studied judgment of the politician that can take full measure of the political consequences of a course of action.[34]

CONCLUSION

As complicated and extensive as the apparatus of national security policy is, the chief lesson of this brief exploration should be that its problems are not unique. The difficulties encountered in creating rational defense and security policies are the same as those impinging on all policy making. Organizationally, the challenge is one of coordinating various segments of a large mission such as defense. Politically, the challenge consists in translating a variety of interests, skills, and values into a pattern of action which is consistent and responsible. Intellectually, the challenge consists in mobilizing the most expert technical judgments, guarding against the human and organizational factors which are bound to taint the pure process of expert calculation, and finally, interpreting and applying this knowledge within the broader context of national needs.

REFERENCES

1. Harry S. Truman, *Memoirs,* Vol. I: *Year of Decisions* (Garden City, N.Y.: Doubleday & Co., Inc., 1955), pp. 506-509.

2. Department of Defense, *Annual Report, 1962* (Washington, D.C.: Government Printing Office, 1963), p. 366.

3. *Ibid.,* p. 373.

4. *Ibid.,* pp. 385, 388.

5. National Science Foundation, *Federal Funds for Science,* XI (Washington, D.C.: Government Printing Office, 1963), p. 49.

6. *Ibid.,* p. 7.

7. For a detailed discussion of the early reorganization proposals and attempts, see Timothy W. Stanley, *American Defense and National Security* (Washington, D.C.: Public Affairs Press, 1956).

8. Truman, *op. cit.,* Vol. II, pp. 52-53.

9. *US Government Organization Manual, 1963-1964* (Washington, D.C.: Government Printing Office, 1963), p. 133.

10. For a detailed summary of the proposals and enactments, see *Congressional Quarterly Almanac,* Vol. XIV (1958), pp. 133-139.

11. Department of Defense, *Annual Report, 1962,* p. 30.

12. For a study of the origin and development of NSC, see Paul Y. Hammond, "The National Security Council as a Device for Interdepartmental Coordination: An Interpretation and Appraisal," *American Political Science Review,* LIV (December, 1960), pp. 899-910.

13. J. C. Heinlein, *Presidential Staff and National Security Policy* (Cincinnati, Ohio: University of Cincinnati, Center for the Study of US Foreign Policy, 1963), p. 48.

14. Quoted in *ibid.*, p. 59.

15. Sherman Adams, *Firsthand Report* (New York: Harper and Row, 1961), pp. 455-456.

16. See Robert S. Rankin and Winfried R. Dallmayr, *Freedom and Emergency Powers in the Cold War* (New York: Appleton-Century-Crofts, 1964), pp. 38-39.

17. *The New York Times,* September 13, 1963, p. 11.

18. Gene M. Lyons, "The New Civil-Military Relations," *American Political Science Review,* LV (March, 1961), pp. 53-63.

19. See John W. Masland and Laurence I. Radway, *Soldiers and Scholars* (Princeton: Princeton University Press, 1957).

20. Department of Defense Directive 1320.5 as quoted in Lyons, *American Political Science Review,* pp. 62-63.

21. See the excellent analysis: "The 'Military Lobby'—Its Impact on Congress, Nation," *Congressional Quarterly Weekly Report,* XIX (March 24, 1961), pp. 463-478.

22. *Ibid.*, p. 464.

23. US Senate, Subcommittee on National Security Staffing and Operations of the Committee on Government Operations, *Administration of National Security.* Committee Print, 88th Cong., 1st Sess., 1963, pp. 11-12.

24. US Senate, Subcommittee on National Security Staffing and Operations of the Committee on Government Operations, *Administration of National Security.* Hearing, Part 5, 88th Cong., 1st Sess., December 11, 1963, p. 359.

25. *The New York Times,* October 5, 1963, p. 1.

26. J. Stefan Dupre and Sanford A. Lakoff, *Science and the Nation: Policy and Politics* (Englewood Cliffs, N.J.: Prentice-Hall, Inc., 1962), p. 15.

27. National Science Foundation, *Federal Funds for Science,* XI, p. 2.

28. *The New York Times,* November 11, 1963, p. 1.

29. Lee A. DuBridge, "The American Scientist: 1955," *Yale Review,* XLV (September, 1955), p. 13.

30. A useful analysis of the scientific skill group is found in Robert C. Wood, "The Scientist and Politics: The Rise of an Apolitical Elite," in Robert Gilpin and Christopher Wright (eds.), *Scientists and National Policy-Making* (New York: Columbia University Press, 1964), pp. 41-72.

31. C. P. Snow, *The Two Cultures and the Scientific Revolution* (New York: Cambridge University Press, 1959).

32. These categories of scientific attitude are discussed in Warner Schilling, "Scientists, Foreign Policy, and Politics," *American Political Science Review,* LVI (June, 1962), pp. 292-294.

33. *The New York Times,* August 21, 1963, p. 14.
34. Don K. Price, *Government and Science* (New York: Oxford University Press, 1962), p. 170.

# CHAPTER 8

# Public Policy and the Public Interest

## THE PUBLIC INTEREST: AN ELUSIVE IMPERATIVE

When called upon to justify their activities, makers of public policy invariably say that what they are doing is in the public interest. When Congress passes a law establishing a new regulatory agency, it usually directs the agency to regulate in the public interest. In this age of democratic consciousness, even the private organization often deems it useful, if not imperative, to proclaim that it is acting in the public interest. Obviously, a term so widely and frequently called upon is of more than descriptive utility. It is nothing less than a statement of ethical evaluation. To say that a given course of action is prompted by considerations of the public interest is to use the concept as both a criterion and mark of moral legitimacy. If we are persistent and ask what, in fact, it is about a given policy that makes it "in the public interest" we are likely to be told that such a policy serves the interests of the public and is, therefore, superior to a policy which serves the interests of less than the public. Aside from the fact that the statement is a tautology, it raises many questions without answering any. It is this feature of the concept of the public interest which has provoked many learned essays suggesting that, because of its hopeless generality and vagueness, we might better discard the term altogether and go on to more profitable investigations.[1]

Nevertheless, it is one purpose of this chapter to suggest that the idea of the public interest, for better or for worse—and, on the whole, I think, for the better—is here to stay. Moreover, ideas —even confused, vague generalities—can have an importance, in spite of their lack of immaculate precision. It should be stated at once that no precise, operational definition of the public interest

192

is possible. Or rather, while a rigorous definition is *possible,* it would be useless as a practical guide since no consensus among policy makers could be achieved that would agree to the use of its terms. If the concept cannot be defined we might try the next best thing by considering its connotations, just as the United States Supreme Court, while refusing to define "due process," does not feel restrained from deciding important issues on the basis of its presence or absence.

The fundamental feature infusing the public interest is the idea of generality as opposed to particularity. That which is in one's interest works, in one way or another, to one's advantage. Thus that which is in the public's interest works to the advantage of the public rather than any particular individual or group. Yet this apparent simplicity masks a deeper complexity because of the undefined nature of "public." There are, for example, very few interests which one could assume to be held by *all* of the public or held in common—though there are surely some. Thus few would argue that physical survival is not an interest held by all the public. But for the practical purpose of making policy, this does not take us far since there are few policies that demonstratively affect all members of society. It might be argued that this is a quibble, and that, after all, sincere men of good sense can make the distinction between an act that is advantageous to society in general as opposed to one that helps a privileged few. Yet if we are going to be practical about this matter, we must conclude that many of the policies we would identify as being in the public interest serve precisely the interests of a *partial* public, perhaps a very small minority. Thus many would argue that public aid to dependent children of widows is indeed in the public interest although this could not be justified by the criterion of generality. An attempt might be made to so justify it by saying that helping children to survive and develop is bound to make a better society, or that anything which contributes to the unfettered development of the human personality is in the public interest. These assertions may be true but they do constitute a further, different element of "public interest" beyond the generality of application. In short, the public interest turns out to be whatever is in accord with the preconceptions and interpretations of the individual or group invoking its spirit.

There are several different sources available from which to draw a basis for the claim that a given course of action is in the public interest. One answer to the question of how the public interest is found is that it is simply the sum of individual interests. What is usually meant by this formulation is that there is naturally a wide range of common interests in society. That is, many individuals have the same interests in common. This is usually the result of a belief in the uniformity of human nature such as that propounded by the seventeenth-century philosopher Hobbes, who believed that all men were basically selfish egoists. However, Hobbes also believed that men were rational creatures who, understanding that selfish egoism, made operational, becomes destructive, realized it was in their greater interest to restrain themselves and cooperate under a generally accepted rule of law. In this way, individuals acting with reason and restraint would come to find an identity of interests in most cases. Thus, to use the common contemporary example, individuals consent to be bound by the restraints of traffic regulations because greater long-run safety for all results. Where the identity of interests is not so easily apprehended on a wide scale, this formulation of the public interest reduces to majoritarianism. That is, the majority takes a course of action and overrides the minority. The problem here, of course, is that some might find it difficult to bestow the accolade of the public interest on all acts of the majority. In view of the ethical connotation of the concept of the public interest, the majoritarian formulation comes perilously close to stating that whatever policy is adopted by the majority in a democracy is morally justifiable.

The fact that the United States is a highly heterogeneous, pluralistic society has led many to reject the action of a possible identity of individual interests in favor of a view which identifies the group as the meaningful exponent of interests. Thus the thread of group analysis that runs from Arthur Bentley at the turn of the century to David Truman in our own times leads to a different formulation of the public interest. According to this view, the public interest is achieved through the process of group conflict, compromise, and resolution of issues. As a description of democratic politics, group theory provides a rewarding analysis; as a means of providing moral justification for specific policies, it falls sadly short of the mark. We might be more sanguine about the

results of group conflict if the groups were evenly mat₍nd
representative, but we know that some are manifestly mor₍er-
ful than others. Regarding policies concerning modern ₍e,
what other groups can compete for influence with the ₍c
community? Some may be prepared to say that the detern
of a scientific elite in the area of national security are *ip*
in the public interest, but then of course this is not policy
lated on the group conflict basis. Furthermore, as Frank
has pointed out, the balance-of-interests formulation loses
tact with a concept of the public interest as a guide to actic

> It ceases, furthermore, even to be a prior standard by wl
> might evaluate the claims of competing interests. The public
> as compromise is no longer an interest that men strive
> longer a guide to policy-making, but a *post hoc* label for the
> ings. Since it does not exist until after the group struggle is l
> won, it can provide no benchmark for policy formation.[2]

A third major variation of the public interest is that view
holds that it is an ethical criterion of policy that cannot be
duced from the wishes, demands, or aspirations of the pec
generally but can only be properly divined by a few qualified pe
ple. This is, in effect, the antidemocratic view of the public inte
est. Its basic assumption is that the average man is not reall
capable of knowing his own best interests and those of society
generally. Thus he needs a spokesman who is able to govern in
his best interests. Holders of this view usually assume that there
is, in fact, an objective identity of individual and community interests. Hence Walter Lippmann defines the public interest to be
"what men would choose if they saw clearly, thought rationally,
acted disinterestedly and benevolently." [3]

What might be called the aristocratic view of the public interest
is held by assorted types of thinkers. Conservatives generally have
a high regard for its formulations since they are disturbed by the
prospect of sudden or rapid change and by pragmatic approaches
to policy that are often motivated by popular demands. Though
literary form may vary, these people normally take refuge in absolute principles of morality and order. Hence, the public interest
may be discovered in the principles of natural law, prescriptive
traditions, or absolute and literally interpreted constitutional provisions. Consequently, the determination of whether a specific pol-

.in the public interest can only be made by those qualified
.rpret the appropriate absolute canons of the moral order,
.er they be scholars, jurists, or simply virtuous, dedicated
en. Occasionally, the aristocratic formulation is prompted,
so much by a belief in immutable and absolute principles of
ality, as by a craving for expertise. In this sense the public
re    is taken to be that which is mechanically effective and
cient. This    ude is sometimes expressed by way of strictures
inst popular or legislative interference with the important work
expert administrators. The chief difficulties with the aristocratic
absolutist view of the public interest is, again, that it fails to
rovide an acceptable working guide for the formulation of policy.
Until a consensus is reached on the appropriate absolute moral
principles to be applied in making policy or the appropriate cre-
dentials of expertise that would permit a few functionaries to mo-
nopolize policy making, the public interest will have little meaning
and inspire little confidence as a criterion.

Although there are other variations on these approaches to the
meaning of the public interest, they are equally unsatisfactory in
application. We return to our original thesis that the public interest
is an undefinable concept. Of what value, then, is a concept so
elusive, so vague as to be little more than a popular slogan? Some
students of public policy have come to the conclusion that the
idea of the public interest performs a valuable function as a great
social myth in democratic societies.[4] The idea of the social myth
as a conditioner of thought and its importance as an inspiration
or stimulus to political behavior was developed at length by
Pareto and Sorel in the early years of this century.[5] The social
myth may be true or not; its power consists in the fact that it is
*believed* to be true. The great attraction in the myth of the public
interest is its intuitive claim to acceptance. Even though it cannot
be defined with precision there is an implacable desire among men
—particularly in a democratic society—to believe that an ethical
norm such as the public interest does in fact exist. Moreover, one
writer has suggested that the public interest is of even greater importance:

> One might say that an essential condition for the existence of a de-
> mocracy is some degree of common conviction that certain achieve-
> ments serve the variety of ultimate values. In other words, the public

interest is the life hypothesis of a pluralistic society—enabling people with different religions, different philosophical convictions, or different subconscious value systems to have a common ground for promoting their various ultimate values. Without this common ground, representing more than an accidental coincidence of individual interests, a pluralistic democracy could not exist.[6]

The real significance of the myth of the public interest as an imperative is that by providing even a very general standard for the evaluation of policy it becomes at least one factor that must be taken into consideration by the policy maker. J. Roland Pennock has said, for example, that it acts as a "spur to conscience and to deliberation," and thus serves as a reminder to the official that there is something beyond selfish, private interests.[7] This is particularly effective as a chastening guide since, from time to time, the context of situations lends greater definition to the public interest. For example, even though it cannot be established by logical definition that the public interest has been violated when a great scandal occurs, such as the Teapot Dome affair, if not all, then nearly all members of society are willing to conclude that a violation has taken place. The very fact that periodically a consensus does develop around a particular application of the public interest as a criterion and judgment persuades the policy maker that there is such a thing.

## DEMOCRACY AND THE PUBLIC INTEREST

In an age when the claims of popular sovereignty are being asserted in every corner of the globe, democracy appears to be the procedural mechanism that is most fitting for the achievement of policies in the public interest. That democracy and the public interest should go hand in hand is hardly surprising since both are great myths grounded on an ethical foundation of the people. And both derive their ultimate justification in an act of faith. Hence the presumption is that democracy, a political system controlled by the people, will produce policies that are in the interests of the people. To understand the exact implementation of democracy —and, therefore, the degree to which the myth of the public interest is made a reality—certain minimum requirements for its operation must be considered.

In the modern state the only possible kind of democracy is

representative democracy. The only rational means by which the representatives of the people can arrive at decisions is on the principle of majority rule. In the United States, laws are passed by majorities, and the election of public officials is brought about by majorities. To be sure, certain issues are deemed so vital that extraordinary majorities are considered necessary, such as in the overriding of presidential vetoes, in the Senate's advice for treaty ratification, and in the constitutional amending process. Nevertheless, these are variations of the majority principle.

Second, the representatives of the people must be forced to face re-election periodically. The theory behind regular re-election is simply that of accountability: the most effectual control exercisable by the people over the policy makers is their opportunity, at regular intervals, to dismiss their representatives.

Third, nearly all people must be represented equally. With the exception of minors, incompetents, and certain types of criminals, all citizens should have an equal right and opportunity to express their political preferences at the polls. In the true democracy there is no place for extraneous considerations at the polls, such as race, class, property qualifications, or other historic bars to suffrage. Ideally, the electoral system should reflect the maxim of "one man, one vote" and not overrepresent one region or social enclave in relation to another. By the 1960s democracy in America had matured to a point where these last legal bars to equal suffrage were being removed by court action.[8]

Fourth, constitutional and legal safeguards are necessary to assure that the democratic process is carried on in an atmosphere of maximum freedom. In the complex and highly organized modern state, paper guarantees which assure formal representation and equal voting rights are of little practical importance if they are not underpinned by effective provisions for the maximum exercise of organizational and persuasive liberties. The traditional rights of free speech, press, assembly, and petition provide a framework within which political parties may organize, interest groups may make their wishes known to government, and government officials may be challenged by citizens. In short, the democratic dialogue must be carried on in an atmosphere free of statist repression or intimidation.

Fifth, since the decision making burden placed upon the citizen in a democracy is a heavy one, the alternatives among which he chooses must be presented with maximum clarity and completeness. He must mandate to the elected leaders of his choice a wide range of discretion in policy making. Therefore, their powers and the institutional matrix within which they operate must be clear to the citizen if he is to make a rational choice. If government becomes so complex, so beset with checks and counterchecks, so divided by competing centers of leadership that the citizen cannot be sure of the consequences of his choices, then a large measure of the substance of the democratic determination is lost.

This is the crisis of democracy in America—and concomitantly, of the quest for the public interest—in the twentieth century. The process of policy making and the sources of effective leadership have been so widely dispersed that traditional notions of responsibility and accountability seem to have lost much of their relevance. To the historic competition between the executive and the Congress for policy leadership has been added the quietly but effectively increasing claims of appointed administrators and even nonpublic advisers in the policy process. Among these latter claimants to, and executors of, the public business, motivations and guiding principles may stem from concepts of public service, professional standards, or ideological imperatives. Whatever their source, they do not always emerge directly from popular initiatives. This is probably inevitable in an age of organizational and technological revolution. It does indicate, however, that traditional attitudes about democracy and the myth of the public interest require thoughtful re-evaluation.

## BUREAUCRACY AND THE PUBLIC INTEREST

Students of government have long been critical, if not skeptical, about the role of bureaucracy in relation to public policy and the public interest. Since the public interest is most often associated with activities which are representative in origin, and since bureaucracy is *formally* the least representative of the public institutions, fears of administrative autonomy unencumbered by considerations of the public interest disturb the composure of some institutional analysts. In consequence, the literature of political science is scattered with schemes devised to place restraints on administrative activity.[9]

Among the solutions to this problem repeatedly proposed, three general types stand out. First, there are those who offer the most extreme cure: get rid of bureaucracy. At first sight this might seem to be a rather pointless prescription since bureaucracy is the only conceivable instrument capable of formulating and implementing the policies modern government is called upon to undertake. But the antipathy of the "root-and-branch" school is in reality a reaction against the *substance* of positive government itself. Getting rid of bureaucracy may be translated into a desire to turn the clock back in more than one sense.

More moderate critics who, on the whole, have accepted the growth and practice of positive government, propose that bureaucracy be brought under the administrative umbrella of the executive. This approach places emphasis on formal, managerial, organizational techniques of control lodged in the Presidency. Such attitudes underlie many of the proposals of the successive Commissions on the Reorganization of the Executive Branch. While such proposals are well intended and offer some measure of improved accountability, they often fail to take into consideration the resistance of informal organization to managerial direction.

Finally, bespeaking the ideological commitment to formal, representative supremacy, another category of reformers argues for stricter legislative supervision of the bureaucracy.[10] A bundle of specific proposals are suggested for accomplishing this, such as the passage of more precise, confining enabling acts by Congress in establishing agencies; more staffing aid for Congress in conducting its oversight function; a reorganization of the committee system to make it more effective in scrutinizing administrative activities; and a more exacting system of auditing. While a tighter system of congressional control over administration might assuage some of the concerns about bureaucratic power, it should be recognized that this pacification comes at a price. Congressional involvement in administration is bound to conflict with such values as day-to-day independence, expertise, and dispatch for which bureaucracy was fashioned in the first place.

It is more than fitting, in a book that deals fundamentally with policy and administration, to conclude with a consideration of the positive side of modern bureaucracy. The best argument *for* bureaucracy—and one made in the context of the myth of the public interest—is that it can make as valid a claim to being representative as Congress can unless one assumes that the only basis of representation is election. It is not here contended that the bureaucrats, as individuals, are more representative of American society than are congressmen as individuals, although this *may* be true as some have contended.[11] In fact, the most recent study of federal executives indicates that they vary considerably from the national norm in education, regional and occupational distribution, and so on, as do such other elite groups as military officers and business executives.[12]

And yet the bureaucrats perform a representative function in a number of ways. They are not constricted by constituency demands and prohibitions as congressmen are and are thus free to represent interests unrelated to geography. They are more specialized and can, thus, develop a greater appreciation of the needs of various interests and the most appropriate means for satisfying those needs. For both of these reasons bureaucracy is able to give representation to groups or interests that would otherwise go *unrepresented*. For example, what limited representation consumer interests receive directly comes from federal agencies rather than Congress. Or, to cite another type of case, minority groups sometimes receive more meaningful representation through federal agencies, such as the Department of Justice or Civil Rights Commission, than they do through Congress.

Since bureaucracy shares in the function of representation as well as policy making in America there is no good reason to assume that bureaucrats are any more immune to the psychological influence of the myth of the public interest than Congress or the President. Hence, to the extent that public policy is formulated and implemented in the public interest, the much-maligned bureaucrat deserves a fair share of the credit.

### REFERENCES

1. Glendon Schubert, *The Public Interest* (Glencoe, Ill.: The Free Press, 1960), Chapter 5. See also Frank Sorauf, "The Conceptual Muddle," in Carl J. Friedrich (ed.), *Nomos V: The Public Interest* (New York: Atherton Press, 1962), Chapter 15, but compare Sorauf, "The Public Interest Reconsidered," *Journal of Politics,* XIX (November, 1957), pp. 638-639.

2. Sorauf, *Journal of Politics*, XIX, p. 630.

3. Walter Lippmann, *The Public Philosophy* (New York: Mentor Books, 1955), p. 40.

4. See, for example, John M. Pfiffner and Robert V. Presthus, *Public Administration*, 4th ed. (New York: The Ronald Press, 1960), pp. 559-560.

5. See Karl Mannheim, *Ideology and Utopia* (New York: Harvest Books, 1936), p. 138.

6. Gerhard Colm, "The Public Interest: Essential Key to Public Policy," in Friedrich (ed.), *op. cit.*, p. 120.

7. J. Roland Pennock, "The One and the Many: A Note on the Concept," in Friedrich (ed.), *op. cit.*, p. 182.

8. *Baker* v. *Carr*, 369 US 186 (1962); *Wesberry* v. *Sanders*, 376 US 1 (1964).

9. For an analytical and critical review of such schemes, see Arch Dotson, "Fundamental Approaches to Administrative Responsibility," *"Western Political Quarterly*, X (September, 1957), pp. 701-727.

10. The fullest statement of this case is made in Charles Hyneman, *Bureaucracy in a Democracy* (New York: Harper and Row, 1950).

11. "The process of selection of the civil service, its contacts, milieu, and income level after induction make the civil service as a body a better sample of the mass of the people than Congress" (Norton E. Long, "Bureaucracy and Constitutionalism," *American Political Science Review*, XLVI [September, 1952], p. 813).

12. W. Lloyd Warner, Paul Van Riper, Norman H. Martin, and Orvis F. Collins, *The American Federal Executive* (New Haven: Yale University Press, 1963), pp. 35, 37, 49, 109.

# Epilogue

As if to confound all counsels of imperfection directed toward the policy-making process in the United States, governmental activism in 1965 achieved new heights—and the chief engine of all this activity was the United States Congress. The reasons for the sharp increase in the public business are neither mysterious nor unusually complicated. They are based simply on the national elections of 1964. Not only did Lyndon Baines Johnson win a landslide victory personally in his campaign for the presidency in his own right, he also carried into power with him extraordinary majorities of activist legislators in both houses of Congress. These two facts were to bring to pass a situation where executive leadership in domestic affairs was exercised by one of the ablest, most experienced and strong-willed legislative tacticians of all times—former Senate Majority Leader Johnson. Correspondingly, the weight of numbers manifest in the congressional liberal majorities made the job of executive persuasion still easier. By August, 1965 major sources of policy controversy extending over the previous generation—primarily in the area of public welfare—had been resolved in favor of the proponents of positive government. A brief catalogue of some of the strides made in the first session of the 89th Congress should be undertaken.

In July the Medicare bill was passed. Henceforth, hospital, nursing home and home-care costs for the aged over 65 would be paid out of the social security system. In addition, voluntary, supplemental medical costs including physicians' fees would be supplied to the aged through public insurance premiums paid at a rate of three dollars per month. The Kerr-Mills program for aid to the blind, needy and dependent children was expanded. Across-the-board increases were made in Old Age Survivors Insurance, retroactive to January 1, 1965. Moreover, coverage was expanded to include physicians and other self-employed groups. Finally, the voluntary retirement age for receiving reduced benefits was lowered to sixty years. The costs of these new programs are to be met by rises in the base of taxable earnings from $4800 to $6600 per year and increases in employer-employee contributions each which will reach 4.95 per cent in 1973 and thereafter.

A new omnibus Housing and Urban Development Act was passed which provides, in addition to increased funds for more public housing units, rent subsidies in the form of cash supplements to low-income families. Extended urban renewal, expanded college housing and urban beautification projects were authorized as part of the new housing package.

In the area of education, $1.3 billion was authorized in federal grants to the states to be disbursed to elementary and secondary school districts comprising large numbers of children from low-income families. Grants were also authorized for building up elementary and secondary school libraries—private as well as public. Community centers were provided under the act, as well as grants for the strengthening of state departments of education. Finally, prospects were good at mid-summer for substantially extended federal aid to the nation's colleges and universities.

Directly aimed at poverty-producing unemployment, the Manpower Development and Training Act was expanded and extended an additional three years.

Substantially increased appropriations were in the offing for the bureaucratic embodiment of the anti-poverty campaign, the Office of Economic Opportunity.

Encouragement was given to consumer spending through a reduction in federal excise taxes—a step partially based upon the salutary results of the $11 billion income tax reduction of the previous congress.

Finally, what appears to be the last *legislative* step in securing equal rights for Negro Americans was taken in July, 1965 when the Administration's Voting Rights Act was passed by heavy majorities in both houses.

As the summer of 1965 wore on, the 89th Congress gave prospects of completing additional legislation recommended by the President in his quest for a "Great Society" in America. Projects for water and air pollution controls, new and liberalized immigration legislation, the repeal of Section 14-b of the Taft-Hartley labor act (permitting state "right to work" laws) were some of the major items of business on the public policy agenda about to be decided.

There is little doubt that a new bench mark has been established in the seemingly cyclical flow of policy often described as a seesaw whose ups and downs depend upon national circumstances of either crisis or benignity and executive leadership, either active or passive. Yet, as the years go by, it is difficult to blind oneself to the fact that both the peaks and valleys of the public business alternate at an ever higher altitude and within an ever narrower amplitude.

# Selected Bibliography

Barnard, Chester I. *The Functions of the Executive.* Cambridge: Harvard University Press, 1948.

Bernstein, Marver. *Regulating Business by Independent Commission.* Princeton: Princeton University Press, 1955.

Berle, Adolf A. *The American Economic Republic.* New York: Harcourt, Brace & World, Inc., 1963.

Blau, Peter. *Bureaucracy in Modern Society.* New York: Random House, 1956.

Braybrooke, David, and Charles E. Lindblom. *A Strategy of Decision: Policy Evaluation as a Social Process.* New York: The Free Press of Glencoe, 1963.

Dahl, Robert, and Charles E. Lindblom. *Politics, Economics and Welfare.* New York: Harper and Row, 1953.

deGrazia, Alfred, and Ted Gurr. *American Welfare.* New York: New York University Press, 1961.

Dupré, J. Stefan, and Sanford A. Lakoff. *Science and the Nation: Policy and Politics.* Englewood Cliffs, N.J.: Prentice-Hall, Inc., 1962.

Etzioni, Amitai (ed.). *Complex Organizations: A Sociological Reader.* New York: Holt, Rinehart & Winston, 1961.

Fainsod, Merle, Lincoln Gordon, and Joseph P. Palamountain, Jr. *Government and the American Economy.* 3d ed. New York: W. W. Norton & Co., Inc., 1959.

Fenno, Richard F. *The President's Cabinet.* Cambridge: Harvard University Press, 1959.

Fine, Sidney. *Laissez-Faire and the General Welfare State.* Ann Arbor: University of Michigan Press, 1956.

Friedrich, Carl J. (ed.). *Nomos V: The Public Interest.* New York: Atherton Press, 1962.

Galbraith, John K. *American Captialism: The Concept of Countervailing Power.* Boston: Houghton Mifflin Company, 1952.

———. *The Affluent Society.* Boston: Houghton Mifflin Company, 1958.

———. *Economics and the Art of Controversy.* New York: Vintage Books, 1959.

Gerth, Hans, and C. Wright Mills (eds., transl.). *From Max Weber: Essays in Sociology.* New York: Oxford University Press, 1946.

Gilpin, Robert, and Christopher Wright (eds.). *Scientists and National Policy-Making.* New York: Columbia University Press, 1964.

Gross, Bertram. *The Legislative Struggle.* New York: McGraw-Hill Book Company, Inc., 1953.

Hacker, Andrew (ed.). *The Corporation Take-Over.* New York: Harper and Row, 1964.

Hammond, Paul Y. *Organizing for Defense: The American Military Establishment in the Twentieth Century.* Princeton: Princeton University Press, 1961.

Harrington, Michael. *The Other America.* Baltimore: Penguin Books, 1963.

Higbee, Edward. *Farms and Farmers in an Urban Age.* New York: Twentieth Century Fund, 1963.

Huntington, Samuel P. *The Common Defense: Strategic Programs in National Politics.* New York: Columbia University Press, 1961.

Jacobs, Paul. *State of the Unions: U.S. Labor Today.* New York: Atheneum Publishers, 1963.

Kerr, Clark, *et al. Industrialism and Industrial Man.* Cambridge: Harvard University Press, 1960.

Kolko, Gabriel. *Wealth and Power in America.* New York: Frederick A. Praeger, Publisher, 1962.

Freeman, J. Lieper. *The Political Process: Executive Bureau-Legislative Committee Relations.* New York: Random House, 1955.

Long, Norton E. *The Polity.* Chicago: Rand McNally & Co., 1962.

Mason, Edward S. (ed.). *The Coropration in Modern Society.* Cambridge: Harvard University Press, 1960.

Matthews, Donald R. *U.S. Senators and Their World.* New York: Vintage Books, 1960.

Musolf, Lloyd. *Federal Examiners and the Conflict of Law and Administration.* Baltimore: The Johns Hopkins Press, 1953.

Neustadt, Richard E. *Presidential Power: The Politics of Leadership.* New York: John Wiley & Sons, Inc., 1960.

Presthus, Robert V. *The Organizational Society.* New York: Alfred A. Knopf, 1962.

Rankin, Robert S., and Winfried R. Dallmayr. *Freedom and Emergency Powers in the Cold War.* New York: Appleton-Century-Crofts, 1964.

Raymond, Jack. *Power at the Pentagon.* New York: Harper and Row, 1964.

Rossiter, Clinton. *Seedtime of the Republic.* New York: Harcourt, Brace & Company, 1953.

———. *The American Presidency.* 2nd ed. New York: Harcourt, Brace & Company, 1960.

———. *Parties and Politics in America.* Ithaca: Cornell University Press, 1960.

Schilling, Warner R., Paul Y. Hammond, and G. H. Snyder. *Strategy, Politics and Defense Budgets*. New York: Columbia University Press, 1962.

Selznick, Philip. *Leadership in Administration*. Evanston, Ill.: Row, Peterson & Co. 1957.

Simon, Herbert. *Administrative Behavior*. 2nd ed. New York: The Macmillan Company, 1961.

Thomas, Norman C., and Karl A. Lamb. *Congress: Politics and Practice*. New York: Random House, 1964.

Truman, David B. *The Governmental Process*. New York: Alfred A. Knopf, 1951.

Waldo, Dwight. *The Administrative State*. New York: The Ronald Press, 1948.

Warner, W. Lloyd, *et al*. *The American Federal Executive*. New Haven: Yale University Press, 1963.

White, Leonard D. *The Federalists*. New York: The Macmillan Company, 1948.

———. *The Jeffersonians*. New York: The Macmillan Company, 1951.

———. *The Jacksonians*. New York: The Macmillan Company, 1954.

———. *The Republican Era*. New York: The Macmillan Company, 1958.

Wildavsky, Aaron. *Dixon-Yates: A Study of Power Politics*. New Haven: Yale University Press, 1962.

Woll, Peter. *American Bureaucracy*. New York: W. W. Norton & Co., Inc., 1963.

———. *Administrative Law: The Informal Process*. Berkeley and Los Angeles: The University of California Press, 1963.

# Index